The Art of the
ENGLISH
MURDER

The Art of the
ENGLISH
MURDER

LUCY WORSLEY

PEGASUS CRIME

NEW YORK LONDON

THE ART OF THE ENGLISH MURDER

Pegasus Books LLC
80 Broad Street, 5th Floor
New York, NY 10004

First Pegasus Books hardcover edition 2014

ISBN: 978-1-60598-634-0

10 9 8 7 8 6 5 4 3 2 1

Printed in the United States of America
Distributed by W. W. Norton & Company, Inc.

'There's the scarlet thread of murder running
through the colourless skein of life,
and our duty is to unravel it, and isolate,
and expose every inch of it.'

Sherlock Holmes

Contents

Introduction

'It is Sunday afternoon, preferably before the war ... You put your feet up on the sofa, settle your spectacles on your nose, and open *The News of the World*. A cup of mahogany-brown tea has put you just in the right mood. The sofa cushions are soft, the fire is well alight, the air is warm and stagnant. In these blissful circumstances, what is it you want to read about? Naturally, about a murder.'

George Orwell, 'Decline of the English Murder' (1946)

In his essay 'Decline of the English Murder', George Orwell describes for us the most satisfying kind of killer. Ideally, he's a solicitor or doctor. He's chairman of the local Conservative Party, or maybe a campaigner against the demon drink. He commits his crime out of passion for his secretary, but he's really driven by fear of public shame: it's easier for him to poison his wife than to go through the public scandal of divorcing her. The archetypal murderer, in Orwell's mind, was a devious but apparently quiet and respectable little man, rather like Dr Crippen.

But it wasn't ever thus. Around 1800, people asked to imagine a murderer would have come up with a much more heroic figure: a gallant highwayman, or perhaps a charismatic career criminal who repents on the gallows. They might even have laid eyes upon him themselves, at one of the many crowded and carnivalesque public hangings. And today, by contrast, our scariest and most enjoyable fictional murderers are much less cosy than Orwell's. They are psychopathic serial killers, nihilistic, motiveless and utterly terrifying.

This isn't really a book about real-life murderers, or the history of crime – although that's certainly part of the story. Instead, it's an exploration of how the British *enjoyed* and *consumed* the idea of murder, a phenomenon that dates from the beginning of the nineteenth century and continues to the present day.

Perhaps appropriately, then, our two bookends will be writers. We'll start in the late Georgian age, with Thomas De Quincey and his essay 'On Murder Considered as one of the Fine Arts'. De Quincey was inspired by the so-called Ratcliffe Highway Murders of 1811, a multiple killing that saw the beginning of the gruesome correlation between lurid reporting of a crime and a massive spike in the sales of newspapers. We'll end at the Second World War, and Orwell's essay, in which he laments the declining 'quality' of British murders and the rise of a different, more violent, less well-mannered, American-style criminal. Both writers, of course, were satirizing the business of enjoying a murder. And a large-scale, profitable and commercial business it was, too.

As the Victorian age wore on, biographies of murderers were among its publishing sensations. In 1849, as many as two and a half million people bought a rather rushed effort purporting to be the 'authentic memoirs' of Maria Manning, the 'Lady Macbeth of Bermondsey', who had helped to kill her lover and bury him under her kitchen floor. In the middle of a cholera epidemic, Manning's story dominated the news. Her execution was attended by thousands, including Charles Dickens, who found it horrific but nevertheless used Maria as a model for his murderess in *Bleak House*.

Maria Manning's execution was one of the last female hangings to take place in public. But even after this date you could still meet murderers face-to-face in the pseudo-scientific 'Chamber of Comparative Physiognomy', otherwise known as the 'Chamber of Horrors', at Madame Tussaud's gallery. Or else you could watch them re-enacting their crimes in street performances, on the London stage or in puppet theatres. Or you could even buy the merchandising, which included – a particular favourite of mine – ceramic ornaments depicting the houses where notable murders had taken place.

While researching this book, I was also making a television series on the same subject and I particularly enjoyed filming the strange and varied artefacts spewed out by a consumer society's response to murder. I was ghoulishly pleased to handle the scales used by Thomas De Quincey to measure out the drug to which he was addicted. I myself re-murdered Maria Marten, the Suffolk mole-catcher's daughter buried in a barn in 1828, by operating the Victoria and Albert Museum's nineteenth-century puppets representing Maria and her killer, William Corder. It was gruesomely thrilling to handle Corder's actual scalp, complete with shrivelled ear. It's on display to the public, as it has been ever since his death, and can be seen in a museum in Bury St Edmunds. It was marvellously horrid to be in the Chamber of Horrors after hours, and to see the wax figure of Dr Crippen released from his cell, and to look straight into his eyes. Such experiences, mixing horror and fun, were genuinely unsettling and genuinely pleasurable.

The murderer's rise to prominence in popular culture and fiction was mirrored, of course, by the rise of the detective. He – and eventually she – was greeted with suspicion and the feeling that it was distinctly un-British to 'spy' on members of the public. Eventually, society grew to rely upon and to respect the professional crime-solver, but the amateur remained more popular in fiction. I especially like girl detectives, having grown up believing that I was Harriet Vane from the Lord Peter Wimsey mysteries reborn. Employing a female sleuth in a novel allowed authors to send feminine characters bursting out of the usual restrictions of class and home. They could follow suspects, wear disguises, spy on other people and use their intelligence to right wrongs. Even the female criminals of the Victorian age, both in fact and fiction, give voice to passions and complaints not usually heard or expressed by women in society.

Now it's pretty obvious that the 'art' of murder – its depiction in theatre, songs, stories, novels or newspapers – reflects society's darkest fears back at itself. The Ratcliffe Highway Murders at the start of our period chimed with fears about the newly expanding city, 'stranger danger' and urban predators in ill-lit streets. But murder becomes more middle class as the nineteenth century matures. New types of poison (and new developments such as life insurance) provided novel means (and motives) for crime. We think of Sherlock Holmes as living in a world of gas lighting and hansom cabs and opium dens, yet actually many of his cases take him to places like Leatherhead, Esher or Oxshott, and houses with names like 'Wisteria Lodge', 'Chiltern Grange' or 'The Myrtles'. To solve these affairs Holmes leaves Baker Street and London behind, travelling out to the Home Counties on the train.

In the earlier nineteenth century, middle-class murderers could count on the deference that the authorities paid to their very station in society to protect them from the law. The later Victorian period saw more and more middle-class murderers, and murderesses, being caught. And eventually they would find themselves – their concern for respectability and appearances – recreated in the works of Agatha Christie, Dorothy L. Sayers, Margery Allingham, Ngaio Marsh and the other great crime writers of the early twentieth century.

Their world was rural and well ordered, with country houses and cottages alike inhabited by readers of the *Daily Mail*. Into its confines, the writers of the detective novel's golden age sowed the seeds of passion and violence. But in their tens of thousands of light novels, a detective character entered the scene, cleared away the body, solved the crime, punished the wicked and neatly tidied up all the loose ends. In the years following the First World War, people wanted leisure reading to numb, not to stimulate, their capacity for experiencing horror.

However, by 1939 something had come to seem a little too cosy about elderly ladies solving puzzles in vicarages. Graham Greene, with his insights into the mind of a killer, and James Bond, the swaggering spy, made them seem completely old hat. The old-fashioned detective may dodder on in fiction today, but since the Second World War he or she has been eclipsed by nastier, more violent colleagues in the thriller section.

Today, one in every three books sold is a crime novel, but many people look down on them as trash, often containing a crude, indeed simplistic, message that good shall triumph over evil. But crime fiction was the relatively unsophisticated genre which taught working-class people how to enjoy reading. And despite its lack of artistic merit, the literature of murder tells us not what people thought they ought to read. It tells us what they *really read*.

It was the very essence of a guilty pleasure. In the pre-war, prelapsarian words of Dorothy L. Sayers: 'Death seems to provide the minds of the Anglo-Saxon race with a greater fund of innocent amusement than any other subject.' Sitting down after a hard day's work, slippers on, guard lowered ... for the last 200 years murder has been the topic to which readers turn for comfort and relaxation.

Let's find out why.

Part One

How to Enjoy
a Murder

1

A Connoisseur in Murder

'I was buried, for a thousand years, in stone coffins, with mummies and sphynxes, in narrow chambers at the heart of eternal pyramids. I was kissed, with cancerous kisses, by crocodiles; and laid, confounded with all unutterable slimy things, amongst reed and Nilotic mud.'

Thomas De Quincey,
Confessions of an English Opium-Eater *(1821)*

During a trip to London in 1804, a student from Oxford's Worcester College began to experience 'rheumatic' pains in his head. They were caused, he believed, by having gone to bed with wet hair. He suffered from an 'excruciating' pain for about 20 days in a row, until by chance he 'met a college acquaintance, who recommended opium'.

Thomas De Quincey remembered with immense clarity for the rest of his life the mundane events of a damp weekend that followed this chance encounter. Although he would only realize it later, this illness, this meeting and this commonplace conversation formed a major turning point upon his life's journey.

> It was a Sunday afternoon, wet and cheerless ... my road homewards lay through Oxford Street; and near 'the stately Pantheon' (as Mr Wordsworth has obligingly called it) I saw a druggist's shop. The druggist – unconscious minister of celestial pleasures! – as if in sympathy with the rainy Sunday, looked dull and stupid, just as any mortal druggist might be expected to look on a Sunday; and when I asked for tincture of opium, he gave it to me just as any other man might do, and furthermore, out of my shilling returned to me what seemed to be real copper halfpence, taken out of a real wooden drawer.

Like so many of his contemporaries, De Quincey greatly admired the poet William Wordsworth, whose description he quotes of the famous Oxford Street assembly rooms called 'The Pantheon'. Few, at the date of his first taste of opium, knew that Thomas De Quincey also had literary ambitions of his own.

As the months passed, the student found himself making further sorties to the big city as a break from his studies, and for a little recreational drug use. His explorations of London's streets, and his trips to the opera, were made stranger and more appealing by doses of the drug available with such ease at any druggist's counter. He found himself traversing immense distances, for 'an opium-eater is too happy to observe the motions of time'. Inevitably, he got lost, but it seemed amusing rather than tedious. In these enjoyable, early days as an opium-eater, he was still in control. 'I used to fix beforehand how often within a given time, and when, I would commit a debauch of opium. This was seldom more than once in three weeks, for at that time I could not have ventured to call every day, as I did afterwards, for *"a glass of laudanum negus, warm, and without sugar".*'

Laudanum was the liquid form of the drug, dissolved in alcohol, often consumed in warmed wine, and, like the pills De Quincey obtained from the druggist, there was nothing shameful or unusual about the sight or use of it in late Georgian London.

Readily available medicines such as 'Mother Bailey's Quieting Syrup', or 'Godfrey's Cordial', or 'Kendal Black Drop' sound beneficent, even health-giving, and yet the ingredient upon which they relied was poppy-based. Mrs Beeton recommended that the wise housewife keep a good stock of opium in her cupboard. De Quincey's fellow users of opiates included the ultra-respectable and the creative: Florence Nightingale, Jane Morris and Elizabeth Barrett Browning. He himself listed the opium-eaters he knew as including 'the eloquent and benevolent —, the late Dean of —, Lord —, Mr. — the philosopher, a late Under-Secretary of State … and many others hardly less known, whom it would be tedious to mention'.

And opium-eating was not limited to high society. De Quincey claimed that in Manchester, the city of his birth, 'workpeople were rapidly getting into the practice of opium-eating; so much so, that on a Saturday afternoon the counters of the druggists were strewed with pills of one, two, or three grains, in preparation for the known demand of the evening'.

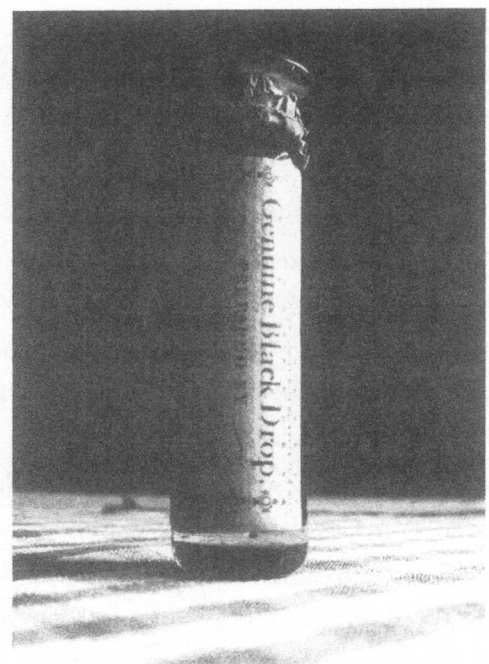

A bottle of 'Kendal Black Drop', a popular
brand of tincture of opium, readily available
at late Georgian chemists' shops.

Opium was cheap, and it was everywhere.

As his larking about in London suggests, Thomas De Quincey
was not a particularly conventional or diligent student. He'd
experienced a period of homelessness before arriving in Oxford. In
a fit of alienation, he'd left home, embarked upon a walking tour of
Wales, spent all his money and got into debt by borrowing against
the expectations he had of a legacy. Estranged from his family, he
ended up living in an empty house in Greek Street, Soho, comforted
only by a prostitute named 'Anne of Oxford-street'.

But De Quincey had immense talent as a writer. After writing fan mail to William Wordsworth, he struck up an epistolary friendship with the writer whose *Lyrical Ballads* (assembled with Samuel Taylor Coleridge, and with some involvement from his sister Dorothy) had become the centrepiece of the Romantic movement.

When he reached the end of his Oxford career, De Quincey performed brilliantly in the first day of his examinations but lost his nerve and failed to show up on the second. Soon afterwards, he departed for the north, to live in the Lake District at what is today called Dove Cottage, a house upon Grasmere formerly rented by his hero Wordsworth.

De Quincey lent money, when he had it, to his new friends in Grasmere. But then he fell into a deep depression after the death of Wordsworth's daughter Catherine, to whom he had become close, and 'often passed the night upon [her] grave'. His use of opium, which at first had been merely an occasional dip into an 'abyss of divine enjoyment', now became a daily necessity. The collection at Dove Cottage still contains a set of delicate nineteenth-century Chinese scales made out of bone, for weighing out opium in powdered form. It's usually very hard to say with certainty to whom such utilitarian items from the past might have belonged, but the wooden case in which these particular scales live is carved with a clear – and rather convincing – 'TQ'. And he must have had frequent need of them. Two hundred and fifty miles distant from London, he described his life as being: 'Buried in the depth of mountains. And what am I doing among the mountains? Taking opium.'

As well as taking opium, he was reading Kant, studying German metaphysics and living on what his fellow gentlemen would have called his 'private fortune'. He spent a good deal on expensive books as well as drugs. One visitor described his rather chaotic living arrangements, which contained 'a German ocean of literature, in a storm, flooding all over the floor, the tables, and the chairs – billows of books'.

But De Quincey's inherited income was too inadequate to fulfil his needs. Financial necessity compelled him to leave behind his indolent ways and start to write essays for periodicals. He found it hard work. 'He has always told me,' wrote his editor, 'that he composes *very slowly*, that his language costs him a great deal of attention.' De Quincey had to persevere, though, for as time went by he acquired further financial obligations in the form of numerous children. He married a farmer's daughter, after having a child with her out of wedlock, and together they would go on to produce eight more offspring.

In 1821, with creditors snapping at his heels, he finally produced the piece of writing for which he is best known. *Confessions of an English Opium-Eater* outlines the bizarre oriental fantasies he had at first enjoyed under the influence of the drug. It made his name almost instantly. The fabulously creative visions he described, combined with the horrific squalor of his addiction itself, were equally shocking and attractive.

Thomas De Quincey's reputation would wane in the twentieth century, as his florid, luscious word games were seen as overblown. With the growth of counter-culture in the 1960s, however, he became celebrated once more as a visionary and an example of a creative drug-user. Those seeking validation for the powers of narcotics point to the fact that De Quincey's best writing is inspired by opium, and that his productivity rose and fell alongside his consumption.

On the other hand, De Quincey himself wrote his *Confessions* explicitly to warn others of the dangers of addiction, and to share the pain of his weaning himself off his dependency. He was not entirely successful in the former. The glamorous example he set seduced, among others, the Brontë sisters' disappointing brother, Branwell, into similar debauchery – without, however, similar achievements. *The Family Oracle of Health*, published in 1824, censoriously noted how:

> the use of opium has been recently much increased by a wild, absurd and romancing production, called *The Confessions of an English Opium-Eater*. We observe, that at some late inquests this wicked book has been severely censured, as the source of misery and torment, and even of suicide itself, to those who have been seduced to take opium by its lying stories about celestial dreams, and similar nonsense.

And De Quincey's own troubles were not eased by his notoriety. People jealous of his success publicized the fact that he had fathered an illegitimate child. His family were evicted from their house for unpaid rent and his wife was threatening to commit suicide. De Quincey was failing to meet the demand for his articles from the editors of *The London Magazine*. Desperate for money, he roused himself to produce some essays for *Blackwood's Magazine*. Among them was a playful, creative, coolly humorous piece called 'On Murder Considered as One of the Fine Arts'.

De Quincey's essay on murder, a 'complex exercise in sinister irony' as his biographer Grevel Lindop calls it, was published in February 1827. The essay purports to have been written by a member of an imaginary new London club, 'The Society of Connoisseurs in Murder', a group who 'profess to be curious in homicide, amateurs and dilettanti in the various modes of carnage, and, in short, Murder-Fanciers'. At their meetings, the members of this club discuss and assess the work of various murderers: 'every fresh atrocity of that class which the police annals of Europe bring up, they meet and criticize as they would a picture, statue, or other work of art'.

The members of the society, like De Quincey himself, were what we might today call achingly cool hipsters. They were well aware that modern times demanded a new level of knowingness and sophistication – in crime, as in everything else. 'In this age,' declaimed one of the club's supposed speakers, 'when masterpieces of excellence have been executed by professional men, it must be evident that in the style of criticism applied to them the public will look for something of a corresponding improvement.'

De Quincey begins his essay by describing a mishap that was universally judged by the connoisseurs to be an unfortunate event of disappointingly poor quality, because in it no one had even died.

A fire had broken out in a piano-maker's workshop, once again in Oxford Street, and close to the home of Mr Coleridge where the author had been attending a party. (This was an in-joke: De Quincey was friends with his fellow opium addict, William Coleridge.) The poet's guests had left off drinking tea to go and look at the fire, but De Quincey (or at least the voice narrating his essay) had been forced, by another engagement, to leave before it had been extinguished. A few days later, he asked his friend Coleridge for a verdict on the entertainment the fire had provided. 'Oh Sir,' said he, 'it turned out so ill, that we damned it unanimously.'

The fire engines had arrived in good time; there were no deaths; the only loser had been the insurance company. De Quincey takes pains to point out that Coleridge was not an evil or unpleasant person: like others of his time, he had simply assumed the right 'to make a luxury of the fire, and to hiss it, as he would any other performance that raised expectations in the public mind'.

And here De Quincey reveals the central phenomenon of his essay (and this book) – murder as a 'performance that raised expectations in the public mind'. The idea that crime, particularly murder, provided *entertainment* was only born in the first decades of the nineteenth century, but it would bloom into one of the greatest mass-market interests of all time.

The 'art of murder' would give rise to sensational journalism, plays, murder-site tourism and memorabilia and the whole body of detective fiction. Its development went hand in hand with 'civilization', gas-lighting, industrialization, life in the city: everything that allowed people to feel safe from nature and its dangers. Barricaded behind locked doors, sitting by the fire, curtains closed, people living in the late Georgian age started almost to miss the violence and death that had once been all too much part of daily life, but which could now, mercifully, be recast in the category of entertainment.

In due course murder would thrill and horrify and delight millions of peaceful people who really, like Coleridge in De Quincey's essay, should have known better. In the words of the satirical magazine

Punch, a truly thrilling novel was written with the intention of 'Harrowing the Mind, making the Flesh Creep, Causing the Hair to Stand on end, Giving Shocks to the Nervous System ... and generally Unfitting the Public for the Prosaic Avocations of Life'.

The idea that murder and pleasure are intertwined – horribly, yet inescapably – has become an important part of modern life. It was a drug-addled, indebted, unreliable dropout who first revealed this to us. But sometimes, of course, it is the outsider – in his own words, 'he came to be looked upon as a strange being who associated with no one' – who can see society most clearly. Thomas De Quincey had put his finger upon an entirely new type of behaviour and skewered it to the page, and, in satirizing it, completely condemned it. Despite appearances, his essay was written entirely against the new practice of 'consuming' crime, as if indeed it were one of the fine arts.

It also identified the exact point at which so much began to change: the horrific events of 1811 known as the Ratcliffe Highway Murders.

2

———◦◉◦———

The Highway

'Murder! Murder! Come and see what murder is here!'
The Marrs' neighbour discovers their bodies (8 December 1811)

Until the end of the eighteenth century, people's attitudes towards murder had been very different. Of course, the crime of killing had existed. But Judith Flanders writes that in the year 1810, out of a population of nearly ten million Britons, only 15 people were convicted of murder. No wonder, for there were no police or detectives in the sense that we know today. But there was indeed a proto-police force based in Wapping, east London, that became involved in the very first 'notorious' or 'horrid' murders. The 'Ratcliffe Highway Murders' were hailed by De Quincey in his essay as 'the sublimest and most entire in their excellence that ever were committed'.

Today, the Highway, as the Ratcliffe Highway is now known, roars with traffic coming into the City from Docklands. One January dusk, after my day's work at the Tower of London, I set off further east, into Wapping, to find the site of the house where

Timothy and Celia Marr, their baby son and their young apprentice boy were killed in 1811.

This was the year in which the Prince of Wales, the future George IV, was appointed Prince Regent, as it had become clear that his father, George III, had descended into debilitating 'madness' and senility. Slaves were revolting in the southern states of America, the British were fighting Napoleon's forces in Spain and closer to home the hand-loom weavers known as the Luddites, deprived of their livelihood by the coming of machines, were using violent protest in the Midlands. It was a time of great upheaval and uncertainty.

Wapping was a busy if impoverished maze of crowded tenements housing the people who serviced the nearby docks. Sailors, boat-builders, victuallers and those aspiring to join those trades all settled here. It was notably rough. The 'Marine' or 'Thames River Police', an early, independent force of professional, paid policemen, was established here in 1798 specifically to deal with the problem of theft from the ships in the Pool of London. They travelled up and down the river in small boats, armed with cutlasses and heavy wooden guns. One of the sights of Wapping was 'Execution Dock', where pirates met their very public end on a gibbet.

Little trace now remains of the area's infrastructure after its bombing in the Second World War, but the dim warehouses lining the alley called Breezer's Hill, now converted into flats, are still topped by winches. The naval character of the area is recorded in street signs for 'Tobacco Dock', 'Rum Close' and 'Cinnamon Street'. According to De Quincey's anonymous (and admittedly unreliable) narrator in the essay 'On Murder', in Regency Wapping 'every third man at the least might be set down as a foreigner. Lascars, Chinese, Moors, Negroes were to be met at every step.' In addition to all these supposedly dodgy foreigners, the settlement was 'the sure receptacle of all the murderers and ruffians whose crimes have given them a motive for withdrawing themselves for a season from the public eye'.

Because of the nature of my mission, and the growing darkness, Wapping seems to me, as I walk east, still to maintain an atmosphere of menace. Along the Highway, I pass Secrets table dancing club, high brick walls topped with spiked metal defences and a huge glowing billboard for a new television drama promising 'A Dark Future'. When I pull out my map to check if I am near the site of No. 29, the home of the Marr family, it is bathed red in the light from a sign in the window of Machine Mart. I am disturbed by a woman with a buggy who bumps into me from behind while coming out of the 24-hour McDonald's attached to the neighbouring petrol station. My map reveals that I am in exactly the right place.

My jumpy journey to Wapping was made in the spirit of murder connoisseurship that Thomas De Quincey identified and condemned, but I find my nerve and sense of irony failing me as I peer down dark, deserted cobbled streets. Wapping is not a dangerous area now. It's known for newspaper production, 1980s yuppie housing and for having a big Waitrose. But the thought of gruesome murder still makes it seem so.

The first of the Ratcliffe Highway Murders took place late at night on 7 December 1811. At the time, the story of the murders was seen to end with a completely satisfactory conclusion, the death of the supposed killer, John Williams. Williams had been arrested later that month and hanged himself in his prison cell three days after Christmas. The Marine Police, the local constables and watchmen and the authorities in general heaved a huge sigh of relief at his decease. It would appear that the murderer had been caught, that peace could return to the streets and that justice could be 'seen' to be done.

A huge procession was mounted to show Williams's dead body to the people of Wapping. On New Year's Eve, his body was taken for burial. A huge crowd, said to number 180,000 people, lined Ratcliffe Highway to watch the cart pass. Contemporary prints show the dead body mounted on the back of a cart, surrounded by watchmen armed with staves, watched by seas of faces on the pavements and crowded into the windows of houses. On the cart with Williams's body were displayed his presumed murder weapons: a chisel, a crowbar and the tool used by ships' carpenters known as a 'pen maul'.

The procession stopped for 15 minutes outside No. 29, the house where the Marrs died. Now a member of the crowd climbed up on to the cart and forcibly turned the dead man's head to look at the home of 'his' victims, confronting him with what he had done. He was eventually taken to a crossroads, the conventional burying place for a suicide. At the junction of the new Commercial Road and Cannon Street, his body was 'tumbled out of the cart', lowered into a grave and 'someone hammered a stake through his heart'.

This last action was to ensure that an unquiet soul would not go wandering. The veracity of the report seemed to be confirmed in

1886, when gas pipes were being buried. At the same road junction, workmen digging a trench discovered a skeleton, buried at a depth of 6 feet, face down and with a stake through its heart.

But despite all this trouble, taken to bring a sense of closure to a troubled community, the startling thing about the Ratcliffe Highway Murders from today's vantage point is just how weak the case for Williams as the culprit seems to have been. Even the Prime Minister, Spencer Perceval, admitted that his guilt 'was still wrapped up in mystery. It undoubtedly seemed strange that a single individual could commit such accumulated violence.'

What was Williams said to have done, and what were the flaws in the evidence for his having done it?

———

Timothy Marr and his family lived above their shop at No. 29 on Ratcliffe Highway. It had a fine painted sign reading 'Marr's Silk, Mercery, Lace, Pelisse, Mantle & Furr Warehouse' above its shuttered bow window. Marr was a former seaman who had only recently, in his mid-twenties, set up in business as a draper. His 22-year-old wife, Celia, had given birth just 14 weeks earlier to a baby boy and had still not quite recovered her strength. Their young male apprentice was a mere 13. They also had a maid, Margaret. Just before midnight (Saturday nights, being payday, were busy in the shop), Timothy Marr directed Margaret 'to go out and purchase some oysters for the family supper'.

Far from being an expensive delicacy, oysters were still the ubiquitous cheap and cheerful street food of Regency London. But, this late at night, Margaret had trouble finding a shop that was still open. She also had to pay a bill at the baker's. When she got back, it seemed that everyone in the house had gone to sleep and she was locked out.

In his essay De Quincey now began to imagine the Gothic and horrific scene. Margaret (or Mary, as De Quincey called her) the maid, out on the midnight street, listened at the door, and heard ... something.

> What was it? On the stairs – not the stairs that led down to the kitchen, but the stairs that led upwards to the single storey of bedchambers above – was heard a creaking sound. Next was heard most distinctly a footfall: one, two, three, four, five stairs were slowly and distinctly descended. Then the dreadful footsteps were heard advancing along the little narrow passage to the door. The steps – oh heavens! whose steps? – have paused at the door. The very breathing can be heard ... there is but a door between him and Mary.

The scene could come from any thriller written between 1811 and 2011. The sense of 'stranger danger', of the murderer having mysteriously got *inside* a secure, workaday, domestic setting, and the defenceless young girl listening in silent terror to his approach are just as fresh and horrifying today as they were to De Quincey's readers.

Margaret banged on the door and the sound aroused the Marrs' neighbour, a pawnbroker. He climbed over the wall between his own and the Marrs' garden at the back, and found the shop's back door open wide. The murderer (or murderers) had fled, but they had left their mark. Inside the narrow passage was 'so floated with gore that it was hardly possible to escape the pollution of blood in picking out a path to the front-door'. Father, mother, apprentice and baby had all been slain. The murder weapon was apparently the bloodied ship's carpenter's hammer – the pen maul – which was discovered in the kitchen.

From this point on, though, events became confused and, ultimately, mishandled. The Thames Police were called in, but these official visitors were accompanied by a whole swarm of unofficial sightseers who wished to see the murdered bodies laid out dead upon their beds. The crime scene was thoroughly contaminated. What forensic and material evidence there was they were not skilled in reading: it took 12 days before anyone noticed that the maul in the kitchen was marked with the initials JP. The Thames Police also struggled to handle a crime which had had no witnesses. And when information arrived in response to a proffered reward, it came – all too neatly – from a woman whose husband was in the debtors' prison, and greatly in need of financial aid. She was the landlady of the nearby Pear Tree Tavern. She reported that she had a lodger named *John Petersen*, representing the initials found on the maul. Petersen was absent away at sea at the time of the murder, but he had left his tools behind him. However, John Williams, another of her lodgers, had had access to the tools, had mysteriously shaved himself clean the day after the crime and had been seen washing what were possibly bloodied stockings at the Pear Tree's pump.

But the information came too late to prevent John Williams – if indeed he was the criminal – from striking again. Twelve days after the first killing, at another public house on what is now Garnet Street, a further massacre took place. This quiet and respectable pub had closed at 11 p.m. Its landlord, John Williamson, his wife Elizabeth and their servant Bridget had all retired to bed. However, the street was disturbed when a near-naked man climbed out of an upstairs window via a knotted sheet.

This was Williamson's lodger, John Turner. He had been in bed when he'd heard the front door banging and the maid calling out. Next, he heard his landlord moaning, and emitting the chilling words: 'I am a dead man'. The lodger heard the sinister sound of somebody walking about below. Creeping down the stairs, Turner saw a tall man bent over the prone body of Mrs Williamson. The horrific sight caused him to rush back upstairs and escape through the window. Amazingly, the Williamsons' little granddaughter, Kitty, just 14 years old, slept through the whole attack and survived.

This second slaughter, so soon after, and so near to the scene of the first, caused a tsunami of terror and panic. Londoners began to feel a new kind of fear. Barricaded behind locks and shutters in their homes, they felt the very modern anxiety that even these defences might not prove stout enough against an urban, predatory killer who struck out at random against law-abiding families, entering homes without warning or mercy. In the country communities that many of them had left behind, one knew one's neighbours. Here in the docklands, with so many strangers about, and with dark, crowded, busy streets ill lit by night, a new kind of menace seemed to be abroad.

———

Given the circumstances, it seems natural that the authorities would want to wrap up the crime as quickly as they could. Indeed, in the opinion of the mistress of detective fiction, P. D.

James, they wrapped it up with unseemly haste, simply to placate public feeling. John Williams was taken into custody: after all, he'd had the opportunity of getting hold of the murder weapon used in the first crime and he had acted suspiciously the day after. There were also rumours that he and the first victim, Timothy Marr, had been former shipmates who had quarrelled. But these were very sketchy grounds. Fortunately for the magistrates, Williams appeared to admit his guilt: after a week in prison, he hanged himself.

The police were quick to announce that the killer had been caught. However, some people remained unsatisfied. There were rumours that Williams's death had not been caused by his own hand. He'd seemed to be in good spirits immediately before it. The death was all too convenient for the authorities and their desire to

The body of John Williams is paraded through the streets of Wapping on a cart before vast crowds. The maul, his supposed weapon, lies by his left shoulder.

reassure and restore order. It was to make a very clear statement that the panic was over that Williams's body was publically paraded as the culprit, clearly and obviously dead.

Yet questions about Williams's guilt, and the handling of the case, remained open and preyed upon the minds of the government. The capital's system of policing had been shown by the Ratcliffe Highway killings to be inadequate. There would not be an immediate, overnight change to the way things were done, but this crime did contribute to the slow but inexorable build-up of the case for a single, coordinated police force.

At the same time, Londoners and indeed the British as a whole lapped up the specifics of the case. It became so widely reported that it has claims to be called the first great modern mass-media sensation. The thirst for information about this particular crime created a new genre of journalism: murder reporting, with all its inaccuracies, gory details and outright condemnation of everyone and everything seeming to stand in the way of a speedy conclusion.

In De Quincey's hands, this very ordinary (and quite possibly unfairly accused) seaman was transformed into a suitably bizarre and charismatic figure. In a parody of the public's image of the killer, he described Williams as having a 'corpselike face', a 'sinister voice' and an oily and snaky demeanour. He had a bloodless ghastly pallor, hair of 'bright yellow, something between an orange and a lemon colour', and 'in his veins circulated not red life-blood, such as could kindle into the blush of shame, of wrath, of pity – but a green sap that welled from no human heart'.

He wore a fine coat of blue, 'richly lined with silk', and he was naturally so courteous that had he accidentally jostled anyone on the crowded streets on his way to commit the crime, he would certainly 'have stopped to offer the most gentlemanly apologies'. He bears little relationship to the person John Williams really was – a rough and ready tar of the docks. He sounds rather like Hannibal Lector.

From the few known facts of the case, combined with terror, speculation and imagination, the fully formed fictional murderer was born.

3

The Watchmen

'One of them would be writing novels, another studying
politics, a third immersed in divinity, a fourth speculating
on the girls that went by, a fifth gnawing his pen for an
unfinished couplet and a sixth playing the fiddle.'

The Examiner, *1811, reveals what London's magistrates were
really doing when they were meant to be catching criminals*

Where were the police?

While Margaret, the Marrs' maid, was knocking on the
door of No. 29, Ratcliffe Highway, the local nightwatchman
passed by. His name was George Olney, and every night, at half-
hour intervals, his beat took him past the Marrs' house. He helped
Margaret to bang on the door, and to rouse the neighbour who
eventually entered the house.

The first police officer to be summoned from the scene after the
discovery of the bodies was Charles Horton, who worked for the
Thames or Marine Police, the small, independent body responsible
for catching criminals in the docks and on the river. The force's

personnel records can still be seen at the Thames Police Museum in the police station at Wapping. They reveal that Horton joined up in 1806, and that he lodged with one Mrs Robinson, a baker. The register also shows that he was issued with a great coat – not really a uniform, but a useful garment for wearing on duty on the river – and he would also have been equipped with a cutlass for personal defence, and a set of handcuffs. (The early Thames Police were obviously not used to arresting many women, because my smallish hands could easily slip out of all the nineteenth-century cuffs I tried on in their museum.)

Horton's actions included taking the bloodied maul away, back to his office (but not examining it closely, otherwise he would have discovered the initials). The Thames Police then offered a reward for information regarding the crime. This was half successful: it did lead to John Williams being identified, but of course it's quite possible that the money itself motivated his impecunious landlady to shop him.

But this was the best that could be hoped for with the current state of policing. Smaller, earlier and simpler communities than Regency Wapping pretty much policed themselves. When a person was accused of a crime, his or her neighbours would appear before a magistrate to save or condemn, on the basis of his or her previous good (or bad) behaviour. An individual's reputation and standing in the community was therefore more important than evidence.

Each parish appointed a single unarmed 'constable' – literally a *comes stabuli*, a 'master of the horse' – who served for one year. His job was to make sure that order was observed on the streets. The office was an ancient one – the word first appears in 1252 – and he was one of four important parish officers, the others being the overseer of the poor, the surveyor of the highways and the warden of the church. His symbol of authority was his truncheon, often provided in a decorative form to act as a badge of office.

The constable usually worked with a group of specialists who looked after the streets after dark. Groups of citizens clubbed together to employ these 'nightwatchmen' to make regular patrols. Their regular calling out of the hour of the clock and a description of the weather punctuated the dreams of Georgian householders. These watchmen, carrying their dark lanterns, were often extremely old and not infrequently took money from criminals to turn a blind eye to their activities. In Covent Garden, central London, we hear that the appointment of aged watchmen was a deliberate practice: the employment of younger men had had to be abandoned 'on account of the connection which subsisted between them and the Prostitutes, who withdrew them from their Duty while Depredations were committing'. (At the same time, though, we should note that the tradition of laughing at the uselessness of nightwatchmen dates from Shakespeare's time – they provide interludes of light entertainment, for example, in *Macbeth*.)

This system began to break down all over Britain as the nation became urbanized. A network of neighbours, constables and nightwatchmen simply could not deal with more serious crimes such as significant thefts or murders. In the early eighteenth century, private individuals who'd been the victims of crime could seek redress by engaging the services of a 'thief-taker', an entrepreneurial individual who offered his services to track down criminals for a fee.

However, the problem with thief-takers was that they knew most of the criminals, and were far too friendly with some of them. Occasionally they would accept a higher counter-bribe *not* to turn a villain in. The most famous thief-taker of all was Jonathan Wild, who had started his London career as a racketeer and dealer in stolen goods. In 1713 he teamed up with an official parish constable in London, Charles Hitchen, and on their nightly 'Rambles' through the city, they extorted money from – rather than protecting – the general public.

Wild, however, managed to maintain an appearance of legitimacy. His house in the Little Old Bailey became, by 1714, 'an Office of Intelligence for lost Goods'. He was careful not to keep stolen property on his premises, but everyone knew that he could help you get back something that had been stolen. And so 'Mr. Jonathan Wild' became 'a considerable Figure in the World', promoting himself as 'Thief-catcher General of Great Britain'.

However, his double game was too tricky to last. His success roused the enmity of his former partner, and now rival, Hitchen. Using the very up-to-date Georgian medium of the published pamphlet, Hitchen accused Wild of high-handed, rough justice, turning in some criminals, protecting others, corrupting all. And so, in 1718, an Act was passed, thought to be aimed specifically at Wild, which explicitly made it a crime to bargain with criminals for the return of stolen goods.

Despite this, Wild remained in business for a good few more years. He was clearly performing a much-valued public service. He eventually fell from grace, though, after his treatment of Joseph 'Blueskin' Blake. This unsavoury character had been a criminal child whom Jonathan Wild had adopted (in the manner of a Fagin) to commit crimes on his behalf. Once 'Blueskin' was caught, however, Wild washed his hands of him. The enraged 'Blueskin' cut Wild's throat. Although Wild survived, people now turned against him. When charged with theft soon afterwards, he found he had lost his ability to talk his way out of trouble. He has hanged at Tyburn, the crowd pelting him with stones.

It was this unsatisfactory situation that caused the writer Henry Fielding to enter the fray. As well as a successful playwright and author of *Tom Jones*, Fielding had a strong social conscience and served as a magistrate. In 1751 he wrote his celebrated work of social science, *An Enquiry into the Causes of the Late Increase of Robbers*. He started keeping a 'Register of Robberies', containing intelligence about crimes committed along with suspicious persons and behaviour, and he encouraged members of the public to report in with information. It was the first time a magistrate had tried to pre-empt crime, rather than just reacting to its consequences after the event.

Fielding also recruited six parish constables to stay in service permanently, for a salary, rather than leaving their posts after the customary temporary term of office. These specially trained 'Bow Street Runners', as the public called them, are often hailed as marking the very beginning of a professional and paid police force. These six men, in blue coats, patrolling the area within six miles of Charing Cross, became a familiar sight on the streets of London.

But they were soon competing with numerous other proto-police forces run by individual parishes. Judith Flanders calculates that in 1790 there were no fewer than a thousand parish watchmen and constables, employed by 70 different bodies. The Thames or Marine Police Force, founded in 1798, was therefore only one of very many. Henry Fielding's work was continued after his death by his blind half-brother, Sir John Fielding, who put his finger on a new problem: competition or non-cooperation between them. 'The Frontiers of each Parish,' he said, were 'in a confused State, for that where one side of a street lies in one Parish, the Watchmen of one Side cannot lend any Assistance to a person on the other side.'

The Ratcliffe Highway Murders definitively showed that this method of policing was inadequate. The reaction of those responsible for law and order in Wapping was confused and incoherent. The head of the Thames Police, John Harriott, had quickly issued handbills promising £20 for information on three men seen loitering outside the Marrs' on the night of the murder. Yet he was castigated by the Home Office for this commendable initiative, and was accused of overreaching his powers. Meanwhile, the magistrates of Shadwell, who were appointed by the Home Secretary, and therefore more 'official' than the Thames Police, offered £50 of their own for the 'discovery and apprehension' of the perpetrator. And, yet again, the Coroner, John Unwin, began to investigate the case by holding an inquest at the Jolly Sailor public house.

Questions were soon raised in Parliament. Why had the Shadwell magistrates overlooked so many clues? Was there any reason beyond xenophobia why so many Irish people had been arrested on suspicion of the murders? Why had Williams been left alone and unsupervised in his cell? The answers were not easy to find. As Spencer Perceval himself said, 'no state of nightly watch, however excellent, could have prevented such a crime. Indeed he hardly knew in what system of police a prevention could have been found.' (Perceval would not live long enough to see what the answer turned out to be. Only five months after the murders, in May 1812, he was assassinated in the lobby of the House of Commons, by a lone gunman with a grudge against the government.)

In the opinion of P. D. James and T. A. Critchley, co-authors of a book on the Ratcliffe Highway Murders published in 1971, a vigorous Home Secretary might have pushed through legislation to create a central police force in the months following the crime. But the Home Secretary was lethargic and unengaged, and faced the widespread attitude that an official police force was only suitable for foreign countries where the people didn't trust each other. Authoritarian governments abroad used their police services to oppress their people. Freeborn Englishmen, people said, would not stand for such an infringement of their native liberty: 'They have an admirable police in Paris, but they pay for it dear enough. I had rather half-a-dozen throats should be cut in Ratcliffe Highway every three or four years than be subject to domiciliary visits, spies and all the rest of [the French police's] contrivances.'

Proposals for a single police force constantly ran up against this belief that the strong arm of the law was as much a curse as a blessing. The state, of course, played a much smaller role in British society than it does today: compulsory schooling only arrived in 1880, old-age pensions had to wait until 1909 and the National Health Service until 1948.

And yet, 18 years later, Parliament finally managed to agree on the solution to London's policing problem: a single central coordinating body to deal with crime throughout the city, to be paid for out of taxes. In 1829, Parliament passed 'an Act for improving the Police in and near the Metropolis', and the job of setting up the new police force was given to the Home Secretary, Sir Robert Peel, who had already reformed the police in Ireland. When, in 1829, the new force was set up, it contained over one thousand men, who became known as 'Peelers'.

The creation of this new force is often seen as a sharp turning point, and yet conscientious historians are at pains to point out that 'before' and 'after' weren't so very different. Some of the same people and practices, and indeed terminology ('constables') continued, and the new force would never have jurisdiction over the powerful City of London, which was protective of its privileges. (Peel was wise in thinking this a battle not worth fighting, and, to this day, the City still has its own separate police force.) Indeed, as far as the statistics can tell us, crime was actually falling, and the perceived need for the police arose just as much from the increased *fear* of crime as its reality. The creation of a police force was part of a wider movement to make cities clean and tidy and orderly. People's all-important *perception* that their streets were safe would be aided by the removal of beggars, the repair of the roads and the abolition of rowdy fairs, as much as the catching of murderers.

But however much historians stress continuity as well as change, the creation of the Metropolitan Police Force was a significant development, and went almost hand in hand with the emergence of the middle class. Terms such as 'working class' and 'middle class' are notoriously slippery, but the Great Reform Act of 1832 did create a new division between the group of people who had formerly all been lumped together as 'the lower classes'.

In 1832, the pool of people allowed to vote in elections was extended from roughly 400,000 to 650,000. Some of the previous system's well-known anomalies – like the so-called 'rotten boroughs' where Members of Parliament were returned by only a handful of voters – were obliterated. Votes were now given to all male property-owners of a certain level of wealth: they had to own land worth £10. Now master craftsmen and successful shopkeepers were voters, with a stake in the status quo. Those just a little bit less wealthy, such as skilled tradesmen, remained outside the political class, and some instead turned to radicalism. There would now be new levels of confrontation between these two classes, with the police on the side of their new friends, the middle class.

Robert Peel's coordinated force was also strikingly different from its ragtag predecessors. It was headed by two 'commissioners', beneath whom – according to a letter of Peel's dated 20 July 1829 – were a Chief Clerk, a Second Clerk and a Third Clerk. The Receiver's office (the head financial post) also had a couple of clerks. Then there were to be 8 superintendents, 88 serjeants and 895 constables.

Most importantly, the efforts of all the policemen in London were now to be coordinated. Runners would travel regularly from station to station, sharing information, and the old *Hue and Cry*, a newsletter about crime, was replaced by the much fuller *Police Gazette* with up-to-date news about suspects. Daily orders for all constables were issued right from the top of the whole organization.

Half of the new 'Peelers' patrolled at night, the other half during the day, and they walked the streets at a steady two and a half miles an hour. Forbidden to sit down anywhere while on duty, they wore a long blue coat with eight buttons and tails. The colour of the coats was important: blue was chosen, not red, in order to distinguish them from soldiers. Nobody in Britain wanted the army on the streets. This was especially true after the horrific Peterloo Massacre of 1819, in which soldiers and hussars reacted in a heavy-handed manner to a peaceful crowd of protestors, slaughtering 11 people and wounding many more.

Around their necks the 'Peelers' wore leather collars to protect them against garrotters. The collars of their coats bore their official number, and, even today, when a police officer's number appears on the shoulder epaulettes of his or her uniform, it's still called a 'collar number'. They wore white trousers of their own purchase – these were not officially part of the uniform – and on their heads they wore six-inch-tall, wide-brimmed top hats: again, to make them look more like civilians, less like soldiers. Their noisy rattles, rather like those once waved by football fans, were intended to make a racket and summon aid when necessary, but were later replaced by the more effective whistle.

Economic security seems to have been the major motivator for constables to sign up. But, even so, the 3rd Class Constables considered themselves to be poorly paid on 16s. 8d. a week. In 1848, a group of ten of them signed a letter complaining about this to their superiors. 'Most of the married men on joining,' they said, 'are somewhat in debt, and are unable to extricate themselves on account of rent to pay and articles to buy which are necessary for support of wife and children.' Over time, though, the police became seen as a stable and increasingly attractive career for people who had been labourers or workers in other trades. Police recruiters could afford to become more selective, and the original requirement that a candidate be at least 5 ft 7 in. tall was raised to 5 ft 9 in.

Of course change and novelty were not always welcomed by the general public, who resented the cost of the new police force and missed their familiar and friendly – if often corrupt – old nightwatchmen. The new 'Peelers' were ordered to be 'civil and obliging' to the public, yet found themselves being insulted in return: popular names for them included 'Raw Lobsters', 'Blue Devils' and 'Peel's Bloody Gang'. This was partly because policemen were obliged to wear their uniforms even when off duty – such was the fear of the infiltration of civil society by 'spies'.

But six years after the founding of the 'Peelers', it was clear that the idea of a single force to serve an entire city was here to stay. The rest of the country followed London's example. The Metropolitan Police Force, the name by which the 'Peelers' were now officially known, was replicated in towns throughout Britain.

However, there was still one piece of the puzzle missing. The original 'Peelers' were concerned only with the prevention of crimes, not their resolution. Not until 1842 was a department of the Metropolitan Police created with the express purpose of *solving* crimes. The Detective Branch, as it was called, originally consisted of just two inspectors, six sergeants and a few constables. Dressed in plain clothes, their existence only became possible once society had got used to, and had started to trust, their uniformed colleagues.

It would take even longer for people to get used to the detectives.

4

The Murder Circuit

'A tragic scene here is display'd
Most frightening to behold
Your hearts will ache, as it will make
Your very blood run cold.'

Verse from a broadside (1855)

To modern eyes, one of the more distasteful aspects of the Ratcliffe Highway Murder was the way that hundreds of people traipsed through the Marrs' house in the days following the crime. They came in order to ogle at the dead bodies of the victims, laid out upon their beds, and they came in huge numbers. *The Times* reported: 'The sensation excited by these most ferocious murders has become so general, and the curiosity to see the place where they were committed so intense, that Ratcliffe Highway was rendered almost impassable by the throng of spectators.'

There were two good reasons why this ghoulish practice was much more acceptable then than now. Firstly, both birth and death were much more part of normal domestic life. Today both processes have been medicalized, and very often shuffled off into a hospital rather than a person's home. Regency people were much more used to relatives dying at home in their own beds, and most women gave birth at home. The laying-out of a corpse in the front room, so that friends and neighbours could come to pay their respects, was normal practice. There was also a strong Irish presence in east London, and the idea of the 'wake' – visiting the home of a dead person in order to see them in their coffin, and contributing money so that the family could hold a gathering with drinking and partying – even now lingers on in Ireland after being forgotten on this side of the sea.

Secondly, justice itself, as we have seen, was still a matter for the community, not for professionals. It was important that any available data could be seen and shared by as many people as possible. This is why the inquest was held at the Jolly Sailor public house, close to the Marrs' house, and why the 12 members of the jury appointed to determine the cause of death were invited to tour the house themselves before they heard anyone's evidence. (They emerged visibly shaken.) The murder of the Marrs was significant precisely because it revealed the limits of this method of solving crimes. This time, hearsay, knowledge of the characters of one's neighbours, and eyewitness reports of what had happened would prove to be inadequate.

That said, many of those visiting the Marrs' house must have also been motivated by a third factor: morbid, salacious curiosity. This wasn't an entirely novel development. After all, even Georgian ladies and gentlemen were used to drawing amusement from grotesque and horrific sights. These included London's 'Bedlam', or Bethlem, or Bethlehem Hospital, an institution constructed in Moor Fields in the 1670s for people suffering from mental illnesses. The governors of the hospital allowed – even encouraged – such visits, because the money paid for entry contributed to the hospital's coffers. A French visitor described the experience, in 1725, of touring the cells, which were:

> reserved for dangerous maniacs, most of them being chained and terrible to behold. On holidays numerous persons of both sexes, but belonging generally to the lower class, visit this hospital and amuse themselves watching these unfortunate wretches, who often give them cause for laughter. On leaving this melancholy abode, you are expected by the porter to give him a penny.

The governors really wanted to attract rich, well-born visitors, potential future patrons of the charity, but for everyone who came the appeal was a mix of entertainment and compassion. The two could be experienced at the same time. A later tourist, the poet William Cowper, wrote that, as well as feeling pity, he too had *enjoyed* visiting the mad:

> I was not altogether insensible of the misery of the poor captives, nor destitute of feeling for them. But the Madness of some of them had such a humorous air, and displayed itself in so many whimsical freaks, that it was impossible not to be entertained, at the same time I was angry with myself for being so.

These feelings – horror, awe, a sense of danger viewed from safety – would come to the fore in the art and literature of the Romantic movement, with its exultation of the sublime, the untamed and the dangerous. They would also become necessary parts of the experience of enjoying a murder.

By the nineteenth century, the upper and middle classes did not need to visit a madhouse to find a thrill: they could simply pick up novels like Mary Shelley's *Frankenstein* (1818) ('If you refuse, I will glut the maw of death, until it be satiated with the blood of your remaining friends'). But their non-literate, working-class contemporaries could experience something of the same from visiting the scene of a crime.

———

In 1823, the year that the second edition of *Frankenstein* came out, the so-called 'Elstree Murder' was committed by boxing promoter, insurance fraudster, gambler and rather incompetent murderer, John Thurtell. His victim was a fellow member of 'The Fancy', the name given to the late Georgian underworld of prizefighters and those who followed them, placed bets upon them and commentated on them.

This was a shifty business, for magistrates were usually unenthusiastic about having potentially rowdy crowds gathering at boxing matches held in their towns. So 'The Fancy' had to rendezvous in open fields. Huge crowds would gather – rather like an illegal rave in the 1980s – to watch an engagement in a roped-off, 8-ft-square ring, and significant amounts of money would change hands as the gambling commenced.

Thurtell had invited one William Weare, who moved in similar circles, to visit a cottage near Elstree, Hertfordshire, for a session of drinking and gambling. His aim was to get his hands on the large sum of money Weare was known to carry. The murderer travelled to Hertfordshire in a hired horse-drawn gig, a vehicle that would later become an iconic image and a powerful visual shorthand for his crime.

During the course of an October evening, Weare was shot by Thurtell, and the murderer and two accomplices then slit Weare's throat. One of these accomplices was William Probert, the owner of the cottage off Gins Hill Lane, an overgrown rural track that later became known as 'Murder Lane'. The three inept criminals threw the body of William Weare into the pond outside Probert's cottage. On second thoughts, though, they decided that this wasn't a safe enough hiding place. So they fished the corpse out again, and a second pond a little way away was chosen instead. Then, in an alarming display of sang-froid, the three went back to Probert's cottage and spent the rest of the night singing songs and eating pork chops.

Their crime – sordid, greedy and unimaginative though it was – nevertheless caught the public's imagination, and it rather brilliantly illustrates the ways in which the location, the setting and even the props of a murder could be enjoyed. The combination of the violence and the everyday domestic detail that emerged as the crime unfolded was gripping to the thousands of readers who followed the case in the press. *The Times* found that the 'cold-blooded villainy in the mode of bringing it about, and the ferocity which accompanied its perpetration, has seldom been equalled', and the publisher James Catnach printed no fewer than a quarter of a million copies of one particular printed broadside giving the latest details about Thurtell's trial.

The transcript of the trial seems almost intended to provide maximum entertainment value. In order to establish the timing of events, Probert's maid was asked:

'Was the supper postponed?'

And her answer was:

'No, it was pork.'

Due to the various bungles in the disposal of the body and the murder weapon, and the lack of sympathy between the three accomplices, Thurtell was easily found guilty and swung for his deeds within three months. He had become a figure of such notoriety that a crowd of 40,000 was said to have gathered to watch his death.

Of course this level of public interest was potentially hugely lucrative. Probert, the accomplice, escaped being hanged for his part in the crime, but he went bankrupt and his cottage and belongings were sold off by his creditors. They were snapped up and the property itself became a tourist attraction. Indeed, a little local circuit developed. The 'curious' began at 'the grave of Mr Weare, in Elstree Church-yard ... and the pond, about a quarter of a mile out of the village'. The second stop was the Artichoke Inn 'in which the corpse was carried, and where the Coroner's inquest was held'. Here the landlord, Mr Field, was on hand to answer questions. He was particularly well informed because he'd been a member of the jury at the inquest. Having had their chat with Mr Field, visitors could then examine the sack used to transport Weare's remains ('the marks of blood which it bears gave it particular interest'.) From the Artichoke

Inn tourists would travel on to the cottage itself, and could barely be restrained from pinching souvenirs to take home. One newspaper reported that 'a twig from the hedge, through which the remains of a murdered man had been dragged, must furnish a treat'. And indeed the hedge had been pulled quite to pieces.

John Thurtell and the Elstree Murder became infamous enough to provide material for a seemingly endless stream of well-known authors. Thomas De Quincey, the philosopher Thomas Carlyle, Charles Dickens, Edward Bulwer-Lytton and, later, Walter De La Mare all had reflections to make. And the Elstree Murder Tour became so well established that five years later even a remote and grand figure like Sir Walter Scott came a-visiting.

Scott extracted maximum romance from the circuit that he made in 1828 of all the notable sites. He started by describing the local 'labyrinth of intricate lanes, which seemed made on purpose to afford strangers the full benefit of a dark night and a drunk driver'. By then, the cottage had been partially demolished, but he carefully inspected the first pond: 'Now only a green swamp, but so near the house, that one cannot conceive how it was ever chosen as a place of temporary concealment for the murdered body.'

He visited the ruins of the cottage, for which privilege he was charged 2s. 6d. by the 'truculent looking hag' acting as custodian.

Scott was by no means the last of the Elstree Murder tourists. Nearly 60 years later, in 1885, a contributor to the publication *Notes & Queries* described another visit to Probert's cottage during which he had found 'an old man clipping the very hedge through which Weare's body was dragged', and been able to visit the very kitchen in which the pork chops had been cooked. And on 24 October

1923, a commemorative meeting was held at the murder scene to mark 'exactly one hundred years to the very hour when the evil deed was done'. Gordon S. Maxwell, a topographer, reported that the weather was disappointingly inappropriate. Instead of 'a clouded sky and a fierce east wind blowing chilly and blusteringly over a scene of desolation', it had been rather a lovely evening.

Enthusiastic murder tourists may have flocked to the cottage for decades to come, but in 1823 it was not in fact necessary to make the journey to Hertfordshire to experience something of the same thrill.

The gig in which Thurtell and his victim had travelled to Elstree had been a choice prize in the sale of his goods. The idea of such a fine and pleasant means of transport being used for such nefarious purposes seems to have piqued people's interest, and few of the broadsides printed about the crime were complete without a picture of the fatal vehicle. In Regency life, a gig was a symbol of respectability, and Thomas Carlyle was particularly struck by the importance attached to it by his contemporaries as the Thurtell case unfolded. In his mind, the gig became a symbol of hollow materialism and a thoughtless grasping after respectability, and he began to refer, in correspondence with his wife Jane, to regrettable conditions such as *gigmania*, *Gigmaness*, *Gigmanhood* and *county gigmanism*.

The original gig was acquired by the New Surrey Theatre in London, to be used onstage in a dramatic retelling of the story of the murder entitled *The Gamblers*. 'Boiled Beef' Williams, the theatre's manager, placed an advert in *The Times* promising that audiences would see the 'identical horse and gig alluded to in the daily press in the accounts of the late murder, together with the table at which the party supped, the sofa as described to having been slept on, with other household furniture, as purchased at the late auction'.

The relish with which Thurtell's story was lapped up seems almost ludicrous today, and yet this crime struck a powerful chord with everyone in Regency England.

William Cobbett, the radical writer, even claimed that his young son was spurred on to learn how to read in order to find out more about the case, at a time when 'all the world was talking and reading about THURTELL'. Thomas Carlyle greatly regretted it once all was over: 'Thurtell being hanged last week, we are duller here than ever.'

He had been rather an amusing murderer, whose blunders and pretensions were a rich source of comedy. Indeed, as Thomas Babington Macaulay noted, 'There is a possibility that Thurtell killed Weare only in order to give the youth of England an impressive warning against gaming and bad company.'

And Thurtell continued to entertain, and to warn by his bad example, even after he was dead. He would soon achieve immortality in wax, in the collection of Madame Tussaud.

5

---◆---

House of Wax

'Methinks it is of ill Consequence that there should be a Murderers' Corner, wherein a Villain may look to have his Figure put more certainly than a Poet can look to a Statue in the Abbey.'

'Mr Pips his Diary', in Punch, *1840*

In 1802, a 41-year-old French woman who spoke no English crossed the Channel without her husband. She was accompanied only by her four-year-old son, and a collection of 30 life-size human portraits in wax. In London, she set up her collection at the Lyceum Theatre in the Strand, and sold tickets for entry to the 'Grand European Cabinet of Figures'. It was the first venue in what would turn out to be a very lengthy tour, and the lady herself would become intimate with England and its ways. Her journey around the nation, with her show in tow, lasted for the next 30 years.

Marie Grosholtz (as she was born) was in 1802 at the lowest ebb of her fortunes. Her profession was an old one, which had the noble aim of bringing the dead back to life. Westminster Abbey contains the earliest and best British models, in wood, and then wax, of kings and queens. In the days before effective embalming techniques, a stand-in figure of the deceased was often made to represent his or her body at the funeral.

These effigies provided a focus for the crowds who gathered to pay their last respects to a king or queen. Placed on top of a coffin, and carried in procession, the effigy allowed them to feel that they were seeing their former monarch for the last time. Some of those at Westminster Abbey today are quite astonishingly old. You can see the face of Edward III, presumed to be taken from his death mask, and carved in wood: he died in 1377. Anne of Bohemia, the wife of Richard II, who died in 1394, still presents us with her long and mournful visage. In 1904 Max Beerbohm described their curious, dignified and moving aura in resonant words: 'They were fashioned with a solemn and wistful purpose. The reason of them lies in a sentiment which is as old as the world, lies in man's vain revolt from the prospect of death.'

The figures in Westminster Abbey that date from the seventeenth century onwards are modelled in wax, rather than wood, and their purpose was slightly broader than for use in a funeral procession. During Charles II's funeral in 1685, his coffin was topped merely by his crown, rather than an effigy. A wax figure was made nevertheless, and put on show for the edification – and, in due course, for the entertainment – of visitors. The figures of his successors, William and Mary, are likewise waxworks in the modern sense: for show, rather than for use in a funeral. In 1685, Johann Schalch, a German showman, received a licence from the Lord Mayor of London to display royal figures, and toured a tableau featuring Queen Mary II on her deathbed. It was said to contain a wonderfully accurate face taken from her death mask.

The desire to show what celebrated, usually royal, people looked like in an age before photography was one impetus behind modelling in wax; the other was the medical profession's growing desire to have wax models of bodies and their organs for teaching purposes. Interestingly, most of the eighteenth-century wax figures made for anatomical purposes were female, often adorned with wigs and eyelashes, and made so as to open up to display wombs and sometimes growing foetuses inside. It was much less common for wax modellers to produce a full-length male figure, and male organs were often fashioned to stand alone. The female models, known as 'Venuses', were venerated as beautiful and even erotic objects, while the masculine gender less often suffered the indignity of being reproduced naked in wax for the scrutiny of medical students.

The effigies of Westminster Abbey fell into neglect in the eighteenth century, were piled up and left semi-abandoned in a side chapel. They became known by the pupils at Westminster School next door as 'The Ragged Regiment'. Out in the wider world, though, the eighteenth century saw waxworks become a popular part of mainstream culture and entertainment.

Exhibitions of waxworks, for which tickets were sold, were by then a solid commercial enterprise. They were connected to the new rationalism of the Enlightenment, which encouraged the classification and codification of human beings, a continuous search for knowledge, and, as Pamela Pilbeam, historian of waxworks, puts it, 'an acknowledgement of the potential of the individual'.

At Mrs Salmon's gallery in the Strand, Georgian London's most famous waxworks venue, one could see kings and queens but also curiosities, such as the famous, hairy, feral child known as 'Peter the Wild Boy'. You could also readily commission a waxwork of yourself or your family: from the 1690s, Mrs Mills, a rival proprietor to Mrs Salmon, who displayed her work at Exeter Change in the Strand, announced to her visitors that they, too, 'may have their Effigies made of their deceas'd Friends on moderate terms'.

In 1770s Paris, the young Marie Grosholtz's mother was working as housekeeper to a Swiss doctor, Philippe Curtius, who had discovered that he had a talent as a maker of wax anatomical models. He would refer to Marie as his 'niece', but it is likely that she was his illegitimate daughter. In due course Curtius opened a 'cabinet de cire', or wax museum, in Paris. Marie entered into an apprenticeship in wax-modelling under Curtius, and evidently showed much skill. She completed her first head – Voltaire – at the age of 17.

It was the start of what would prove to be a tremendous career. In pre-Revolutionary France, Marie later claimed, she had won the patronage of the French royal family, and even visited Versailles to give lessons to the doomed Louis XVI's sister Elizabeth. But it has to be said that her memoirs, written many years later, and with the help of a ghost writer, probably exaggerated her royal and aristocratic connections.

Dr Curtius's gallery, however, was a great commercial success and he found his services in demand even after the Terror began. The Parisian mob required wax heads of their heroes, to carry on sticks through the streets, and they also wanted their decapitated enemies, fresh from the guillotine, to be recorded in wax. It was

Marie who undertook this gruesome task for the Convention, and in 1793 she took death masks of the executed Louis XVI and Marie Antoinette. Her model of the murdered Marat was displayed in Paris in a tableau with the celebrated bath and the assassin's dagger still sticking out of his body.

But the years following the Revolution did not prove kind to the waxworks business. Curtius died in 1794, Marie found it hard to stay on the right side of the Revolutionary authorities and visitor numbers declined. She had married one Monsieur Tussaud in 1795, but nevertheless within ten years had made her way alone to Britain.

Late Georgian London was a good choice of destination for Marie Tussaud. It would prove to be a paradise for showmen and performers of all kinds. The promenade – walking up and down, observing the fashionable folk and the clothes they wore – had become the pastime of the age, and visitors to pleasure gardens like Vauxhall liked nothing more than to ogle other people. Even better, then, to visit a waxworks: here it was not impolite to have a good stare.

But Madame Tussaud did not at first have a permanent venue. She kept her show on the move around Britain, rarely sticking to schedule because an announcement that departure from (say) Birmingham had been delayed due to excessive numbers still visiting was an excellent way to drum up business. Eventually, as Marie entered her seventies, the show settled down, permanently, in premises in Baker Street, London. It had three main themes: France (because of Madame's background), Royalty and, of course, Horror.

What would become the notorious 'Chamber of Horrors' was known, at first, as simply 'the Other Chamber'. It specialized in

Revolutionary horror from France: the models of guillotined heads that Marie had brought with her and a small replica of the guillotine itself. But these were supplemented over time, not only by representations of British murderers but also by artefacts belonging to them. Tussaud's agents were quick to arrive during trials and after executions to make financial offers for items of interest.

In its permanent, Baker Street, home, Madame Tussaud's flourished. In her history of the institution, Pamela Pilbeam points out that its surge in popularity coincided with the reduction in the number of public hangings, as if people turned to wax to replace a lost pleasure. She also notes how carefully the Waxworks was positioned to take advantage of the burgeoning travel networks of London. Horse-drawn buses could bring people to the door from all the railway stations on the 'New Road': Paddington, Marylebone, Euston, King's Cross and St Pancras. None of them was more than two miles distant, and a trip to the Waxworks, while not cheap, made a convenient day out in the capital for the suburban dweller.

Marie Tussaud died in 1850, but still remains present in her own gallery in waxen form. Her family continued to run the business. As the century wore on, though, a certain middle-class disapproval of the ghoulish nature of the 'Chamber of Horrors' began to be expressed. It was heightened by the acquisition of a celebrated collection of instruments of torture in 1872. 'It panders to a morbid, unhealthy, unfeeling curiosity,' one pressman moaned.

And yet, horror and murder made financial sense to Madame Tussaud's. In 1890, a new model of Mrs Pearcey drew 31,000 visitors on Boxing Day alone. Eleanor Pearcey had bludgeoned the wife and child of her lover to death in Kentish Town. Madame Tussaud's had

Punch magazine regrets the British tendency to hero-worship
murderers, in a caricature of Madame Tussaud's gallery.

acquired the child's pram and even – a touch of genius – the sweet
the baby had been sucking at the time of its death.

Madame Tussaud's Waxworks tried to hide its financial success
behind an educational fig leaf, and certainly learning lay somewhere
in its mission. Marie Tussaud had aimed to convey the authentic
flavour of a person, for example presenting her figure of Napoleon
alongside a real tooth of his, real hair, and various other personal
possessions. The exhibition's catalogues were instructive in tone,
and claimed to 'convey to the minds of young Persons much

biographical knowledge – a branch of education universally allowed to be of the highest importance'. Madame Tussaud would have been pleased by an early press review of her gallery which did indeed advise those in charge of 'young persons to take them to see this exhibition, as the view of so many famous characters in history must make them desirous to open the pages of history'.

Unlike earlier waxworks shows, there were no nude figures or erotica, and in 1842 *Chambers's Edinburgh Journal* reported that 'you must not allow yourself to associate [Madame Tussaud's] in your mind with those tawdry and tinselled spectacles which are often seen in provincial towns; there is nothing paltry, or mean, or got-up looking about it, but, on the contrary, everything bears evidence of the excellent judgement of liberality of the indefatigable conductor, Madame Tussaud'. Indeed – the ultimate sign of respectability – 'the linen, laces, etc.' are changed 'every week or two, so that they are all beautifully clean'.

But what determined whether a model would stay, or leave the display, was careful observation of the number of visitors who stopped before it for a closer look. Very few of the models were placed upon pedestals, and visitors could get close enough to touch. This pattern of stoppage was carefully monitored, with various wildfire celebrities or 'ephemerals' being retired after a few weeks. Other, perennial favourites ('immortals') were constantly retouched, refreshed and occasionally remodelled over many years. Queen Victoria was the most popular figure of all.

The 'Other Chamber' was renamed the 'Chamber of Comparative Physiognomy' in 1860. This gave it the gloss of the contemporary pseudo-science of phrenology, the now discredited Victorian practice of deducing people's characters from their physical appearance and physiognomy, and for measuring the bumps of the cranium to diagnose temperament and mental abilities. But its popular name was the 'Chamber of Horrors', and its fame, fear and mysterious magnetism became so great that during the First World War, trainee soldiers were frequently set the 'initiative test' of hiding and spending the night there. This caused such inconvenience that Madame Tussaud's was forced officially to ask the War Office to stop the practice.

'Jack the Ripper' would never appear among the murderers, as he was never caught. The modellers of Tussaud's prided themselves on the accuracy of their depictions, which were based on sittings in the studio, where that was possible (for non-murderous models), or else on sketches made in court or, in due course, on photographs.

As photography was banned at the Old Bailey, photographs were hard to obtain. The chief modeller in the later nineteenth century, John Theodore Tussaud, great-grandson of the founder, was said to work from pictures taken secretly during the course of murderers' trials by journalists who had cameras hidden within their hats.

At Madame Tussaud's, a true picture was painted of the type of personalities that the general Victorian public wanted to meet. This was quite different from the pantheon of great men celebrated by the nation in Westminster Abbey, received at Windsor Castle by the Queen, or commemorated by statues in town squares. In 1918, W. R. Titterton, a writer on London topics, summed up what the Waxworks really meant in the Victorian age: 'You perceive that this is some sort of holiest of holies, the nearest Victorians got to a cathedral, with its saints enriched within.'

It turns out that what the lower middle and working classes most wanted to do, in their leisure time, was to come face-to-face with murderers. And if that wasn't possible, they wanted to read about them.

6

True Crime

'Murder, though it hath no tongue,
Will speak with most miraculous organ.'

Shakespeare, Hamlet

In 1811, at the time of the Ratcliffe Highway Murders, Thomas
De Quincey noted the curious and irrational behaviour of one of
his neighbours in Grasmere. Even in the peaceful Lake District, the
killings had caused an 'indescribable' panic. The little old lady who
lived next door to De Quincey 'never rested', he said,

> Until she had placed eighteen doors ... each secured by
> ponderous bolts, and bars, and chains, between her own
> bedroom and any intruder of human build. To reach her,
> even in her drawing room, was like going, as a flag of truce,
> into a beleaguered fortress; at every sixth step one was
> stopped by a sort of portcullis.

How had De Quincey's neighbour managed to work herself into
such a fearful state in remote Grasmere? A frenzy of fear that swept

the nation was achieved by the newspapers, as one of the chief ways that people consumed murder was through print.

The easiest and cheapest way to find out about murder was the broadside. This very simple kind of newspaper, often just one piece of paper, was printed on one side only. It lay just within the financial reach of even the working man or woman.

Though only just. The rise in prosperity and living standards that one could have expected the Industrial Revolution to provide for everybody in Britain from the eighteenth century onwards failed to filter down to the workers until about halfway through the nineteenth century. The 1840s were known as 'the Hungry Forties' and it's no surprise that in the first few decades of the 1800s Britain teetered on the edge of riot and disorder. The people who provided the manpower to operate the new factories and cities found themselves being employed in new ways, but still living in the old squalor and poverty.

The notion that a man's wages could support a stay-at-home wife and family would only really hold true from the 1850s onwards. Until then, low-paid urban workers lived in crowded conditions, ate poorly, and often, when times were hard, dipped temporarily into criminal pursuits such as thieving or prostitution. When times were good, they enjoyed watching cockfights, betting on prizefights, or attending melodrama at the huge and illegal theatres of east London.

Despite their low and precarious standards of living, these people had higher standards of literacy than their agricultural forbears. Exactly how many of them could read is difficult to ascertain, but in 1840, 60 per cent of the people getting married were able to sign their own names in the parish register. This figure – a very basic indicator of writing skills – had remained the same for the previous hundred years. As historian Rosalind Crone tells us, reading was taught *before* children moved on to writing, leading us to believe the figure for readers must have been much higher.

The beginning of the nineteenth century also saw a great increase in the educational opportunities available to the children of working people. There were Sunday Schools, and National Schools, many of them set up by evangelists who promoted reading skills alongside new and unconventional forms of religion.

It also seems very likely – if hard to prove – that the range and variety of cheap printed materials now becoming available to these people spurred them on to read more. For example, the hugely popular *Penny Magazine*, covering topics from art, history and society, and illustrated with attractive engravings, sold 200,000 copies a week by 1832. If you consider that each copy must have been passed on among friends and neighbours, it probably had a readership of about a million.

Broadsides, the basic way in which you could read about current affairs, developed out of a tradition of scurrilous, subversive and sometimes even radical pamphlets, which had long kept up a commentary of catcalls on the doings of the rich and respectable. By the nineteenth century, though, broadsides were dwelling more and more often on violent crimes like murder. In some ways this seems paradoxical, because the number of executions was in decline. The historian V. A. C. Gatrell, however, argues that as hangings became rarer, they became more relished as not-to-be-missed events, and therefore caused more significant spikes in sales.

A 'stunning good murder', as it was called, would be covered by the broadsides in a certain predictable way. The first reports of the crime would appear, briefly, on a quarter-sheet of paper, or the smallest possible edition of this particular form of journalism. Soon, bigger half-sheets would appear, with more details of the crime itself, and also of its investigation. The climax would be the day of the execution, when a proper 'broadsheet', a whole piece of paper, would be printed, summarizing everything so far, plus an account of the execution. It often had a striking picture of the gallows as well.

The most infamous crimes were honoured with the publication of 'books', consisting of more than one broadsheet folded together. The printers discovered that they could sell 'books' about old murders, too, at the time a new one occurred. It seems that once people were in a murder mood, they wanted as much of it as they could get. The sales could be very significant indeed: in 1849 they rose to the almost incredible figure of two and a half million copies of a book on the crimes and deaths of the husband and wife murderers Maria and George Frederick Manning.

And you didn't even have to know how to read in order to join in the fun. Rosalind Crone describes the activities of the specialized London street-sellers whose product was the news. They were ultimately trying to sell broadsides, but in order to catch the attention of the crowd they would call out, perform or even sing the main story of the day. Henry Mayhew, one of the co-founders of *Punch*, was also the compiler of a tremendous work of oral history gathered from people on the streets of London in the 1840s. One of his interviewees was a street 'patterer'. Posted on a street corner, he kept up a lively constant 'patter' of verbal information, and worked with a partner to perform dramatic mini-reconstructions of crimes: 'He always performs the villain, and I take the noble characters. He always dies, because he can do a splendid back-fall, and he looks so wicked when he's got the moustaches on.'

These two were 'standing patterers', who took up a fixed spot on a street corner. They were complemented by 'running patterers', who moved constantly through the crowds, shouting out details of what was in their broadsides. Emphasizing words such as 'horrible', 'barbarous' and 'murder', they made a vital contribution to the very distinctive aural landscape of the Victorian city.

There were also 'chaunters', or 'singing patterers', whose sales technique was music. They incorporated the stories of a crime into a song or chant. All three types of patterer would converge on the prison on the day of an execution, contributing greatly to the noise and energy of the scene. 'Where they came from was as much a mystery to the inhabitants [of a town hosting a hanging] as whither they disappeared when the last dying speech had been sold,' recollected one Victorian gentleman. The patterers turned up in such large numbers because, of course, on hanging days they could expect to make their greatest sales.

No horrible detail was overlooked by the printers of the broadsides, and their careful technical language and close observation is strikingly similar to the police procedural fiction of today. The crime scene incorporating the body of Mrs Lees, murdered by her husband William in 1839, was described like this:

> there were several gashes on her face, and a deep wound on the throat separating the jugular vein, there was also a

bruise on the right eyebrow, which appeared to have been inflicted by the same blunt instrument from which it appears that the murderer, after striking his hapless victim with a stick or piece of wood and rendering her perfectly senseless, completed by cutting her throat.

The illustrations usually showed the criminal and victim in the throes of the crime, with melodramatic poses and spurts of blood. Today they appear comical, because so unconvincing, and yet also horrific, when you stop to consider what is actually being shown.

But despite the sensationalism, the broadsides ultimately had a moral message. The gallows confession of the repentant criminal was almost always included, though inevitably made up, because of the need to have it printed and ready by the time of the actual execution. Writing these 'confessions' was a specialized job. 'I wrote Courvoisier's sorrowful lamentation,' explained one man who wrote for the cheap printers. 'I wrote a pathetic ballad on the respite of Annette Meyers. I did the helegy, too, on Rush's execution,' he continued, tossing off a list of murderers' names. Rush's 'was supposed, like the rest, to be written by the culprit himself, and was particular penitent'.

Reading through a series of broadsides, it's striking that all the confessions are penitent and the lamentations sorrowful. Each crime closes, satisfyingly, with the confession and final punishment of its perpetrator. We have no real idea whether these murderers did indeed repent on the gallows and regret their crimes. We cannot even know if some of them were truly guilty. But no reader of broadsides could have been left without the impression that to turn to crime leads inevitably to shame, repentance and death.

———

The mixture of fear and pleasure produced by reading about true crime applied to fiction as much as factual writing. There had existed since the eighteenth century a separate school of fiction, the Gothic novel, devoted entirely to creating feelings of horror, revulsion, awe and excitement.

The quintessential work in the genre was Ann Radcliffe's *The Mysteries of Udolpho* (1794). During the course of this long, intricate and frankly implausible story, the young and orphaned Emily St Aubert is imprisoned in a remote castle. Its hectically plotted pages are packed with sublime scenery, malevolent characters and feisty heroines. Indeed, Radcliffe's novels have been described as 'the verbal equivalent of Salvator Rosa and Claude Lorraine' in art. Poor Emily becomes the captive of the evil, haughty and brooding Montoni (an Italian brigand masquerading as an aristocrat, who has also murdered her aunt) but finally flees just before he can force her to sign over to him all her property.

Udolpho was hugely popular. Radcliffe received an astonishing £500 for her work, in an age when the average fee for a copyright to a novel was £80. Radcliffe herself was a figure of some mystery: she broke off publishing novels at the height of her success, and eventually died of asthma, at her home in Pimlico, in 1823. Various inaccurate but more exciting stories circulated about what had happened to her (and, wisely for the purposes of sales, she did nothing to correct them). She'd been confined, mad, it was said, to

Haddon Hall in Derbyshire, or else maybe she'd died, in 1810, 'in that species of derangement called "the horrors"'.

By the end of the eighteenth century, though, Gothic novels such as Radcliffe's were looking dated. Jane Austen's first completed work, *Northanger Abbey* (written in 1798–9, but published only posthumously in 1817), is a send-up of the genre and *Udolpho* is Austen's target.

The overfanciful Catherine Morland, who by the age of 17 is firmly 'in training for a heroine', finds herself on a visit to a country house, Northanger Abbey itself. She is addicted to novels with titles like *Mysterious Warnings* or *Necromancer of the Black Forest*. At Northanger Abbey, based on her reading of Ann Radcliffe, she firmly expects to find dark passages, secret rooms, locked chests containing clues and, ultimately, some piece of evidence to show that her host, General Tilney, has murdered his dead wife. Instead, the house is warm, welcoming, light and refurbished in the modern style, and the naïve Catherine finds only embarrassment and shame when her Gothic fantasies are revealed. 'Consult your own understanding, your own sense of the probable, your own observation of what is passing around you,' says General Tilney's son, a young man whom she much admires. 'Dearest Miss Morland, what ideas have you been admitting?'

But the cool, sophisticated humour of Jane Austen was lost upon those who, like Catherine Morland, had a cheap and lurid taste for horror and mystery. Had she been born a decade or two later, and belonged to a lower social class, Catherine Morland would have been an avid reader of the so-called 'Penny Blood', a downmarket version of the Gothic novel.

Brought out in instalments, these trashy 'Bloods' became an important feature of publishing after 1828. Each week you could buy the next eight pages of the story, illustrated by a woodcut, for a single penny. (Meanwhile, a lofty, three-volume, middle-class novel would cost you over a pound.) From the 1830s, the first generation of working-class people who'd learned to read at school became avid consumers of literature.

Real, hard-core 'Penny Bloods' were often set in the past, and bore some sort of relationship to supposedly real events. They included the *Calendar of Horrors*, published between 1835 and 1836, and a long-running publication called *The Lives of the Most Notorious Highwaymen, Footpads, &c., &c.* Both purported to be a history of true crimes and mysterious happenings, but were in fact largely fictional. In the latter, various genuine highwaymen are introduced, and then go on to share adventures together, despite having lived at different times in the eighteenth century.

'Penny Blood' writers often wrote extremely quickly, infrequently revised their work for publication and bulked it out with all kinds of plagiarized and extraneous material. Their plots were implausible, their characterizations crude and their locations usually included prison cells, haunted castles, sinking ships and desolate heaths. 'More blood, much more blood' was the instruction issued to his writers by one 'Penny Blood' editor.

It may not sound particularly edifying, yet, a generation earlier, devotees of 'Penny Bloods' would not have had any access to literature at all. And the genre quenched a great new thirst. It's been estimated that in the year 1845 the publishing house of Lloyd's, based in Fleet Street, sold half a million copies each week of the various magazines and 'Penny Bloods' it produced – and each one of these would have been read by several people, bringing the total number of readers into the millions. Henry Mayhew, recorder of the lives of the London poor, found an interviewee who described how the reading of 'Penny Bloods' was a shared and sociable experience: 'on a fine summer's evening a costermonger, or any neighbour who has the advantage of being a "schollard", reads aloud to them in the courts they inhabit'.

Costermongers were people who sold fruit, vegetables or other perishable goods on the London streets. (A 'monger' is a 'seller', and 'costards' were a type of apple.) And Edward Lloyd, the publisher, stated himself that these people constituted his audience. He wished to lay 'before a large and intelligent class of readers, at a charge comparatively insignificant, the same pleasures of imagination which have, hitherto, to a great extent, only graced the polished leisure of the wealthy'.

Successful 'Penny Blood' writers needed dedication, a good nose for the kinds of story that ordinary, unpretentious people liked to read and a wealth of invention. They did not need a fancy education, or artistic aspirations – quite the opposite, in fact. Many of them were driven to their work by financial desperation, and some of them had lives no less sensational than their fiction.

George Augustus Sala, a favourite young writer of Charles Dickens's, was typical. Originally a hard-working 'Blood' writer, he cut his teeth on these products before going on to become a celebrated journalist and leader writer for the *Daily Telegraph*. Described as 'a red, bloated, bottle-nosed creature', he also had a seamier side to him: when times were hard, he produced both

'Bloods' and pornography. Towards the end of his life he wrote *The Life and Adventures of George Augustus Sala*, an autobiography fittingly described by the *Oxford Dictionary of National Biography* as 'notoriously unreliable'. The adventures he writes about include going to Russia, being imprisoned for debt and reporting from the American Civil War.

Another 'Blood' writer was Edward Bulwer-Lytton, whose most famous opening line you've almost certainly heard before: 'It was a dark and stormy night'. The son of a general, he was seduced in his youth by Lady Caroline Lamb, the former lover of Lord Byron (and the lady who had dubbed the poet 'mad, bad and dangerous to know'.) Lady Caroline was 18 years older than Edward, and embarrassed him by rejecting him after a brief affair. He was then cut off by his family when he married a celebrated but penniless Irish beauty. He had to support himself by producing fiction of all kinds, and in fact was extremely successful at it and made a great deal of money.

Bulwer-Lytton's novel *Pelham, Or the Adventures of a Gentleman* (1828) was a huge hit, and was so beloved by George IV that the king ordered copies to be kept at each of the royal residences. The eponymous 'gentleman' leaves behind a life of leisure to become an amateur sleuth, determined to clear a friend from a charge of murder. In 1832, Bulwer-Lytton's *Eugene Aram*, the story of a Georgian murderer, told with some sympathy for his plight, became another bestseller.

But the apparent immorality of making a murderer into a hero turned literary London against Bulwer-Lytton. At the same time, his relationship with the romantic Rosina, his wife, soured, and when he stood for Parliament she herself publically denounced him at the hustings for mistreating her. Following a course worthy of one of his own characters, he had her committed to a lunatic asylum, before embarking on a career as an MP and, ultimately, being raised to the peerage.

Elsewhere in his enormous scrapbook of impressions of life on the London streets, Henry Mayhew described how the people he met devoured such fiction as Sala's and Bulwer-Lytton's. 'You see's an engraving of a man hung up, burning over a fire,' said one 'intelligent costermonger' of its appeal, 'and some costers would go mad if they couldn't learn what he had been doing, who he was, and all about him.'

By the time of Queen Victoria, the 'Penny Blood' had morphed into the 'Penny Dreadful', and maintained its large sales figures. The stories that unfolded retained quite simple contrasts between good and evil, with violence and murder woven into a view of the world that was nostalgic for the simple pleasures of a rural past.

The story of Sweeney Todd, the demon barber, for example, expressed deep concerns about the problems posed by a new kind of life in the city. In this tale, originally called 'A String of Pearls' after a lost necklace, a succession of customers seat themselves in Sweeney's chair for a shave, before being ejected down a trapdoor into a prison below. There, their bodies are cut up and a local businesswoman in partnership with Sweeney makes them into pies.

Sweeney Todd reflected the concerns of people who had moved to the city in search of work, and who were now living an unfamiliar urban life. Most of the customers were in the barber's shop only because they were looking for someone else, having lost their friends among the crowds. On top of that, city dwellers could not know exactly what was in the tasty fast food (pies) that they bought so cheaply on the streets. Fears of tainted meat were profoundly felt in the age when tinning or canning was in its infancy. Indeed, poor little Fanny Adams, the victim of a Victorian child-murderer, would lend her name both to the expression 'Sweet FA', meaning something small or negligible, and also to the unpopular tinned mutton given to sailors: it tasted so bad they thought they must be eating a child.

The story of Sweeney Todd even, it's been argued, tapped into a new fear about what would happen to Londoners' bodies after they died. No longer could they hope to rest peacefully in a grassy village churchyard. The urban deceased would be crammed into crowded city burial grounds. And as people knew from the real-life exploits of Burke and Hare, the Edinburgh body-snatchers who committed murders to sell the corpses to medical schools, there was a commercial demand even for corpses.

The fact that violence, horror, prostitution, madness and murder continued to form such a large part of people's reading matter seems at odds with our impression of a society that was growing increasingly respectable and prim. Is there something contradictory about the unabashed pleasure that the buttoned-up Victorians took in murder?

The explanation put forward in 1972 by Richard Altick might at first sight seem convincing. In his seminal book *Victorian Studies in Scarlet*, he argued that the Victorians' love of murder was a product of 'their intellectually empty and emotionally stunted lives, so tightly confined by economic and social circumstance'. Reading about a murder gave them, he argued, 'a ready channel for the release of such rudimentary passions as horror, morbid sympathy, and vicarious aggression and for the sheer occupation of minds otherwise rendered blank or dull by the absence of anything more pleasing'.

This notion that the Victorians were the prisoners of etiquette and respectability, leading circumscribed lives of hard work, actually emerged very soon after Victoria's reign ended. In particular, it was down to Lytton Strachey, with his immensely influential book, *Eminent Victorians* (1918). Strachey defined the generation just gone as straitlaced, pompous and slightly laughable. He found them hypocritical, anxious and false. But of course, as with all historians, his work says just as much about his own time as it does the past. Strachey was a member of the Bloomsbury set, a group of writers and painters who defined themselves as freethinking, radical and iconoclastic. How better to develop this image than to attack others for being different?

Even at the time, some people recognized that Strachey had painted an unbalanced, if powerful, picture of an age. The *Times Literary Supplement* immediately suggested that he was wrong to mock: 'we live in a world that [the Victorians] built for us, and though we may laugh at them, we should love them, too'. Historians of the nineteenth century, even to this day, have continuously repeated this caveat. Strachey's image of the Victorians as being collectively and seriously repressed was so powerful, and so striking, even if untrue, that it somehow stuck.

In the 1970s, when Altick argued that consuming horror provided the Victorians with a release from the mundane nature of their lives, he was partly still under Strachey's spell and partly reflecting the values of his own time. This was the decade in which historians sought to suggest that the prosperity of the Industrial Revolution had been bought at an enormously high price. To tell the story of the nineteenth century as a journey from an agrarian economy to a capitalist one, from country to city, from community to anonymity, from good to bad, was a story that chimed with the spirit of the 1970s.

Today, historians are at pains to point out how Victoria's subjects were not seething with passion buried below a bland surface: their sensations, pleasures and vices were just as vivid to them as ours are. In fact, as Rosalind Crone argues, the Victorians shared a love of violence and blood with their Georgian grandparents, equally avid attenders of boxing matches and public hangings. And, indeed, the Victorians might well have found something very familiar in our own modern obsession with brutal horror films and violent computer games. This pleasure taken in violence is timeless; it just takes different forms and emphases depending on the technologies and economy of an age. In the nineteenth century, the rise of literacy and the fall of the price of print allowed a love of blood to flourish in new ways. But it was always there – and still is today.

7

Charles Dickens, Crime Writer

'We shall never forget the mingled feelings of awe and respect with which we used to gaze on the exterior of Newgate in our schoolboy days. How dreadful its rough heavy walls, and low massive doors ... made for the express purpose of letting people in, and never letting them out again.'

Charles Dickens, an essay on the criminal courts

On 13 November 1849, a young writer and four of his friends rented a room in a house near Horsemonger Lane Gaol in Bermondsey. They wanted to get a good view of that day's execution of a villainous couple, the murderers Mr Frederick and Mrs Maria Manning. Their crime had been to kill Maria's lover, and to bury him beneath their kitchen floor, and *The Times* reported that at least 10,000 people had come to watch them swing.

Most of the crowd attended for pleasure, but the writer judged that there was something degrading and animal about the relish he saw being taken all around him: 'Upturned faces, so inexpressibly odious in their brutal mirth or callousness, that a man had cause to feel ashamed of the shape he wore, and to shrink from himself, as fashioned in the image of the Devil.'

He and his party had set out to enjoy the spectacle, but it had turned out to be disgusting and disappointing. The murderers, he thought, had 'perished like beasts'.

Charles Dickens had always been fascinated by crime and its consequences, and his interest pervades his novels. Dickens isn't easy to categorize, and fails to fit comfortably into any single genre. But one strand of his work that's often underappreciated is that which overlaps with the type of books known as 'Newgate Novels'.

These novels were set in the London underworld, in and about the world of Newgate Prison that had so attracted Dickens as a boy. Built in the 1780s in a style designed to strike fear into the heart of the offender, Newgate was the site of public hangings and it had the dubious distinction of providing training to all the nation's hangmen.

Stories about crime and criminals had for a long time been published in a collection known as *The Newgate Calendar* (subtitled *The Malefactors' Bloody Register*). It started out simply as a list of the criminals who had been executed at Newgate, but subsequent editions were padded out with peripheral information and context about their life and crimes. Almost inevitably, reality became embellished and, indeed, glamorized. In the timeless journalistic manner, the regurgitation of the gory details is justified on moral grounds by an editorial voice that condemns each fact even as it relishes it.

By 1774, you could buy a standard five-volume compendium of all the most popular stories. Respectable middle-class readers found the whole idea of reading fiction with thieves and murderers as

The forbidding entrance to Newgate Gaol.

heroes to be repellent, and yet it was said that, after the Bible and *The Pilgrim's Progress*, *The Newgate Calendar* was the book most likely to be found in an ordinary working person's home.

The subject matter was attractive and addictive, and many authors used the *Calendar* as a jumping-off point for stories of crime set in the London world dominated by the prison. In a similar vein, another long-running series called *The Mysteries of the Courts of London*, which was published between 1844 and 1848, had more than 40,000 subscribers.

In the hands of the right author, the 'Newgate Novel' could become great literature. Charles Dickens was not one who aimed at producing high art, or a social climber who placed himself above his subjects. Indeed, although he hated to mention it in later life, he had worked for part of his boyhood in a blacking factory during a period of parental poverty. He climbed his way back to respectability, but he well understood that he closely escaped falling further and becoming 'a little robber or a little vagabond' himself. He therefore knew something of life on the London streets, and kept up his knowledge even after his great successes by walking out and talking to the kinds of people who populate his work. Not all of them were on the right side of the law.

Oliver Twist (1838) was Dickens's second novel, and the very title points to the fact that this is a crime novel: to 'twist' – in thieves' language – means to hang for a crime. The young hero, Oliver, becomes a member of a gang of boy criminals. And yet, as Judith Flanders points out, he is also designed to appeal to the middle-class readers who bought novels. Although he doesn't know it, Oliver has been exiled from a much higher social class and ends up in the workhouse because of the cruelty and neglect of his relations. He naïvely and unwittingly joins Fagin's gang rather than being born into it. And, indeed, Dickens does not glamorize the criminals in *Oliver Twist* as a true 'Newgate Novelist' would have done. Sikes and Fagin are clearly bad, sordid and wrong.

Oliver Twist, though, is characteristic of the 'Newgate Novels' in being closely linked to a real-life crime. Eliza Grimwood, a murdered woman, appears in *Oliver Twist* as Nancy, the victim of murderer Bill Sikes. In real life, Eliza's poise and elegance meant that she was known as 'The Countess', but actually she was a prostitute from Waterloo. She was also 'about twenty-five years of age, of sober habits, and had saved a little money'. In 1838, she set off from her lodgings in Waterloo in search of clients, whom she picked up around the theatres in Drury Lane across the river. Eliza shared her room with William Hubbard, her lover and pimp, who would leave it when Eliza was working. One particular night, Eliza returned to her room accompanied by a tall man 'who had the look of a foreigner, and dressed like a gentleman'.

But the following morning, coming back to the room, Hubbard claimed to have found it empty, except for her dead body. It was an appalling sight. Even the professional and experienced policeman who investigated the case confessed to Dickens: 'when I saw the poor Countess (I had known her well to speak to), lying dead, with her throat cut, on the floor of her bedroom, you'll believe me that a variety of reflections calculated to make a man rather low in his spirits, came into my head'.

Eliza's horrible fate sparked a good deal of attention, both from journalists and fiction writers. *Eliza Grimwood*, for example, written by Alexander Somerville, was a 'Penny Blood' giving a glamorous riff on her life and death. As well as 'biographical notices of her fair companions', the work also promised the usual cast of 'Penny Blood' characters from high and low: 'sketches of dukes, lords, Hon. M.P.'s, magistrates and her murderer'.

In real life, William Hubbard, suspected of killing Eliza, got off. In fiction, Dickens, who was always on the side of fallen women and streetwalkers, made it clear that he thought the murderer should pay for his deeds. In *Oliver Twist* the evil Bill Sikes is served just retribution for murdering Nancy: haunted by remorse, chased by a furious mob, he is eventually killed while trying to escape.

In later years, Dickens carried out a great number of hugely popular and profitable dramatic readings from his work in lecture halls and theatres, and the murder of Nancy was always well received as the very climax of the performances. This was done in defiance of a ban placed upon dramatic versions of the story of *Oliver Twist* by the Lord Chamberlain. The censorship was motivated by a concern for public order and the morale of Londoners. The authorities did not want the real murder of Eliza Grimwood to be given any more notoriety by its being shown on stage. They wanted it to be forgotten, and for all the fuss to die down. But Dickens, through *Oliver Twist*, and even more through his readings, kept an echo of the memory of 'The Countess' alive.

———

Dickens' life-long interest in social justice took a new direction in 1850 when he began to write more and more often about the Metropolitan Police. Embarking upon a series of articles in the magazine he edited, *Household Words,* he set out to present this new profession to his middle-class readership as respectable, admirable and, indeed, quite as glamorous as the thieves had appeared to be in old-style 'Newgate' fiction. He took it upon himself to promote London's detectives to the world, explaining that the force: 'proceeds so systematically and quietly, does its business in such a workman-like manner, and is always so calmly and steadily engaged in the service of the public, that the public really do not know enough of it, to know a tithe of its usefulness'.

In an essay called 'The Modern Science of Thief-Taking', Dickens described the Detective Branch in similarly awe-struck terms: 'forty-two individuals, whose duty it is to wear no uniform, and to perform the most difficult operations of their craft'.

The creation of the Detective Branch was, as we have seen, not universally welcomed. Its members were seen as upstarts, busybodies and spies. Dickens did them a great service by depicting them differently. He transformed the members of this newly established profession into crime specialists, people with unique qualities and abilities.

To them, a crime scene presented 'tracks quite invisible to other eyes'. In a room where a jewel robbery had taken place, for example, a skilled detective might trace the hallmarks of a particular gang of criminals simply 'by the style of performance'. In one of his essays for *Household Words,* Dickens shows a detective in action, addressing the couple whose jewels have been lost. The couple themselves epitomized the sort of well-off readers of *Household Words* who might well have resented the intrusion of a detective into their comfortable world. After examining the crime scene, the detective gives his verdict:

'All right, Sir. This is done by one of "The Dancing School!"'

'Good heavens!' exclaims your plundered partner. 'Impossible, why our children go to Monsieur Pettitoes, of No. 81, and I assured you he is a highly respectable profession. As to his pupils, I –'

The Detective smiles and interrupts. 'Dancers', he tells her, 'is a name given to the sort of burglar by whom she had been robbed; and every branch of the thieving profession is divided into gangs, which are termed "Schools"…'

Dickens became such a fan of the detectives that in 1850 he invited the entire squad to attend a party in the office of *Household Words*. Over brandy and water ('very temperately used indeed') and cigars, the staff of the magazine and the detectives made 'a review of the most celebrated and horrible of the great crimes that have been committed within the last fifteen or twenty years'. One of those present, an inspector whom Dickens calls 'Wield', would have a particularly notable effect on Dickens's writing in the 1850s. Inspector Field, as he was really called, had joined the force in its very earliest days in 1829. His career had seen steady progress, and he had ended up as the head of the newly formed Detective Branch on its formation in 1842.

Dickens captured his friend's real-life physical tics with a novelist's trick of bringing a character to life: 'A middle-aged man of a portly presence, with a large, moist, knowing eye, a husky voice, and a habit of emphasising his conversation by the air of a corpulent fore-finger, which is constantly in juxta-position with his eyes or nose.'

In a subsequent essay, called 'On Duty with Inspector Field', Dickens follows his favourite policeman on a regular night's work, as he makes his rounds of the ill-famed St Giles area of London.

Here an enormous 'rookery', or mass of overcrowded housing, covered the area now surrounding the Centrepoint building next to Tottenham Court Road tube station. It was one of the worst slums in Europe. Henry Mayhew described the parish in 1860 as consisting of 'nests of close and narrow alleys and courts inhabited by the lowest class of Irish costermongers ... the synonym of filth and squalor'.

The journalist and 'Penny Blood' writer George Augustus Sala also revelled in the horror of St Giles. His prurient tone places him firmly in the character of the middle-class people who enjoyed 'slumming it', or visiting these areas for a salacious thrill, and who treated their inhabitants, with unattractive condescension, as a sub-human species:

From a hundred foul lanes and alleys have debouched ... unheard-of human horrors. Gibbering forms of men and women in filthy rags ... hang around your feet like reptiles, and crawl round you like loathsome vermin, and in a demoniac whine beg charity from you. One can bear the men; ferocious and repulsive as they are, a penny and a threat will send them cowering and cursing to their noisome dens again. One cannot bear the women without a shudder and a feeling of infinite sorrow and humiliation. They are so horrible to look upon, so thoroughly unsexed, shameless.

Eventually, like the lancing of a boil, New Oxford Street was cut through the depths of the slum.*

Dickens's tour of St Giles with Inspector Field begins with the clock of St Giles church striking nine, and his arrival at the Police Station House nearby. There he discovers a host of lost souls: a boy who can't find his way home to Newgate Street, an inebriated woman, a quiet woman imprisoned for begging, a watercress seller, a pickpocket and a drunken male pauper.

Dickens and Field then set off on Field's nightly round of the area. Dickens is amazed and impressed by Inspector Field's lack of fear, his knowledge of his beat and his knack of getting what he wants. 'I should like to know where Inspector Field was born,' he muses. 'In Ratcliffe Highway, I would have answered with confidence, but for his being equally at home wherever we go.' Inspector Field invades lodging houses and slums, brutally turning out nests of thieves from their beds in search of malefactors.

Saint Giles's church strikes half-past ten. We stoop low, and creep down a precipitous flight of stairs into a dark close cellar. There is a fire. There is a long deal table. There are benches. The cellar is full of company, chiefly very young men in various conditions of dirt and raggedness. Some are eating supper. There are no women or girls present. Welcome to Rats' Castle, gentlemen, and to this company of noted thieves!

---

* St Giles is also the location of the opening scene, where we meet one of the book's many prostitutes, in Michel Faber's magnificent homage to Victorian fiction, *The Crimson Petal and the White* (2002).

Inspector Field searches the cellar, and soon has the young men standing up and respectfully taking off their caps. He knows each and every occupant. His is the hand 'that has collared half the people here, and motioned their brothers, sisters, fathers, mothers, male and female friends, inexorably to New South Wales ... Inspector Field stands in this den, the Sultan of the place'.

The year following their night-time jaunt through the slums of St Giles, Dickens would fictionalize his friend, placing him, as 'Inspector Bucket', into the novel *Bleak House* (1852). Inspector Bucket captures the murderous maid, Hortense, who is herself based on Maria Manning.

Although the overarching theme of the novel is the condemnation of the ponderous, slow and therefore unjust Court of Chancery, and although the murderess and the policeman are minor characters, Dickens is nevertheless often credited with writing, in *Bleak House*, what may be described as the first detective novel. His character Hortense murders a lawyer and frames her employer, Lady Dedlock, for the crime. Inspector Bucket, originally employed to investigate Lady Dedlock, follows the clues and catches the murderess.

Dickens himself would deny the link between the real-life Inspector Field and the fictional Inspector Bucket. After all, a novelist wishes to be known for his or her imagination, not for journalistic observation. But the link of the lifted finger points to the connection. Like Field's, Bucket's 'fat forefinger seems to rise to the dignity of a familiar demon. He puts it to his ears, and it whispers information ... he rubs it over his nose, and it sharpens his scent.'

Just as John Williams, in the mind of De Quincey, became literature's first glamorous murderer, Inspector Field has a good claim for providing, in Dickens's work, the model for the first fully formed professional detective in fiction.

8

———◆———

The Ballad of
Maria Marten

'There's nothing beats a stunning good murder, after all.'

*Ballad-seller commenting on his
profession's most profitable moments*

Far distant from the noisome slums of St Giles, the peaceful
Suffolk village of Polstead is a quiet and picturesque place
amid fields and woods.

The village has a lovely medieval church on a knoll grazed by
sheep, an idyllic pond and a green with a comfortable pub called
the Cock Tavern. In 1828, however, a particularly brutish and nasty
crime took place here. In the graveyard of the church, a wooden sign
tells the visitor that the body of Maria Marten is buried somewhere
close by. Poor Maria, the victim of the celebrated Murder at the Red
Barn, was only 25 years old. The wooden sign is necessary because
her actual gravestone has disappeared (more on this shortly).

The people who live in Polstead today aren't particularly interested
in this local murder, and would rather forget about it. Indeed, when
I was there, a passing local family told me that the village doesn't like

to talk about Maria. 'You won't find we're keen,' the father said. Yet her presence is still clearly felt: in the plaque in the churchyard, at her cottage (clearly signposted as 'Maria Marten's') and in the prominent signpost marking 'Corder's House', the home of her killer, William Corder. That same afternoon, others tweeted that I might as well give up looking as I wouldn't find the remains of the Red Barn. Indeed, I was already well aware that they had vanished.

Maria was the daughter of a mole-catcher and had two illegitimate children with different fathers. In time, as Maria's tale became embroidered in the retelling, this somewhat disreputable back-story would be glossed over. Many later accounts make her out to have been an innocent, pure and virginal young maid of the village. In 1827, though, she gave birth to a third baby, fathered by William Corder, who lived in a much bigger and grander Elizabethan house over near the pond. The son of a prosperous yeoman farmer, Corder had a slightly dodgy reputation and criminal contacts in London. But, again, in order to make a better story, he would later be elevated into the more straightforward and recognizable role of village squire.

Corder seems to have promised Maria that they would marry, or at least elope together, and an assignation was made at the 'Red Barn', a structure on the hill behind Maria's house. This barn, later so illustrious in fact and fiction, took its name from its partially red-pantiled roof. But also, it was said, its position allowed it to catch the rays of the setting sun, which nightly turned it a bloody and ominous red.

After leaving for her assignation – some said dressed in men's clothes as a disguise – Maria was never seen alive again. William Corder likewise left the village. Letters arrived at intervals for

Maria's family, claiming that the happy couple were now settled on the Isle of Wight. Maria had hurt her hand, the letters stated, which was why she had not written herself.

Next, contemporaries believed, a providential or supernatural intervention worked its beneficent magic. Maria's stepmother had a dream in which it was mysteriously revealed to her that Maria was not, after all, in the Isle of Wight. This dream or vision would feature heavily in retellings of this particular tale, and provided a key part of its popularity. The stepmother woke up believing that Maria was in fact still very close to home, buried in the barn behind the house. Maria's father, convinced by his wife, went to have a look, and there indeed he discovered his daughter's body. There were enough identifying marks to confirm that it was her, and around her neck was a green handkerchief that had belonged to William Corder.

It proved quite easy to catch Maria's killer, who had by now settled down in London with a wife he had acquired since leaving Polstead. (In a bizarre twist, Corder had found this wife through advertising for a spouse in *The Times*.) William Corder was brought back to Suffolk for his trial, which took place, amid enormous publicity, at the Shire Hall of Bury St Edmunds. Corder's defence claimed that the media had massively prejudiced his trial by assuming his guilt. Whether this was true or not, they ultimately failed to protect him. After all, his rather unconvincing line of defence was simply that he hadn't done it. Once condemned to death, he did finally come out with a confession of sorts, but even then he claimed that it had been an accident: he had threatened his lover with a gun, and fired it only because of a trembling in his fingers.

Corder's sentence decreed that he should not only be hanged – a process that took a good ten minutes, even with the hangman pulling down upon his legs – but also that his body should be dissected and 'anatomized'. Despite the requests of his new wife for the return of her husband's corpse, it was taken back to the Shire Hall, opened up by the slitting and peeling back of the skin and laid out upon a table. According to the papers, no fewer than 5,000 local people came trooping through the building to see the body.

The next day, science took precedence over spectacle and the body was carefully dissected for the edification of a group of young medical students from Cambridge. They were particularly interested in studying it in the light of the new 'science' of phrenology then in vogue, so a careful cast was taken of Corder's head, for future reference. That cast is now in Moyse's Hall Museum, Bury St Edmunds, where the curator, Alex McWhirter, showed it to me. It's rather a distressing sight. The nose and lips are horribly swollen, as the blood vessels in these organs had burst during the process of hanging.

The murder in the Red Barn created an enormous sensation in contemporary East Anglia, and cast an unusually long shadow over what historians call 'material culture': everyday things like knick-knacks, pictures, song-sheets and artefacts. Almost immediately, this rather sordid, rural tale of betrayal and violence struck a chord with the British public, each of whom seemed to want a tangible keepsake to remind them of the story.

For the broadside and ballad-sellers at the execution itself, William Corder would be long remembered as a great boon to their trade. The most popular item for sale was Corder's 'last confession', a detailed screed reportedly taken down by witnesses the night

William Corder's head modelled
just after death, and showing the
swollen lips and nose that were
the effects of his hanging.

before he died. One 'patterer' retained fond memories of the sales
frenzy that swept through Bury St Edmunds: 'I got a whole hatful
of halfpence at that ... a gentleman's servant come out, and wanted
half a dozen for his master, and one for himself.'

Corder's 'Last Dying Speech and Full Confession' was published
alongside a song called 'The Murder of Maria Marten', which
became one of the most popular ballads of 1828. It wasn't just a
local sensation, as copies of this particular ballad still survive from
named printing presses in London, Wales and even Scotland. Such
was its reach and popularity that it must have been the contemporary
equivalent of a number one single.

95

At least four different ballads about William Corder are known to have been written and printed at the time of his trial but 'The Murder of Maria Marten' is the best known. People purchased the printed words on a piece of paper, and learned the tune either from listening to the ballad-seller or from their friends who already knew how the music went. 'Our servants are constantly loitering in the street,' complained a late Georgian journalist, 'to learn the last new song ... You would be surprised, sir, could I enumerate the number of women-servants whose money has been squandered in the purchase of our Grub-street harmony.'

Or, alternatively, people may well have sung 'The Murder of Maria Marten' to any handy tune that they knew already. Tunes were constantly recycled with different words (just as, conversely, words could be sung to different tunes).

When I met Vic Gammon, a historian of folk music, to learn this particular ballad, I was pretty sure that the tune to a song about a murder in 1828 would be unknown to me. I was astonished to learn, though, that I was already perfectly familiar with it, and could start singing it right away, for one of the best-known tunes to which 'Maria Marten' was sung pops up in one of Ralph Vaughan Williams's fantasias on English folk songs, 'Five Variants on Dives and Lazarus', for harp and string orchestra. The composer was an avid collector of folk songs and ballad tunes who travelled the countryside collecting music and writing down old tunes which might otherwise have been lost. He wrote his fantasia on folk songs as a commission for the British Council, and it was first performed in the Carnegie Hall, New York, in 1939. The occasion was a century distant in time, and three and a half thousand miles distant in space, from Polstead and the Red Barn. But the piece opens with the best-known of the melodies to which 'Maria Marten' could be sung.

Ballads like 'The Murder of Maria Marten' tumbled off the busy printing presses in the Seven Dials area of London, the centre of the cheaper end of the publishing business. Many of them shared common features, for instance beginning with the words 'come all, come all', as the singer announces his presence and gathers round an audience. In the case of 'Maria Marten', the song begins:

Come all you thoughtless young men, a warning take by me
And think upon my unhappy fate to be hanged upon a tree.

Then, at the conclusion of the song, comes the conventional, sorrowful adieu, in which the murderer bids goodbye to the world:

Adieu, adieu, my loving friends, my glass is almost run,
On Monday next will be my last, when I am to be hang'd;
So you young men who do pass by, with pity look on me.
For murdering Maria Marten I was hang'd upon the tree.

Enormous relish is taken in the ghastliness of the crime ('After the horrid deed was done, she lay weltering in her gore; Her bleeding mangled body he buried, under the Red-barn floor'). Yet alongside the fun to be found in the horror is the clear social purpose served by this song on everyone's lips in 1828. It sent a strong moral message to the listener, a warning to the nation's hot-headed young men, advising them against succumbing to their basest instincts.

Words and music were not the only souvenirs. Equally as durable as the ballads and broadsides – and equally available to anyone with the cash – were the cheap and colourful Staffordshire ceramic models of the players and the barn itself, intended to be displayed on the nation's mantelpieces. Marten and Corder, represented in ceramics, were usually shown in the early stages of the story, still in love, hand in hand, meeting at the barn for their assignation. These were poignant scenes, showing an apparently happy courtship, with their real meaning – impending doom and death – only to be decoded by the well-informed viewer. (One almost wants to shout out, 'Maria, run away!') The figurines were objects that simply didn't work without background knowledge, and they seemed perfect for creating conversation and sociability.

Ceramic figures like these, apparently so bizarre today, illustrate an important development in Victorian cultural life: the crumbling of the notion that art was not something that could be owned by working people. In the seventeenth century, only the super-rich could afford to decorate their homes with paintings and sculpture. One of the great changes in interior decoration of the eighteenth century was the filtering down of the practice. When so many more people, as the result of trade and industrialization, began to have the spare cash to flash on soft furnishings or figurines, the Georgian concept of *taste* emerged. As a member of the middling rank in society, you needed to decorate your house not only expensively but in a way that revealed knowledge of antiquity, history and contemporary fashion.

But Georgian working people still lacked the spare cash to trick out their parlours with anything but the most functional items. One of the greatest visual changes to the homes of working people in the nineteenth century lay in their being able for the first time to afford items whose function was purely decorative, expressions of taste, and preferences, and personality.

So now mantelpieces began to be crowded with cheap, perhaps gaudy, but very personal items, such as ceramic figurines. They were selected for no other reason than that they pleased the owner, and formed part of his or her view of the world. These figurines were talking points; they showed characters that nearly everybody could recognize – yes, even notorious murderers – and represented a world of entertainment and intrigue beyond the daily grind.

Rather more exclusive than the china ornaments were the knick-knacks made from the timbers of the Red Barn itself. The very structure of the building was ripped up and sold off in pieces. There was a local newspaper report of a man 'seen passing through Polstead with a bundle of boards from the barn ... it was his intention to take them to London to make a variety of articles for sale as curiosities'. One such article is the little snuff box in the shape of a shoe, which still remains at Moyse's Hall Museum, Bury St Edmunds. Maria's missing gravestone suffered the same fate as the barn: it can no longer be seen as sightseers chiselled it away.

Even more desirable were items explicitly associated with the crime: one-offs, pieces that nobody else could have. In this category might be placed the lantern, also at the museum, which, it is claimed, was used by Maria's father when he discovered the body. Alex McWhirter, the curator, doubts that this was the actual lantern Mr Marten used, but it reveals how every possible association with the crime could be milked. Even more excitingly,

THE RED BARN

Seems to have taken its name from the tiles that cover part of it, and consists of a long wheat barn, with two divisions for corn; between which is the floor for threshing out the corn, and whereon the waggons are driven in harvest time, on one side tiled, and on the other a chaff-house, also tiled. Behind the barn is a projection or lean-to. and round a farm-yard, yet further in the rear, a thatched shed for shelter of the cattle in wet weather. The long roof of the barn was also thatched. There is a gate at the end of the yard, dividing the thatched shed.

A newspaper illustration of The Red Barn showing its lower
timbers missing because they had been sold as souvenirs.

the museum also has the truly authentic pistols with which Corder fired the deadly shot.

The most gruesome and valuable mementos of all are constituted from the actual body of the murderer. One of the highlights of the Moyse's Hall Museum is the celebrated 'skin book'. It's a volume, written by a *Times* journalist, about William Corder's life and death, and looks just like a normal book. Open it up, however, and a note on the inside of the cover tells you that its leather binding is in fact made out of the 'skin of the murderer', taken from his body, tanned and cured by one of the surgeons from the local hospital after the public dissection was over.

And then there was William Corder's own head, which somehow found its way into the hands of showmen and became a source of enormous entertainment and profit. When it was displayed by a stallholder during the annual two-week St Bartholomew's Fair in London soon after the trial, he took more than £100, twice the yearly salary of a shopkeeper or clerk. The display of human remains for money was not uncommon: in 1856, when the police were debating if the bodies of convicted criminals should be returned to their families, one inspector advised against it: 'I should rather fear that they will be inclined to exhibit' the corpses, he said, for financial gain.

William Corder's scalp eventually made its way back to Bury St Edmunds, where it still forms one of the highlights of the town museum. When I took it from its case to handle and examine it, I experienced a mixture of macabre pleasure and guilt at interfering with the remains of a human being. The scalp is now black, crispy and shrunken, but in a terribly creepy detail it still contains the fuzz of Corder's short, ginger hair, and still has one little round ear attached.

After the anatomization, William Corder's skeleton ended up for many years in the museum of the Royal College of Surgeons, but in 2004 his remains were removed from display and cremated. The fate of his skeleton perhaps seems the more civilized option. But it has to be said that William Corder's shrivelled ear does a great deal for the visitor numbers of the local museum in Bury St Edmunds. Its curators told me that every single week some local person with a dim memory of seeing it in childhood comes in specifically to ask if it's still there.

9

Stage Fright

'Of *Hamlet* we can make neither end nor side, and nine out of ten of us ... would like to be confined to the ghost scenes, and the funeral, and the killing off at the last. *Macbeth* would be better liked if it was only the witches and the fighting.'

London costermonger quoted by Henry Mayhew (1861)

The murder in the Red Barn produced a significant range of souvenirs and artefacts for collectors, but it also had an unusually interesting afterlife as a story told on stage. In 1830s London, visitors to St Bartholomew's Fair could choose between several alternative peepshow performances of the death of Maria Marten. The proprietors of peepshows always found murder a profitable subject. 'People is werry fond of battles in the country,' said one of their number to Henry Mayhew, 'but a murder wot is well known is worth more than all the fights.'

The peepshow, or its close companion the puppet show, did not yet have its modern-day connotations of light comedic entertainment for children. Many puppet shows were staged with all the weight and seriousness of tragedy. In fact, this was the medium by which people living in rural England were able to experience the best plays to be seen on the London stage, and the serious, adult-orientated puppet show was a vastly popular form of entertainment.

The Victoria and Albert Museum contains a pair of rather beautiful marionettes of William Corder and Maria Marten that were originally used to recreate her murder on stage. They are among 35 marionettes in the museum's collection, which were once possessions of the Tiller-Clowes Company, who ran a touring puppet theatre. Their 'Maria' had a wonderful special feature described in an inventory of their puppets as 'hair to come away'. This probably meant a lock of hair that could be lifted up by its own special and separate string. It might have been added to allow William Corder to drag her about by the hair in the course of killing her, or it could simply have been to allow Maria's hair to stand on end in fright. 'Maria Marten' puppets also often had a 'blood string', a string that was pulled out of their body at the moment of death, with a piece of red cloth attached to represent a sanguinary gush.*

I have had the pleasure of operating the museum's puppet of William Corder under the supervision of its curator, Cathy Haill, and found myself taking an inappropriate level of enjoyment in causing him to kill his Maria once again. It's almost impossible

---

* To see this in action, it's worth visiting the Victoria and Albert Museum's website to see a wonderful performance of the climactic killing, featuring the historical marionette puppets and the voices of actors Bill Nighy and Diana Quick: www.vam.ac.uk/content/videos/m/video-maria-marten-or-murder-in-the-red-barn.

today to imagine the mindset where a puppet like Corder could be used to express pathos or horror rather than comedy, but that was his original purpose.

Shows like those put on by the Tiller-Clowes Company were completely portable. A wooden theatre frontage with canvas sides would be packed into wagons (or, later, vans) and driven from fair to fair. Once erected, up to 200 spectators could be packed inside, or a really big puppet theatre could seat 600. On the stage the marionettes appeared within their own miniature proscenium arch. Their features were exaggerated so that each of the five or six 'stock' characters could be easily recognized: the old woman, the policeman, the villain, the handsome young man and the heroine. The William Corder I handled has a villainous moustache, bulbous staring blue eyes, with bold and sinister black rims. He also has a red dot at the inner point of each eye: a make-up technique recommended in early greasepaint manuals for the making of a living actor's eye look whiter and fresher. 'Maria Marten', on the other hand, wears a virginal white dress, has yellow ribbons in her hair and lovely pink cheeks.

The text of the play *Maria Marten, or Murder in the Red Barn* that was used by the Tiller-Clowes Company indicates a conventional theatrical performance, and the audience would have expected exactly the same level of drama, excitement, tragedy and horror. 'Oh, William, behold me on my knees,' says Maria, as she begs for her life. A stage direction follows: 'she tries to escape. He seizes her – throws her round', until finally, 'he dashes her to the earth, and stabs her. She shrieks and falls. He stands motionless till the curtain falls.'

Puppet performances continued throughout the nineteenth century, until finally brought to a halt by improvements to public transport – once people could travel to their nearest town with ease, they became less interested in having the travelling theatre come to them – as well as the growth of the cinema. The First World War proved the death blow to the old puppet show families. With the young men removed, there was no one to carve the puppets, perform the shows, or drive the van. When puppetry was revived after the war, it returned as much more of an entertainment for children.

The story of Maria Marten was so popular, though, that it remained prominent even in the dwindling repertoires of late nineteenth-century puppet troupes. It had all the characteristics of *melodrama* in the technical sense: an implausible, over-the-top, formulaic but extremely lively and participatory form of theatre which flourished with both mechanical and human actors, in both informal and formal settings.

In the London theatres the story of the Red Barn became the most celebrated work of the age that the genre of melodrama could offer. One of the defining features of melodrama is the role, in the story, of 'fate' or 'destiny'. The doom-laden red sunset said to have given the Red Barn its original name seemed almost deliberately identical to a melodramatic lighting effect.

Victorian melodrama was ghoulish in the extreme: acts of violence, drawn out, prolonged and magnified so as completely to avoid any sense of realism or authenticity. Today it seems almost impossible that it would have been taken seriously. And yet, to its audience, it wasn't a joke. Rosalind Crone explains how the reaction of the spectators was a very important part of the show. They would hiss the villain, and shout out curses against the murderer when he was captured. Closure, the righting of wrongs and the healing of the wounds in the community were all important aspects of watching a murder on stage. Melodrama allowed people to let off steam.

Real-life murders formed the basis of only a small percentage of the plays that showed people dying or committing crimes, but the playbills telling people what was on at the theatre would be pasted upon London walls alongside the broadsheets recounting real-life crimes. The boundary between fiction and fact was blurred. The play called *Ruth Martin, the Fatal Dreamer*, performed in 1846, clearly drew on Maria Marten and her mother's dream without being faithful to the facts, as did another spin-off called *The Red Farm*.

But real melodrama could only be seen in a specialized form of theatre. The Victorian theatrical business was divided in two. Firstly, there were the proper, authorized theatres of the West End, the so-called Theatres Royal. Only they were authorized to stage dramas, tragedy rather than melodrama, and did so with the approval of the Lord Chamberlain. Then, there was a thriving counter-culture in the form of the 'minor' or 'illegitimate theatres'. Forbidden from performing canonical works, they turned instead to other forms of entertainment such as musicals, burlesque, pantomime or murder shows. The two types of theatre, so very different, ran alongside each other until 1843, when finally the Theatres Act decreed that any theatre could perform any kind of show, so long as it was licensed.

Theatres weren't just for the well-off – indeed, until much later in the century, the Victorian middle classes often looked down on the theatre, considering it vulgar. And yet theatre managers wanted their venues to be thought of as safe, well-regulated and respectable as well as cheap. In November 1846, the manager of the Victoria Theatre claimed his patrons included 'the industrious Mechanic'. 'HERE for a small amount saved from his earnings,' the manager somewhat pompously declaimed, 'He can witness an excellent and superior Entertainment and go cheerfully to his work on the morrow, with the consciousness that he has not purchased a too-dearly-bought gratification.'

Melodrama required a particular, stylized form of acting, intended to get the story out from the stage to a huge auditorium containing perhaps one thousand people. One nineteenth-century theatre handbook gives instructions for expressing despair. The actor: 'Rolls the eyes and sometimes bites the lips and gnashes with the teeth ... [the body] strained and violently agitated. Groans, expressive of inward torture, accompany the words.'

No wonder *Punch* satirized the melodramatic actor, who 'is murdered at least twice a week, commits parricide several times in the course of the year, and is torn by remorse every night at about nine o'clock'.*

The writers of these plays had to keep churning out the stories, and, inevitably, many of the plots had similarities and overlaps. As with 'Penny Bloods', the main intention was to show ordinary people, just like members of the audience, caught up in dramatic events, and, ultimately, for good to triumph. Most importantly,

---

* Charles Dickens, a frequent theatregoer, captured the special style of delivering speech employed by the actors in a melodrama: 'I ster-ruck him down and fel-ed in er'orror! ... I have liveder as a beggar – a roadside vaigerant, but no ker-rime since then has stained these hands!'

argues Rosalind Crone, a melodrama had to tell 'a nostalgic story, its plots looking back to a perceived golden age in which the simplicities and innocence of rural or village life were preferred to the corrupting, anonymous city'.

Despite the cheap thrills, and the fact that it took place in 'illegitimate' theatres, melodrama was not a subversive form of entertainment. If a wicked master seduced an innocent girl, he was punished. In dramatic versions of *Maria Marten*, the facts were often simplified. Maria Marten's illegitimate children are not mentioned, William Corder becomes an out-and-out cad with no motive apart from evil: he is a 'nasty, mean, ugly, sulky fellow'. The dialogue is terrifyingly straightforward: when Maria begs for mercy, William replies: 'Nay ... 'tis in vain, for I am desperate in my thoughts, and thirst for blood.'

The stage directions next tell us that: 'He again tries to stab her. She clings round his neck. He dashes her to the earth and stabs her. She shrieks and falls. He stands motionless till the curtain falls.'

The emotions would be heightened by the tremendous swellings and wailings of the orchestra. Another version of the text includes some specific directions for the music: as William Corder is seen digging the grave in preparation for Maria's arrival at the barn, 'villain's music' is played. While Maria begs for her life, 'tremolo strings' are to be heard. When finally he kills her, there is artificial 'thunder and lightning'.

The actual moment of murder in a melodrama would sometimes even be repeated at the demand of the audience. One particular actor named 'Bricks' was a dab hand at death, as appears from an account of a performance published in 1867. Bricks portrayed a particularly long-drawn-out expiration with great skill, so much so that the audience:

> Applauded him most lustily, and when they had finished cheering, one of them, led away by his enthusiasm, stood upon his seat, and ... roared out at the topmost pitch of a very strong voice, 'Die again, my bold Bricks! Die again!' The cry was answered by the rest of the gallery and Bricks enthusiastically rose to his feet and did 'die again'.

This description of the absolute *involvement* of the audience is telling. A good melodrama drew theatregoers into a collective emotional response. The modern equivalent would be a football match, or a pop concert, where the performance itself is only part of what people pay for. They really buy tickets to experience – and to express – powerful emotion. When Bill Sikes killed Nancy in a performance of *Oliver Twist*, one spectator remembered how:

> Nancy was always dragged round the stage by her hair, and after this effort Sikes always looked up defiantly to the gallery ... He was always answered by one loud and fearful curse, yelled by the whole mass like a Handel Festival chorus ... no expression of dynamite invented by the modern anarchist, no language ever dreamt of in Bedlam, could equal the outburst.

The Lord Chamberlain was very worried about murder appearing on stage, particularly when it was derived from real crime. 'Representations of real murders on the stage appear to me to be very undesirable,' he wrote in 1862. 'It only gives the Public a morbid feeling and encourages mischievous thoughts in their minds.'

But he was wrong. Far from celebrating crime, melodramatic performances gave their audiences an outlet for condemning it, and everyone must have left the theatre feeling happier and safer in the knowledge that the villain was dead.

However, the Lord Chamberlain was right in saying that melo-drama was, by 1862, on the decline. Tastes were moving away from this bold, unsubtle form of acting, not least because the design of theatres themselves was changing. Stalls replaced the pit, the lights were dimmed during the performance (this hadn't been done before) and the audience was expected to be quiet. The half-price show at 9 p.m., standard practice in melodrama days, was abolished, so people who couldn't get away from work in time for the earlier performance, or who couldn't afford a full-price ticket, found it impossible to attend.

The working people who had enjoyed melodrama so much began to desert the theatre at this point, and it became a more middle-class place of resort. In order for the audience to continue to smoke, drink and talk during the performance, a new form of entertainment – the music hall – sprang up to accommodate the former fans of melodrama. But here murder was no longer on the menu.

10

The Bermondsey Horror

'Old and young, pray take a warning
Females, lead a virtuous life.
Think upon the fateful morning
Frederick Manning and his wife'.

Ballad sold and sung at the execution
of Frederick and Maria Manning

The culmination of this earliest phase in the history of murder came in 1849. A case known as 'The Bermondsey Horror', it had all the trappings of a 'stunning good' murder. And it was also one of the final few to end with an old-fashioned hanging in public before a vast crowd.

You would think that a sordid death involving a love triangle in Bermondsey would cause far less of a stir than the terrible cholera epidemic sweeping through London that hot summer. By September, the epidemic had claimed more than 10,000 Londoners' lives, including two of the witnesses who had been due to give evidence at the trial of Frederick and Maria Manning.

Following the story of the Mannings, though, was a welcome alternative to worrying about one's health. It became a national obsession. 'At this moment,' suggested *Punch* in September 1849, 'refined, civilized, philanthropic London reeks with the foulness of the Bermondsey murder.' The cholera, a far more frightening 'Bermondsey Horror', might come and grab anybody at all. Yet it was comforting to think that only the immoral and unworthy were likely to be discovered buried, as the Mannings' victim was, beneath a kitchen floor.

The case also had a very attractive cast of criminals: two for the price of one, husband and wife, apparently working as a team (although the husband tried to blame it all on his wife). Maria in particular was a wonderful villainess, with a few quirks that caused her quickly to be forced into the mould of Lady Macbeth.

She was born in Switzerland as Marie, and later Anglicized her name to Maria. She had lived the high life as a lady's maid, travelling abroad and staying with her mistress in grand country houses. This association with high society caused a frisson. The cast-off clothes from her mistresses allowed Maria to amass rather a spectacular wardrobe: after her capture, she was discovered to possess 11 petticoats, 9 gowns, 28 pairs of stockings, 7 pairs of drawers and 19 pairs of kid gloves. She dressed far above her station as a former servant, and most striking of all was her figure-hugging, black satin gown.

Maria had hoped to marry one Joseph O'Connor, a man rather older than herself and considerably richer. O'Connor had amassed his wealth through lending money, and various dodgy dealings down in the docks where he worked for the Customs and Excise

Department. But he dallied and toyed with Maria and failed to make her his wife. She fell back instead upon Frederick Manning, not a particularly prepossessing choice of husband. He had been a guard on a railway train before losing his job, and had then failed in business as a publican. Maria supported them both, working as a dressmaker, and probably regretted her marriage. The couple were clinging on to the lowest levels of respectable, middle-class life, and their grip was very tenuous indeed.

But the wealthy Joseph O'Connor was still on the scene. The two men competed for Maria's attentions, and O'Connor was often to be found at the Mannings' home, No. 3, Miniver Place, Bermondsey. Passions ran high, and on 9 August O'Connor failed to return home to his lodgings after a roast chicken dinner at Miniver Place. The Mannings had shot him and finished him off by bashing in his head. The police surgeon later calculated that O'Connor had been hit 17 times with a crowbar. The couple had then put his body in quicklime in an attempt to make it decompose speedily, and buried him beneath the slabs near their kitchen fireplace. Once the body was discovered, O'Connor's identity would be confirmed by the dentist who had made his false teeth, which had been left in his mouth. The Mannings were rather inept criminals, it has to be admitted.

And now, perhaps realizing this, dissention broke out between them. The two of them ran, and in opposite directions. With considerable coolness, Maria made the first move. She went to O'Connor's house and stole his share certificates. She also made off with the joint wealth of herself and her husband and took a train to Edinburgh. Frederick, meanwhile, fled to the Channel Islands.

The Metropolitan Police were on the case, and their speedy solution would greatly boost their prestige. After O'Connor's disappearance, two constables were sent round to No. 3, Miniver Place. PC Barnes, number 256 from K division, and PC Burton, number 272 from M division, found the house empty: 'the nest was there but the birds had flown'. But they noticed something odd about the kitchen floor. Further investigation revealed the body of O'Connor, now blue and in a state of some decomposition.

The constables' superiors were quickly on to the trail of the killers. Maria Manning had sent her luggage off separately for storage, but the police were not distracted by this red herring. They were able to track down the cab driver who had taken the lady herself to Euston. Travelling under the name of Mrs Smith, she had departed by the 6.15 a.m. train for Edinburgh. The Metropolitan Police sent a telegraph message to their counterparts in Scotland, asking them to be on the lookout for their suspect.

When Maria tried to cash in the stolen shares in Edinburgh, she aroused suspicion at the stockbroker's office. Although she claimed that she lived in Glasgow, she had a foreign accent. A wire to London confirmed in no time that she matched the description of the suspected killer, and she was apprehended. It all unfolded with a smoothness and efficiency – a modernity – that provides an extreme contrast to the Ratcliffe Highway case nearly 40 years before.

While all this was happening, Maria's hapless husband had been drinking himself into a sorry state in Jersey. He, too, was captured and brought back to London. His first words after his arrest were aimed at the wife who had outwitted him: 'Is the wretch taken? … She is the guilty party, I am as innocent as a lamb.' (At least, that's how the respectable papers reported it. It's possible that he used a word worse than 'wretch'.) During the journey back to London, he had to be taken off the train at Vauxhall, one stop before the terminus, to avoid the enormous crowd that had gathered to see him at Waterloo.

The Times ran no fewer than 72 different stories about the case, and, during the trial, Maria in particular gave wonderful entertainment through her unusual, unwomanly behaviour. As well as the murder, she had stolen money and double-crossed her husband. She had also committed a further series of 'crimes', not against the law, but against *propriety*. She was unattractively cold and composed in court – 'almost as motionless as a statue, and was never seen, throughout the day, to turn her eyes towards her husband' – and people were affronted by her manner. 'She does not exhibit the slightest emotion,' onlookers recorded.

And then the verdict was announced. Frederick Manning turned down the customary offer for the accused to address the court. But Maria seized it, and let loose with a violent harangue against the legal system, the judge and the British people. Her impressive clothes – 'a black or dark dress, fitting closely up to the throat' – only added to the impression of a frightening, powerful and dominating woman. 'Jezebel', she was called, or 'The Lady Macbeth of Bermondsey'. In a final blow to her reputation, Maria was a sexually active woman who had lived with two men – even, apparently, with two men at the same time. She seemed somehow to be *even worse* than a male murderer. As her husband's barrister summed it up at her trial: 'History teaches us that the female is capable of reaching higher in point of virtue than the male, but that when once she gives way to vice, she sinks far lower than our sex.'

Under Queen Victoria, respectability, propriety and chastity were values on the rise, and Maria Manning transgressed them all.

———•———

The joint execution of the Mannings upon the roof of Horsemonger Lane Gaol was one of the most hotly anticipated of the nineteenth century. A whole three days before the set date, the nearby streets were cleared and barricaded off, in expectation of a crowd that was estimated to number 30,000. Five hundred policemen were present to keep order.

Going to a public hanging had many of the same qualities as a trip to see a tragedy at the theatre. There were the crowds, the food- and drink-sellers, and better seats for those rich enough to afford them. The owners of houses near the gaol not only sold seats in any window with a view, but even erected scaffolding against their frontages to accommodate many more. Contemporary descriptions of the crowds at hangings often stressed their disreputable and lower-class character. But in fact respectable commentators omitted the fact that many middle-class and even aristocratic people were also present.

Salesmen at a hanging would now hawk about broadsides as if they were programmes for a play.* Once the expectant spectators

———

* An inspector in the Metropolitan Police in 1866 made the parallel explicitly. It was his duty to mix 'frequently with crowds, at theatre and different places [...] it appears to me that they look upon a theatrical scene precisely in the same way as upon an execution'.

were gathered, programmes in hand, the hanging followed an inexorable narrative arc. It began with the solemn ascension of the condemned to the scaffold, followed by his or her moving last words and lamentations. Then came a period of growing suspense, as the end drew near, and the crowd speculated upon whether or not the drop would work successfully the first time. The final denouement was the horrific jerking of the body.

Maria Manning did not disappoint in the semi-theatrical role she now assumed, displaying her unwomanly self-confidence and scorn to the end. It was reported (whether true or not) that she had insisted upon having an unworn pair of silk stockings for her final costume, and, in a last moment of role reversal, she 'walked to her doom with a firm, unfaltering step'. Meanwhile, her husband had to be carried by two gaolers as he was so 'feeble and tottering'.

The sight of Maria's death left a lasting impression on many in the crowd. Charles Dickens described her body as 'a fine shape, so elaborately corseted and artfully dressed, that it was quite unchanged in its trim appearance as it swung slowly from side to side'. She would live on in popular imagination, transformed into the character of Hortense, the murderous maid in *Bleak House*. Like Maria, Hortense is an uncomfortable, edgy character, who helps the lawyer Mr Tulkinghorn to uncover the secrets of her employer, Lady Dedlock. 'I don't know what Mademoiselle Hortense may want or mean, unless she is mad,' Tulkinghorn says. When Tulkinghorn dismisses Hortense and fails to find her another job, she shoots him, and attempts to frame Lady Dedlock herself for the murder.

Like Manning, Hortense came to stand for fear, social disorder and the unknown. *Bleak House*'s narrator, Esther Summerson, thought Hortense 'seemed to bring visibly before me some woman from the streets of Paris in the reign of terror'. Even more disturbingly, it's hinted that Hortense is a lesbian, and thereby even outside the sexual control of men. Dickens shows her as a wild beast, with a 'feline mouth'. She pants, like a tigress, or else paces about, 'a very near She-Wolf imperfectly tamed'. ('You are a vixen, a vixen!' says her victim.) Hortense is one of Dickens's few effective grown-up female characters, and perfectly captures the middle-class fear that even the trusted servant living beneath one's own roof could in fact be a murderer.

Maria Manning also achieved lasting fame at the Waxworks. In Madame Tussaud's gallery, *Punch* noted, she stood 'in silk attire, a beauteous thing to be daily rained upon by a shower of sixpences'. The moral poison of this display, the writer thought, seeped out 'from the Chamber of Horrors, contaminating not only Baker Street, but all London'. Despite – or, perhaps, because of – the immorality she represented, her effigy became one of the 'immortals' of the gallery, remaining on display for well over a century. She was still there, on my very own first visit to the Chamber of Horrors, in the 1970s. And in a final, brilliantly weird detail, the gallery also displayed a model of Manning's notorious Bermondsey kitchen.

———

As we have seen, Dickens took a good deal of trouble to enjoy the Mannings' execution, hiring a room, inviting friends, organizing refreshments. But in the end he found the occasion distressing and it caused him to become a vociferous opponent of public hangings. In his opinion, the crowd, baying for blood,

The figure of Maria Manning displayed
in Madame Tussaud's gallery, dressed in
her celebrated black satin dress.

was uncouth, frightening and uncivilized, and displayed tremendous 'wickedness and levity'. In a letter to *The Times*, Dickens described how:

Thieves, low prostitutes, ruffians and vagabonds of every kind, flocked on to the ground, with every variety of offensive and foul behaviour. Fightings, faintings, whistlings, imitations of

Punch, brutal jokes, tumultuous demonstrations of indecent delight when swooning women were dragged out of the crowd by the police with their dresses disordered, gave a new zest to the general entertainment.

All in all, Dickens thought that:

When the two miserable creatures who attracted all this ghastly sight about them were turned quivering into the air, there was no more emotion, no more pity, no more thought that two immortal souls had gone to judgement, no more restraint ... than if the name of Christ had never been heard in this world.

Dickens soon started up a campaign against the practice of public hangings. But it was a form of spectacle that was already on the decline. The Mannings' execution had drawn such a great deal of attention in part for the very reason that hangings had become something of a rarity.

The change had been inevitable since 1823 and the repeal of the set of laws known today as 'The Bloody Code'. By 1800, there were more than 200 different crimes punishable by death. Many of these had been added to the statute book over the course of the eighteenth century, and were crimes against property: crimes carried out, essentially, by the poor, against the rich. You only had to steal goods worth twelve pence to run the risk of death by hanging.

The year 1823 had seen the passing of the 'Judgement of Death Act', which greatly reduced the number of capital crimes. From now on, the only criminals who would be punished by death were those guilty of treason or murder. Those convicted of property crimes were to be transported instead. It has long been traditional among historians to ascribe the change to a humanitarian and tolerant spirit among law-makers. But V. A. C. Gatrell finds our ancestors less sentimental than that, claiming that the legal system simply couldn't cope with the huge number of hangings. The penalties were reduced simply to get justice moving again.

Either way, the reduction in the number of hangings was accompanied by a change in the nature of the criminals hanged. The eighteenth-century hanged man or woman was very often an Everyman or Everywoman, someone who had perhaps stolen goods worth a few pence and had the bad luck to be caught. There was a sense that anybody could accidentally become a criminal; that culpable weakness lurked in every human being. That is why the 'loveable rogue', the 'Robin Hood' figure and the gallant highwayman are stock figures in Georgian culture.

From 1823 onwards, though, only *really bad* men and women would be hanged. These people were seen as profoundly flawed, and fundamentally different from the spectators of their deaths. This essential otherness, this difference from the rest of us, is an essential angle of the glamorous murderer created by Thomas De Quincey.

Dickens in 1849 was acting, as he so often did, as a barometer of popular public opinion. If he thought that the spectacle of a hanging had grown distasteful, then so too would his enormous number of readers. People who believed themselves to be civilized no longer felt the need to experience the punishment dealt out to the guilty. They began to trust the proper authorities to see that done.

The law took a little time to catch up, but change it did, and the last public hanging took place in 1868. Capital punishment continued, but invisibly, behind the walls of prisons. And this was a vital precondition for the classic detective story to emerge. Detective fiction, unlike melodrama, or 'Penny Blood' fiction, didn't care about retribution. Its concern was more the *solution* of crime.

Murderers themselves, the detectives who hunted them down, and the authors who processed real life into fiction: all were about to reach a new level of sophistication.

Part Two

Enter the Detective

11

Middle-Class Murderers and Medical Gentlemen

'Fie on these dealers in poison, say I: can they not keep to the old honest way of cutting throats?'

Thomas De Quincey, 'On Murder' (1821)

The Ratcliffe Highway Murders took place beneath the high walls of London's Tobacco Dock, while Frederick and Maria Manning lived in cholera-stricken Bermondsey. John Williams, the seaman, and Maria Marten, the mole-catcher's daughter, never brushed with high society. The events and characters of the first part of our story seemed a world away from the secure, prosperous homes of the West End. But once the 'great' murders of the earlier nineteenth century had given readers a taste for lurid death, the activity of enjoying a murder became increasingly acceptable higher up the social scale. Victorian murder became something of a middle-class pastime, and began to take place – both in real life and in fiction – at the heart of the supposedly safe haven of the respectable home.

By the second half of the nineteenth century, the murder rate, as far as we can identify it, was once again falling: from 1.7 per

100,000 people in the 1860s, to 1 per 100,000 in the 1890s. Most crime continued to take place among the poverty-stricken and desperate, and criminals were most frequently young men accused of theft. Yet a murder in a well-to-do family was far more attractive to journalists and authors. We start to hear less about stabbing, bludgeoning and the cutting of throats, and much more about madness, bigamy and poison. And the archetypal murderer's weapon of choice was something fairly ubiquitous in the Victorian home: arsenic.

Historian James Whorton describes the poison's devastating effects if swallowed:

> it produces a sharp, burning sensation in the stomach and oesophagus (usually about 30 to 60 minutes after ingestion), and then profuse vomiting and diarrhoea lasting for hours. Ultimately, the poison damages the heart and other viscera, but typically death comes only after 12 to 24 hours, or even longer. Statistics from the 1800s suggest that about half of those poisoned died.

Unfortunately for the health of the Victorians, arsenic was also a very useful chemical. It was commonly used for killing rats, in colouring green wallpaper and in fixing the bright new dyes that caused mid-century fashions to flare brightly with colour. Its insidious effects could be extremely debilitating: sometimes invalids got better during a trip to the seaside simply because they were no longer breathing in toxic fumes from their bedroom wallpaper at home.

And it was very readily available. 'On account of the facility with which it may be procured in this country, even by the lowest of the vulgar,' wrote one toxicologist in 1829, 'it is the poison most frequently chosen for the purpose of committing murder.' Completely odourless, it could easily be slipped into food or drink. In France, arsenic was known as *poudre de succession*, or 'inheritance powder', and until 1836 it was impossible to detect whether arsenic was present in a dead body. Its effects were almost indistinguishable from those of cholera.

That year, however, a chemist named James Marsh published an article in the *Edinburgh New Philosophical Journal* titled an 'Account of a method of separating small quantities of arsenic from substances with which it may be mixed'. This was the so-called 'Marsh Test', a method of detecting arsenic, and the discovery would have far-reaching effects, raising people's awareness of this silent, secret killer.

The 1840s became a decade characterized by a new fear of being poisoned. The journal *Household Words* claimed that 249 people had been poisoned to death between 1839 and 1849, but that only 85 murderers had been convicted. Poisoning was 'a moral epidemic more formidable than any plague', claimed the *Pharmaceutical Journal*. Likewise, *The Times* believed that many deaths by poison escaped the notice of doctors, and one of its writers pointed out the peculiar horror of a poisoning: 'domestic treason' was implied, the poisoner presenting the smiling face of spouse, friend or doctor.

But a big dose of arsenic was a crude and violent way of finishing someone off, and once the Marsh Test had been created, the murderer was in danger of detection if the remains of his victims were examined. It was much more sophisticated and slick to administer poison drop by drop, causing the victim's health to decline over time, so that the final *coup de grâce* would arouse no suspicion. The 'clumsy method of poisoning by large doses of arsenic', as the *Pharmaceutical Journal* put it, was about to give way to poisoning 'as an exact science'.

One of the most prolific poisoners of the period (at least among those caught) was Mary Ann Cotton, who seems to have successfully killed three husbands, fifteen children or step-children and a lodger. Her motive was to benefit financially from insurance policies taken out in their names. Suspicion was aroused when, after the death of one of her little boys, she visited the insurance company's office even before calling on the doctor. She was found guilty and hanged at Durham Gaol.

Many believed (albeit without particularly convincing proof) that the new and vigorous industry of life insurance was growing hand in hand with sales of deadly arsenic. Such was the concern that, in 1850, Parliament decided that the lives of children under three years old could not be insured for more than £3.

But the most sensational poisoner case of the nineteenth century was that of William Palmer, of Rugeley. Its notoriety was due to the fact that – like Harold Shipman in the twentieth century – every affluent newspaper reader felt that he or she could easily have become one of his victims. For Palmer was a doctor.

Born in Staffordshire in 1824, Palmer trained as a chemist in Liverpool, studied medicine in London and obtained his licence from the Royal College of Surgeons in 1846. He then returned to his native Rugeley to practise. Palmer struggled to live within his means,

Dr William Palmer of Rugeley, poisoner.

and also seemed terribly unlucky in his family life. He married, and his mother-in-law came to join his household. She soon died in mysterious circumstances. Four of Palmer's children then died, of 'convulsions'. These deaths didn't seem unusual at first – infant deaths were much more common at the time – but when his wife died, too, at the age of 27, it seemed that Palmer was shedding relatives with remarkable rapidity. He had insured her life for £13,000.

Palmer attempted to take out another life insurance policy on his brother, who suffered from alcoholism, but now his actions were beginning to arouse suspicion. The insurance company sent Dickens's friend, Inspector Field, to Rugeley to investigate what was going on (Scotland Yard detectives were available for private hire by anyone with the money to pay). Field concluded that the company should not pay up, as Palmer had been encouraging his brother to drink himself to death. Meanwhile, he'd also begun an affair with his housemaid, with whom he had an illegitimate child. It seemed that Palmer's life was slipping out of his control.

Financial security could, perhaps, have been restored if Palmer's final plot, against another friend, John Parsons Cook, had succeeded. Cook was a rich if weak-willed young man, who was Palmer's betting buddy. After a very successful day's gambling together at the horse races in 1855, Cook was flush with funds. But instead of enjoying his triumph, he felt rather sick, and was overheard to claim that 'that damn Palmer has been dosing me'. Cook retreated to the Talbot Arms Inn, in Rugeley, to recuperate. Luckily, it seems, this inn was situated opposite Palmer's house, so Cook's friend was on hand to provide treatment. But the patient's condition only improved when Palmer was called away to London.

On Palmer's return, the pattern of sickness returned too. Cook seems repeatedly to have fallen ill after drinks given to him by his doctor: after the brandy, a cup of coffee, and after the coffee, a bowl of soup. (Palmer is often credited with introducing a novelty into the English language: the friendly offer of a drink, 'What's your poison?' Rather disappointingly, however, its first recorded use dates from well after his death.) Poor old Cook eventually expired, vomiting and writhing, his entire body convulsed by his agonising final throes.

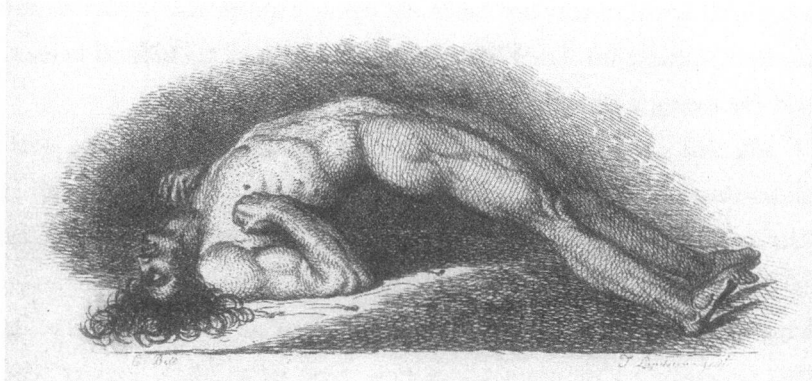

The death throes of Joseph Cook were much discussed. The arching of the body could have been the result of tetanus, or strychnine poisoning.

It later emerged that Palmer had been a frequent purchaser of strychnine, although the two chemists who'd sold it to him had both failed to record the fact – as they were obliged to by law – in their shop's 'Poison Books'. And, once Cook was dead, Palmer was able further to exploit his standing as a doctor. Even though Cook had accused Palmer of poisoning him during his last, painful hours, the doctor was allowed, as a courtesy, to attend his friend's post-mortem.

It was a procedure flawed from start to finish. The coroner's assistant, Charles Newton, had been drinking, and Palmer exploited the general atmosphere of disorganization to jostle the person charged with removing Cook's stomach so that its contents were spilt on the floor. Later, it seems that Palmer tried to bribe the courier charged with taking the stomach to the London train to make it go missing, and when it arrived in London for analysis the jar in which the stomach had been placed was found to have been tampered with: its top had been slit open. Palmer also wrote to the coroner, asking for Cook's death to be ascribed to natural causes, and enclosing a ten-pound bribe.

All this came out at Palmer's trial, which was followed with enormous interest and enthusiasm. The *Law Times* would call it 'the longest, greatest, gravest and most important criminal trial of the nineteenth century'. It piqued the interest of a generation who believed that poison and poisoners were everywhere. It also brought to prominence a new type of medical expert: the analytical chemist.

The prosecution's job was to prove that Palmer had used poison. A vast array of expert witnesses now appeared in the courtroom, some to make the case, others to refute it. These people and their expertise were unfamiliar to the reading public, but now they stepped forward into the limelight and into the newspapers. Numerous pictures of the 'analytical chemists' appeared in the press, and their testimony was reproduced, word for word, for the nation to read over breakfast.

'Expert witnesses' in toxicology had begun to appear in trials in the eighteenth century, but it was the development of the Marsh Test for arsenic that gave the specialist chemist his role in murder cases. From 1836, when the test was established, it gradually became clear that it needed to be conducted by a qualified chemist, and not simply by the doctor who performed the post-mortem. The test itself was dangerous: indeed, by the year 1900, no fewer than eight scientists had themselves died from inhaling the fumes while performing it. In the media glare of Palmer's trial, specialist toxicologists such as Alfred Swaine Taylor, of Guy's Hospital in

London, and William Herapath, of St Peter's Hospital in Bristol, became the faces of an exciting new profession.

The aim of 'the Medical Gentlemen', as they were called, was ambitious: it was to make the corpse speak. They claimed, in their laboratories, to be able to read invisible evidence from the dead body that could tell the story of a crime. As one writer put it of the contemporary toxicologist, his work caused 'the vulgar to marvel at the mysterious power by which an atom [of poison] mingled amidst a mass of confused ingesta can still be detected'.

But Dr William Palmer's case was filled with suspense because, despite their best efforts, these magicians of the modern age failed to prove that there was strychnine in Cook's stomach. Taylor, the most prominent among all the toxicologists, was on the prosecution side. But he was unable to identify strychnine in Cook's body, finding instead only a little bit of antimony, a heavy metal. This latter drug was indeed poisonous, but it was also a constituent of many medicines, and its presence did not prove murder. The difficulty was that strychnine was extremely hard to find. It was, as Taylor said, 'so speedily absorbed in the blood that in the course of an hour after the administration no chemical test at present known could detect it'.

Taylor, a well-known expert witness and the author of a book called *A Manual of Medical Jurisprudence*, was particularly good at combining legal precedent and knowledge of the workings of the law with chemistry. Unlike others, he understood the different standards of 'proof' required in the courtroom and in medicine. 'A court of law,' he wrote, 'requires to know whether arsenic [for example] was present and was the cause of death, rather than whether it was mixed with traces of bismuth or lead, a fact which however interesting in a chemical, is wholly unimportant in a medico-legal way.'

At Palmer's trial, though, William Herapath, a pioneer of arsenic testing, provided Taylor with a worthy adversary. The two of them were in competition for status and success, and Herapath led the team of ten medical witnesses for the defence, all of them arguing for the weakness of the process of identifying strychnine in the body.

However, despite the absence of evidence for strychnine, Palmer was still convicted. The evidence of the poison purchase, Palmer's parlous financial situation and his suspicious behaviour at the post-mortem all told against him. The work of Taylor and the medical experts for the prosecution was bolstered by the testimony of the chambermaid at the inn who witnessed Cook's death: the arching of his spine as he died, the stiffening of his limbs and the wild look in his eyes were all considered compatible with the poison theory.

Palmer was hanged on 14 June 1856, before a crowd of 30,000 at Stafford prison. On the scaffold, he apparently teased or taunted those following his case with these words: 'I am innocent of poisoning Cook by strychnine.' Did he mean he was altogether innocent? Or was he hinting at the use of some other poison? It was a wonderfully titillating moment, and there are still residents of Rugeley today who believe that Palmer, their local hero, was innocent.

Taylor seemed to have won the tussle between the toxicologists. But despite his star status among the medical witnesses, his failure to find any evidence of strychnine in Cook's body damaged his reputation. In subsequent editions of his *Manual*, which had been published before the Palmer trial, he took the trouble to include several pages justifying his actions. And years later, Herapath would get his revenge. In 1859, Taylor made an unfortunate mistake in the trial of one Thomas Smethurst. He'd relied upon just one type of test for arsenic, when it would have been wiser to check his results with the multiple methods by then available. Herapath wrote to *The Times*, accusing Taylor of 'a bungle', and claiming that 'no sound chemist' would have certified 'to the presence of arsenic by such an analysis'. It's amusing to hear these lofty and respectable men of science doing each other down, but it also shows how they, along with the science they represented, were still feeling their way, testing and promoting different means of determining the truth.

———

As the historian Ian Burney has pointed out, poisoning was a crime that was peculiarly attractive to the Victorian imagination. Murder by poisoning fitted in with much that was novel about their contemporary society. People now lived in cities, cheek by jowl with strangers, at a distant remove from their kin and friends. Poison was administered remotely, impersonally. It wasn't a crime of passion, but instead embodied what might even be considered to be typical Victorian virtues: forethought and meticulous planning.

Poison was unnatural and invisible, like many of the chemicals that made the Victorians' world comfortable and convenient by comparison with the past. It could only be detected by modern medical professionals with skills and subtlety as advanced as those of the poisoner himself. As William Baker, a coroner, said in 1840:

'In the rude ages, the means resorted to ... was always of a bold and violent description, and left its traces behind, but now villainy is so refined ... that the murderer leaves scarcely a clue to his discovery.'

The fathers of prosperous families who were living the Victorian ideal – a big, respectable town house, servants, wife's life insured – were particularly affected by the story of poisoners like William Palmer. He even looked like one of them. In physical appearance, Palmer was likened to 'John Bull': the archetypal red-faced, bluff, hearty Englishman.

And yet, at the same time he had enormous debts, he was addicted to betting on horses, he had voracious and improper sexual appetites. In short, he was a man with a secret darkness at the heart of his apparently successful life. William Bally, one of the phrenologists who examined Palmer's head, claims to have read exactly this from the bumps of the murderer's skull: 'a man who, as a rule, would be respectful, polite and even charitable; but one who, for any preconceived object, would act most cunningly and secretly, perfectly indifferent to honour or truth.'

To middle-class readers of the newspapers, the respectable sounding Dr William Palmer was the first in a run of a new and horrifying type of murderer, who seemed to have access to their very own drawing rooms. Sir Arthur Conan Doyle may have had the last word on the specific threat he presented. 'When a doctor goes wrong,' said Sherlock Holmes of Palmer, years later, in *The Adventure of the Speckled Band*, 'he is the first of criminals. He has nerve and he has knowledge.'

12

—◦◦◦—

The Good Wife

'The men of the middle classes do not choose that their females should work for money, so we have no option but … the monotonous round of home-pursuits – busy idleness, unremunerative employment.'

Anonymous female writer in The National Magazine, *1857*

As we've seen in the case of Maria Manning, the Victorians found it hard to know what to think about murderesses. The female members of middle-class families were supposed to be pure, virtuous, most influential within, and best confined to, the domestic realm. What was a murderous woman, then? She must be crazed, wanton, or suffering from some horrible sickness. This was necessary to protect her father, husband and male associates from accusations that they had failed to keep her in check. It was impossible that she could look or behave like a normal person.

And if she *did* look and behave normally, what then? Despite the difficulties that lie in revisiting and attempting to resolve cases more than a century old, it seems perfectly possible that a couple of the celebrated poison cases of the later nineteenth century involved women who actually managed to get away with their crimes. This was in part because, despite the considerable evidence against them, people simply couldn't quite believe that a well-born, well-spoken, attractive young female could have committed murder.

———

In 1857, when she was only 22, a young lady named Madeleine Smith was accused of poisoning Pierre Émile L'Angelier, a young man from a lower social class. Brought up in upper-middle-class Glasgow, cosseted by her parents, Madeleine began her relationship with L'Angelier when she was 19 and recently returned home from boarding school. Conventionally for her background and station, Madeleine's education had been devoted to preparing her for life as a wife. This was, in many ways, a training in the art of deception. In many boarding schools, the mistresses read all the pupils' correspondence, with the result that the girls would bribe servants to deliver private letters. 'Concealment and deception prevail in girls' schools,' ranted *Fraser's Magazine*. 'Girls learn to grasp after show and pomp; and, as women can rarely acquire these for themselves, they are taught to look at marriage as the means of making their fortune.' It was true too of life beyond the schoolroom: Madeleine's success or failure would be measured by the speed and splendour of her engagement.

Despite his romantic name, L'Angelier was far from being the rich, dream husband Madeleine's parents desired. Originally from Jersey, he had spent some time in France, and was now a clerk in a shipping firm. His friends in Glasgow described him as being moody and dissatisfied with his lot. He met Madeleine in the only possible place where such an intersection of the classes could happen: out on the public street. Attraction sparked between them immediately, and they went on to exchange over 60 letters, which were smuggled out of Madeleine's parents' house by a maidservant. Madeleine showed herself to be pragmatic to the point of cold-heartedness in arranging all this. She blackmailed a family servant into delivering the letters, by threatening to reveal that this maid had an unauthorized young man of her own.

Madeleine and L'Angelier (they called each other 'Mimi' and 'Émile') also had secret meetings during which their physical relationship progressed beyond the point – for a Victorian young lady – of no return. She took issue with the very real expectation that she should marry well. 'It was expected that I would marry a man with money,' she wrote to Émile, but 'I take the man I love. I know that all my friends shall forsake me, but for that I don't care.'

When Madeleine's side of this correspondence emerged during the course of her trial, it caused a sensation. It showed that even a middle-class girl could want, indeed enjoy, sex. 'I am now a wife, a wife in every sense of the word,' she wrote to Émile on 27 June 1856, although they had not of course actually undergone a wedding ceremony. 'I can never be the wife of another after our intimacy,' she promised, reassuring herself that: 'Our intimacy has not been criminal, as I am [his] wife before God, so it has been no sin our loving each other.'

However, Émile never married his Mimi. Over time she cooled towards him – something else that young ladies were not supposed to do – and tried to fob him off with various excuses. Her parents, unaware of their daughter's relationship, were putting pressure on her to marry, and she feared they might discover everything. Finally, Émile learned from a third party that Madeleine's parents had arranged for her to marry someone else who was much more suitable, one of her father's business associates.

It seems that Madeleine feared that her cast-off lover, hurt and angry, had the power to ruin her life by revealing all about their relationship. She certainly begged him not to, writing: 'Émile, for God's sake, do not send my letters to papa. It will be an open rupture. I will leave the house. I will die …'

In March 1857, they had several more assignations – tearful and tortured, one imagines – Madeleine inside her parents' house and talking to Émile through the kitchen window. At one of them she gave him a cup of hot chocolate; afterwards he suffered from an upset stomach. Two days after their final meeting, he died.

It was the discovery of Madeleine's letters at Émile's lodging house that drew her to the attention of the police. They also found her name in a chemist's 'Poison Book', which revealed that she had made two recent purchases of arsenic. The poison could have been intended, as Madeleine claimed, to kill rats, or else as a facial treatment. But it could also have been a way of ridding herself of a grave, and potentially life-wrecking, embarrassment.

Madeleine's letters themselves were not read out during her trial, and now we see how a descending veil of decency began to obscure the true details of her actions: 'All objectionable expressions, all gross and indelicate allusions were carefully and studiously omitted … that the feelings of the prisoner might not be overwhelmed by such a terrible publicity.'

And, despite the damage to her reputation, Madeleine Smith got off. She was a young, attractive, romantic figure, and aroused a great deal of sympathy. She simply didn't look like a murderess. Reports of her behaviour in prison made her sound well brought up and innocent: she spent her time 'in light reading, with occasional regrets at the want of a piano'. Even the phrenologist appointed to 'read' Madeleine's character from the shape of her skull found her admirable, with a propensity for mathematics. 'Owing to her strong affections and healthy temperament,' he wrote, 'she will make a treasure of a wife to a worthy husband.' This was a sharp contrast to the conclusions reached on William Palmer. One suspects that these phrenologists tended to be influenced by the impression they had formed of the person before even feeling his or her head.

The young and attractive Madeleine Smith,
whose guilt was 'not proven'.

The Scottish jury voted the accusations against her 'not proven', the announcement was cheered in court and the world at large glowed with compassion for Madeleine. Among women, she became 'quite a heroine'. The *Northern British Mail* claimed that her fellow females regarded her as:

> a thoughtless but most interesting and warm-hearted young woman – one who in the simplicity of her heart, in her first love affair, abandoned herself to the man of her choice, with an amount of confiding love and outspoken artlessness of purpose, which, censure or regret as they may, they cannot regard without sympathy and admiration.

To many, it was all Émile's fault, for seducing her.

The tradesmen of Glasgow even raised a subscription so that the now-glamorous Madeleine would have some money upon which to live. Newspapers bandied around the figure of £10,000. This was raised for the intriguing young girl who may or may not have killed Émile (the verdict of 'not proven' was quite as good as 'not guilty'). Meanwhile, as Judith Flanders points out, Émile's poor old mother, whose son was dead and who had been left with absolutely no means of support, was also given a gift by the public. She received just over £89.

It's tempting to see Madeleine's rebelliousness, her increasingly dangerous choices, as being motivated by boredom with a restrictive, unexciting, middle-class domestic life. The idea that nineteenth-century life was split into separate spheres of influence, public and private, male and female, the powerful and the powerless, can easily be created with choice quotations from advice and etiquette manuals.

But in reality it disguised a more complicated picture. The Victorians defined 'work' as an activity that took place outside the home. Therefore, much of what Victorian women did in running houses and contributing to family businesses seemed invisible to the eyes of outsiders. Indeed, to appease the pride of their husbands, many women pretended to work less than they really did.

Even if it was often ignored, though, there was a powerful image in contemporary culture of the ideal female as calming, decorative, exerting a moral influence through virtue, rather than an active influence through the toil of her hands or brain. Madeleine Smith seemed unenthusiastic, or at least ambivalent, about this vision of her future – but it was an ideal that eventually saved her.

This story of a young girl hiding from the consequences of her crime behind the conventional view of Victorian womanhood seems almost too good to true, bringing out as it does all the clichés about nineteenth-century society. Historians of the period are at pains to point out that the supposed neuroses and anxieties about the body that make up such a significant part of our popular idea of Victorian middle-class life are merely a twentieth-century construct. For example, the celebrated myth that the Victorians thought piano legs immodest and covered them up in special fabric sleeves has long been exploded. Of course not every Victorian female teenager was virginal, nor was every married woman in comfortable circumstances kept happy and busy by domestic duties, church attendance and bringing up her children. Yet neither were they all seething with repression and passions unfulfilled. We still remember women like Maria Manning and Madeleine Smith because they made contemporaries ask questions of themselves about what was womanly, and what was not.

———

Florence Bravo, the heroine of the so-called 'Balham Mystery' or 'The Murder at The Priory', was an even more intriguing character than Madeleine Smith. Young, rich and beautiful, Florence was also rather a poor picker when it came to men. Her first husband, Alexander Ricardo, whom she'd married at 19, gradually revealed himself to be a violent and unfaithful alcoholic. 'I was very happy with him when we first met,' Florence recalled, 'but he gradually became more and more abusive – always attacking me and saying terrible things.'

The feisty Florence wouldn't stand for this. In the teeth of opposition from her family, she left her husband, claiming ill health, and retreated to a hydro in Malvern to recuperate. The hydro Florence attended was run by Dr James Gully, a man with a magnetic personality. Then in his sixties, but vigorous and energetic, he worked hard on behalf of his female patients, whose problems were frequently emotional as much as physical. On Florence's behalf, he now negotiated with her family for a financial settlement upon which she could live. Florence repaid his kindness by falling in love with him, and they embarked upon a physical relationship.

Florence now had the financial means to live a more exciting life within reach of London. She rented a new home, The Priory, a grand house in Balham, and persuaded Dr Gully to take a house

The beautiful, rich and young Florence
Bravo, who may have got away with
poisoning her husband.

of his own nearby. But their affair petered out after Florence had
a miscarriage.

She wanted the respectability of being married once more,
and again, in 1875, she chose badly. Charles Bravo was young,
handsome and an ambitious barrister. However, it seems pretty
clear that he married Florence merely for her money. Tensions arose
almost immediately, because the 'Married Women's Property Act'
had just been passed (1870), which allowed Florence to insist upon
maintaining control over her very considerable estate.

Charles, baulked of what he wanted, treated her with bullying and violence. Florence miscarried again, this time with Bravo's child, and was terribly ill. Yet he insisted on sleeping with her and on having his rights as her husband and master.

One night in 1876, Florence's horrible second husband retired to bed, having taken a drink of water from the glass always placed by his bed. When he called out a little later, he was discovered to be writhing in agony, vomiting and passing bloodied stools. He spent the next three days in this distressing condition. He'd been poisoned with antimony. Tasteless when dissolved in water, it causes failure of the kidneys and liver, leading to headaches, depression, violent retching and – in Charles's case – death.

But it would be very hard to prove what had happened. The doctor who attended the dying man believed that someone had administered poison. 'I was not satisfied then and I am not satisfied now,' he said, during the trial; 'someone in the house knew the truth.' In this unhappy household, though, with its secrets, collusions and a cast of servants devoted to their mistress, no one broke ranks and told him. Florence herself was questioned in court, but there was not enough evidence to charge her with the crime. One intriguing fact did emerge, though: Dr Gully, Florence's former lover, who still wished her well, had been meeting up with Florence's lady companion, Mrs Cox, to pass on a strange medicine in a bottle marked 'poison'.

The fullest study of the case, by James Ruddick, concludes that Florence was indeed guilty, and that she could not have acted alone. He proposes a female alliance, between Florence and her servant, Jane Cox, with Florence committing the actual deed of the poisoning and Jane covering up for a mistress.

There are several interesting possible explanations as to why Florence might have poisoned her husband with antimony. Some Victorian women used it, and similar drugs, as a crude method of birth control. In 1885, a woman called Adelaide Bartlett was accused of murdering her husband with chloroform. Not so, she said, she had simply used it to send him off to sleep, so that he wouldn't have sex with her and make her pregnant again.

A drop of antimony in the drink and an unruly husband would fall sick and vomit. It could even have been a defence Florence had used in her first marriage to an alcoholic: a spiked drink that made him nauseous would prevent him either from drinking any more or from assaulting her. Perhaps Florence didn't even mean to kill him, which would account for her behaviour after his death. She convinced all the doctors and policemen that she was genuinely distraught.

But was she? Ruddick argues that it was hard for people to spot female deception in an age when women deceived men constantly, and Florence benefited from the same assumptions that prevented people from imagining Madeleine Smith as a murderess. Florence herself was something of a renegade, toughened by circumstances. Like Madeleine, she had been brought up to see marriage as the goal of her life, and yet she had the misfortune to marry two successive husbands who had wronged and abused her. So, again like Madeleine, she broke the rules: first, by leaving her first husband, and taking an older lover, Dr Gully. She then went against the grain once more when she insisted on keeping control of her own money in defiance of her second husband. Perhaps she was indeed using drugs to control him – she wouldn't have been the first woman in her time to do so – and the most charitable explanation is that her power play simply went wrong.

Of course it's too crude to see Victorian murderesses as proto-feminists, playing the system to defend their rights as individuals against husbands, fathers and men who treated them as pieces of moveable property. And yet it's a more sympathetic way of looking at a group of women whom many of their contemporaries would have thought simply wicked.

Victorian women reading about the case surely did so with a shudder of horror and fear, knowing that their interest would be considered morbid and prurient by their male relatives. One newspaper condemned the female spectators who avidly followed the trial of Madeleine Smith, who dishonoured their sex by 'eagerly drinking in that filthy correspondence'. A novelist came down similarly upon women 'brought up in refined society ... who pride themselves on the delicacy of their sensibilities' and yet who 'can sit for hours listening to the details of a cold-blooded murder'.

It was ghoulish, yes, but how else could they learn about a woman who, perhaps like them, took a lover? And enjoyed sex? And fought back against a violent husband? Murderesses had something to teach. When female newspaper readers could read the reported words of Florence Bravo – 'I told him that he had no right to treat me in such a way' – and see her go unpunished, something small but significant changed in society.

As the historian Mary Hartman put it in her definitive study of Victorian murderesses, the female readers avidly consuming the reports of murder trials 'could understand the frustrations and terrors that drove the accused, for they had travelled some of the same dark paths themselves'.

13

Detective Fever

'The tempest ... bursts out, in its full fury, to hurl parents, children, servants into one common, inevitable, and promiscuous destruction.'

Joseph Stapleton, The Great Crime of 1860 *(1861)*

In 1860, a particularly puzzling murder took place near the village of Rode (then called Road) in Wiltshire. Road Hill House was a substantial mansion built in the 1790s. On the night of 29 June 1860, the house was made secure as the family went to bed. The garden, in which a dog prowled, was surrounded by high walls. The doors and shutters were barred. The 12 people who slept in the house that night were completely sealed off from the world. They included Samuel Kent, an ambitious but indebted inspector of factories, and his second wife, Mary, who had formerly been his household's governess.

The relationships between the nine blood members of the Kent family (they had three live-in servants) were complex but important for understanding the background to the crime. Mary had come to prominence during the illness, some say insanity, of Samuel's first wife, also called Mary. The four children of Samuel's first marriage were now treated with less affection and respect than their young half-sisters and brothers, the three children of his second.

That night, a boy of nearly four years old, Savill Kent, son of the second Mrs Kent and one of the favoured children, was silently removed from his cot in a first-floor bedroom. It was done without waking the nursery maid and his sister who were sleeping in the same room, and without disturbing his mother and father in their bedroom next door. The killer took the sleeping boy down the servants' stairs at the back of the house. The next morning, Savill was nowhere to be found. After a few hours of searching, and of growing panic, his body was discovered in the chamber beneath an outdoor privy. His throat had been slashed so deeply that his head was almost completely cut off.

The investigation that followed was macabrely inept. Textiles and clothing provided a series of seemingly important, but indecipherable, clues. The nursemaid came under intense suspicion, because she changed her story about the exact moment when she noticed that the blanket had gone missing from the boy's bed. Then, a breast-cloth (an item worn beneath a Victorian corset) was discovered down the privy along with the boy's body. It was tried for size (like Cinderella's slipper) against the chests of the females of the house, but only the servants, not the young ladies. But there were hierarchical distinctions even among the female family members. The 16-year-old Constance became a suspect, because one of her nightgowns had gone missing in the wash. It was argued

The draper's shop run by the Marr family, in the Ratcliffe Highway, East London, scene of their slaughter in 1811. As De Quincey tells it, their maid, Margaret, heard the killer moving about within as she knocked in vain on the green door.

The Residence of the late
MR MARR,
RATCLIFFE HIGHWAY,
where he was dreadfully murderd with his Wife, Infant Child, & Apprentice, on the 7th Day of December 1811.

A member of the Marine Police in his official-issue greatcoat, with his cutlass, lantern and gun. Rather like a private security guard, he had to prevent theft from the ships moored in the Port of London.

Smartly dressed 'Blue Devils' or 'Raw Lobsters', as the constables of Robert Peel's new Metropolitan Police Force were nicknamed. They wore blue on purpose to avoid confusion with the red coats of the army.

Edwardian police officers demonstrating disguises for undercover work. Sherlock Holmes borrows his own skill in changing his appearance from the real-life Eugène Vidocq, the man behind the first official detective squad in France.

Dragging the pond for the body of William Weare, 1823. The pond became one of the stops on the celebrated 'Elstree Murder Tour'. The yellow gig, the vehicle in which the murderer travelled, is an emblem of this particular murder.

This mug commemorates the murderer John Thurtell who killed William Weare and threw his body into the Elstree pond. Knick-knacks like this were often souvenirs from an enjoyable day out at a public hanging. Thurtell's own was attended by 40,000 people.

Madame Tussaud's gallery of waxworks in Baker Street still contains a figure of its founder, the original Madame, who brought her travelling exhibition from Paris to London in 1802.

Her exhibition specialized in celebrities of the French Revolution, royalty, and horror. She'd modelled the heads of its victims as they came off the guillotine, including those of Marie Antoinette and Louis XVI.

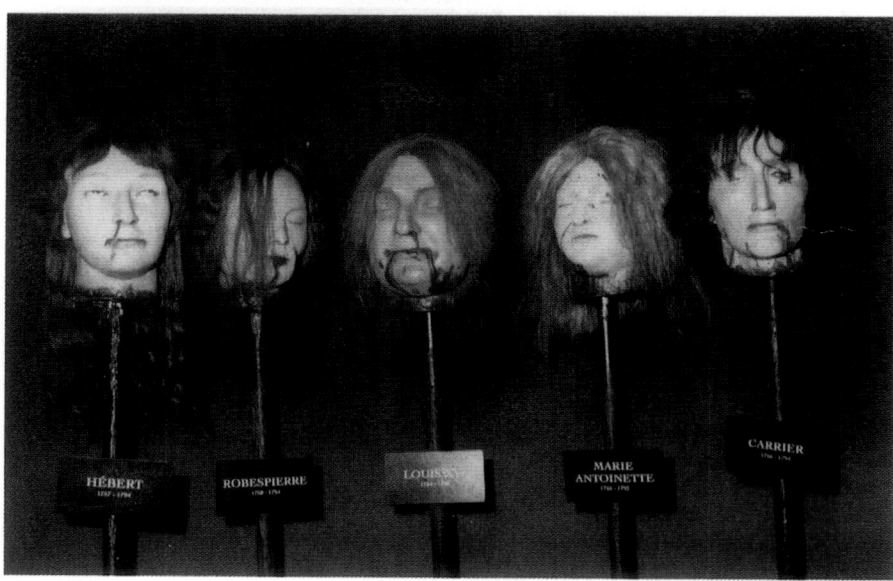

Broadsides about murderers usually featured a picture of the crime itself. Today they may look almost laughably naïve – note the lady's severed legs in the coal scuttle – but contemporaries enjoyed their hard-hitting, horrific nature.

A much more harrowing image of criminals at the gallows, by Théodore Géricault, 1820. It's an unusual image because artists at a public hanging often concentrated on the spectacle of the vast crowd rather than those about to die.

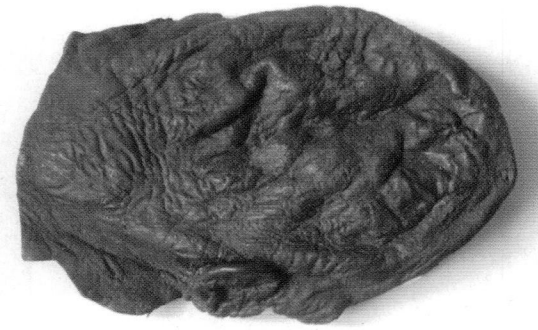

The most powerful of the many souvenirs from 'The Murder in the Red Barn': the scalp of its perpetrator, William Corder, with his little shrivelled ear at the bottom. The skin also retains a fuzz of short, ginger hair. It's the star exhibit at Moyse's Hall Museum, Bury St Edmunds.

This looks like an ordinary book about the life of William Corder, who committed 'The Murder in the Red Barn', but its extraordinary binding is made out of the skin of Corder himself.

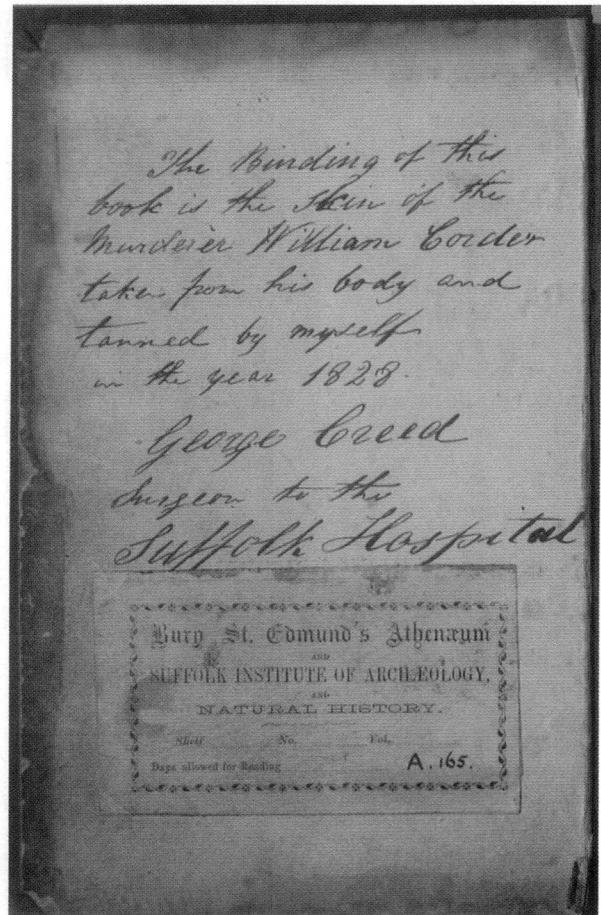

The inscription in this book (right) reveals that Corder's skin was removed and tanned by one of the surgeons at the Suffolk Hospital after his execution in Bury St Edmunds in 1828.

Ceramic models of crime scenes, like 'The Red Barn' shown here, and figurines of the murderer and his victim, were displayed on many nineteenth-century mantelpieces.

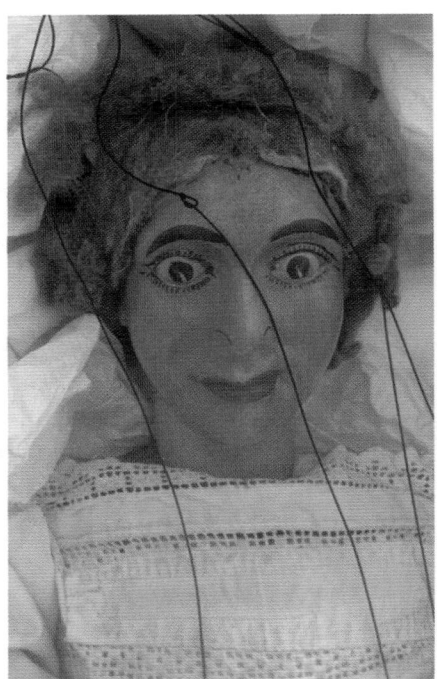

This marionette puppet of murder victim Maria Marten belonged to a travelling puppet show company that performed her death as a play in villages across East Anglia.

You can tell that this puppet of Maria's evil murderer, William Corder, is a villain, by his murderous-looking moustache and his heavy black eyeliner.

A good melodrama, like those based on the wildly popular 'Murder in the Red Barn', contained recognizable stock characters such as the village maiden and the dastardly villain. It would always end with wrongs righted and cheers from the audience.

The new Detective Branch of the Metropolitan Police was set up in 1842. Inspector Charles Field would become its most celebrated officer.

Charles Dickens was a great admirer of Inspector Field. As a journalist, he wrote articles puffing up the new Detective Branch. As a novelist, Dickens made Field into his character Inspector Bucket in *Bleak House*. Here, Bucket raises his 'corpulent forefinger' in speech, just as Field did in real life.

Inspector Bucket.

Bleak House.

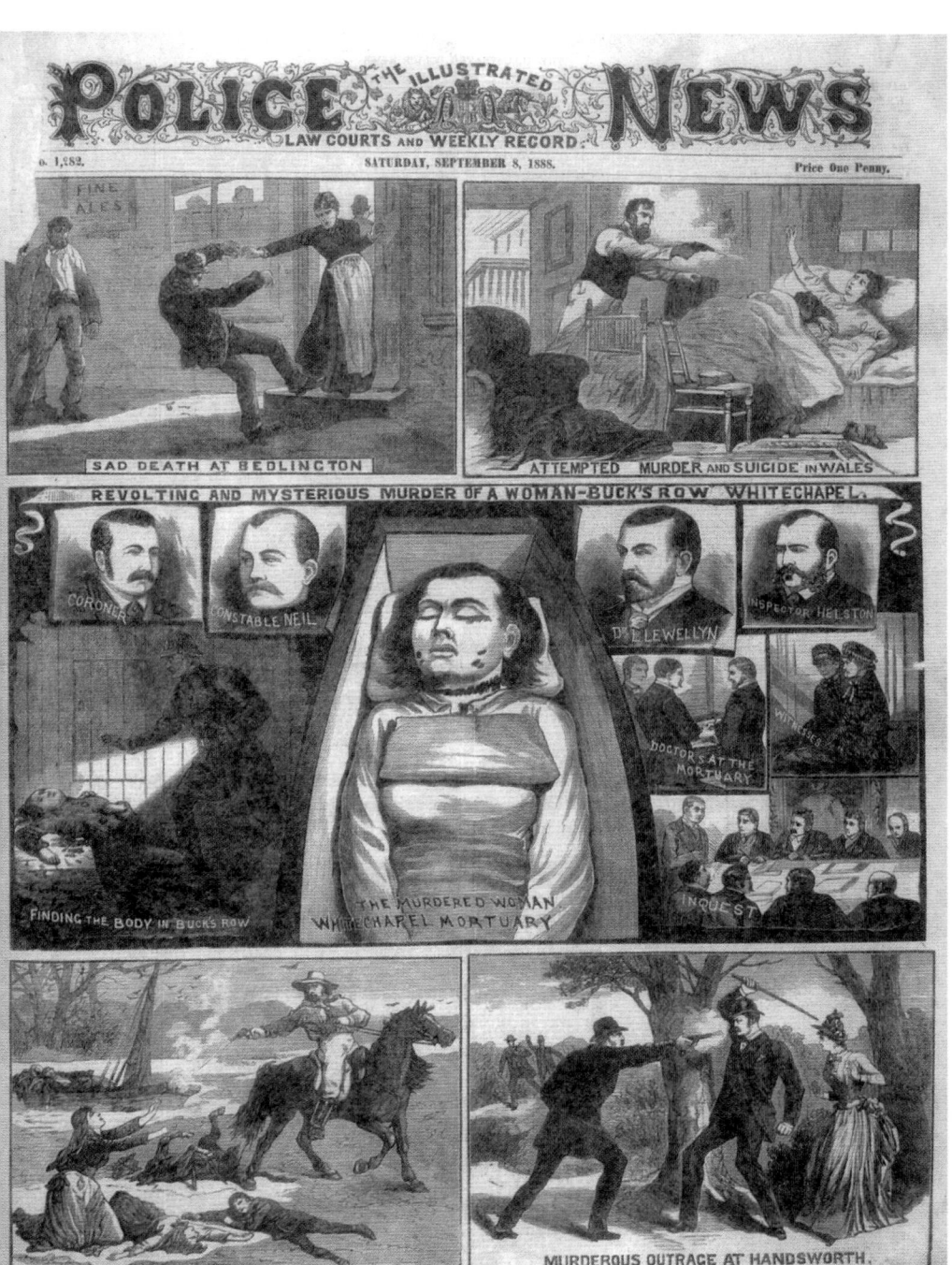

Members of the early police force were greeted with suspicion and fear, but by the time of the 'Jack The Ripper' case the Metropolitan Police were well established. Yet prominent failures like this, and the Road Hill House case, undermined their reputation.

The medicine chest said to belong to the archetypal murderer of the 1850s, the poisoner Dr William Palmer. 'I am innocent of poisoning Cook by strychnine,' he said on the gallows, taunting the crowd with what was possibly a confession to having used some other drug.

Road Hill House in Wiltshire, location of the original 'country house mystery' with its closed cast of family and servants. The killing of a little boy here in 1860 would echo throughout the decade's 'sensation' novels.

The actor Richard Mansfield transforms himself from the evil, crouching Mr Hyde into the good and upright Dr Jekyll. His performance was so frightening that 'strong men shuddered and women fainted and were carried out of the theatre'.

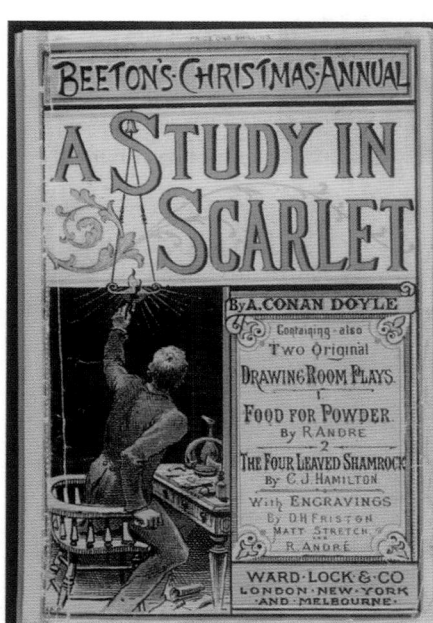

Sherlock Holmes made his first public appearance in 1887. In this story, he's seen beating a corpse with a stick. He was researching post-mortem bruising in the course of his innovative work as a forensic scientist.

The cover of W. S. Hayward's *Revelations of a Lady Detective* (1864) shows a rather racy lady lifting up her skirt and smoking. She excels at her work because 'the woman detective has far greater opportunities than a man of intimate watching'.

After the brutality of the First World War, Hercule Poirot caught on because he was the opposite of an action hero: 'the neatness of his attire was almost incredible; I believe a speck of dust would have caused him more pain than a bullet wound'. In contrast, Sidney Paget's illustrations (below) showed that Sherlock Holmes was no stranger to violence, and was quite capable of chasing and even shooting criminals.

"IT'S NO USE, JOHN CLAY."

'The Detection Club' was founded in the 1930s to promote and celebrate the profession of crime novelist. Its members included Dorothy L. Sayers, seen here at a Club meeting, with a broad smile and glass of beer.

Dorothy L. Sayers in the arms of her creation, Lord Peter Wimsey, who brought her financial stability and fame. This humorous sketch by a friend glosses over the fact that in real life Sayers was much less lucky than her fictional characters in finding lasting love.

SLEUTHS ON THE SCENT

DETECTION Club in Gerrard Street, West End, is favourite meeting-ground of detective-creators and literary crimesters. Above, a group of eager sleuths. Mr. E. R. Punshon, left, Miss Ianthe Jerrold and "Anthony Gilbert." Right, Miss Dorothy Sayers, seated, Miss Helen Simpson at back.

Bodyless head in lower half of picture belongs to author Milward Kennedy. Behind him, investigating mystery, is E. C. Bentley.

This rough magic I here abjure — as my Whimsy takes me.
(Signed) LADY PETER.

STRONG POISON

THE 9 TAILORS

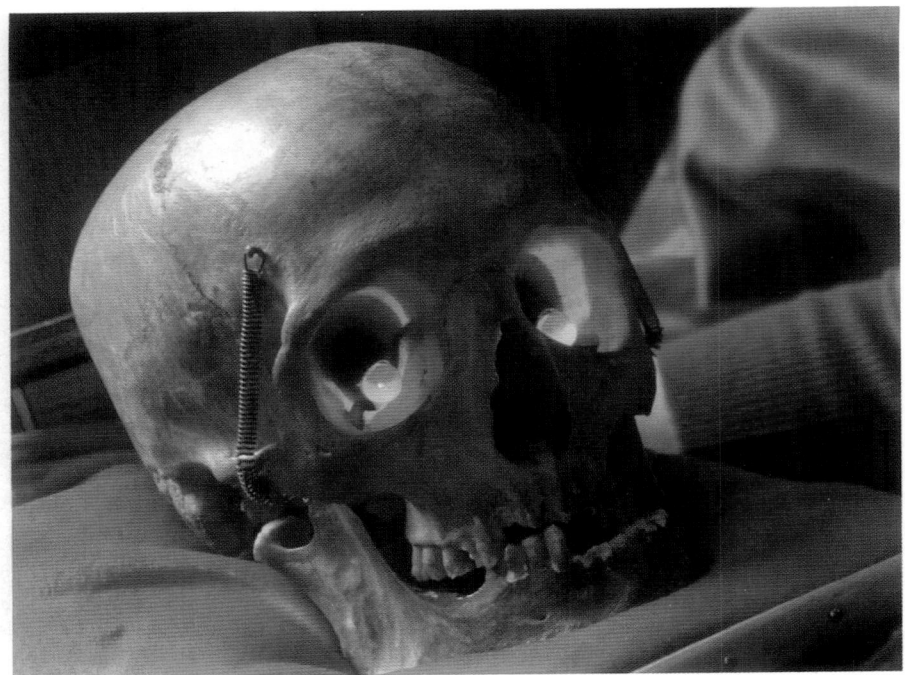

'Eric the Skull', with his glowing red eyes, is the property of 'The Detection Club', and is still used to this day at the ritual initiation of new members. ('Eric' was recently discovered to be female.)

The 'Golden Age' of detective fiction saw murder treated rather like a crossword puzzle. Here's a book of murder puzzles 'to be solved from given data', and a jigsaw showing a crime scene.

MATCH FOUND IN THE BISHOP OF BUDE'S CABIN ON THE MORNING OF 9.3.36.

Murder, by the 1930s, had become something of a parlour game, with very little blood or violence. You could even buy your own 'Murder Dossier', a set of printed clues including photographs of cigarette butts or even actual matchsticks, with the solution in a sealed envelope at the back.

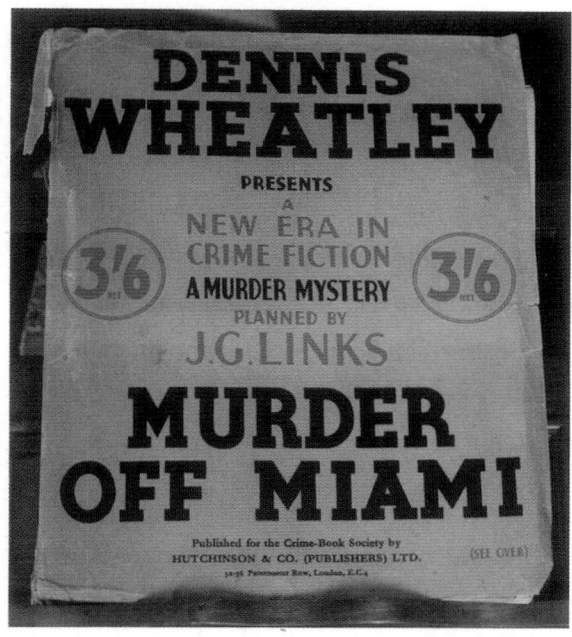

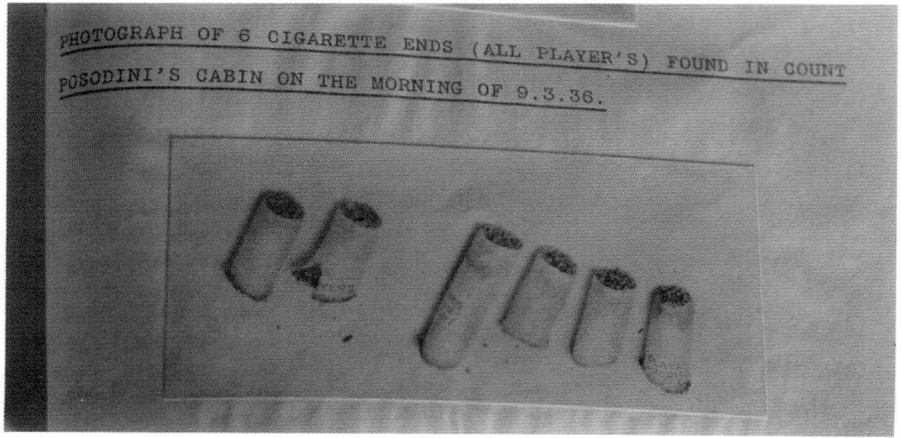

PHOTOGRAPH OF 6 CIGARETTE ENDS (ALL PLAYER'S) FOUND IN COUNT POSODINI'S CABIN ON THE MORNING OF 9.3.36.

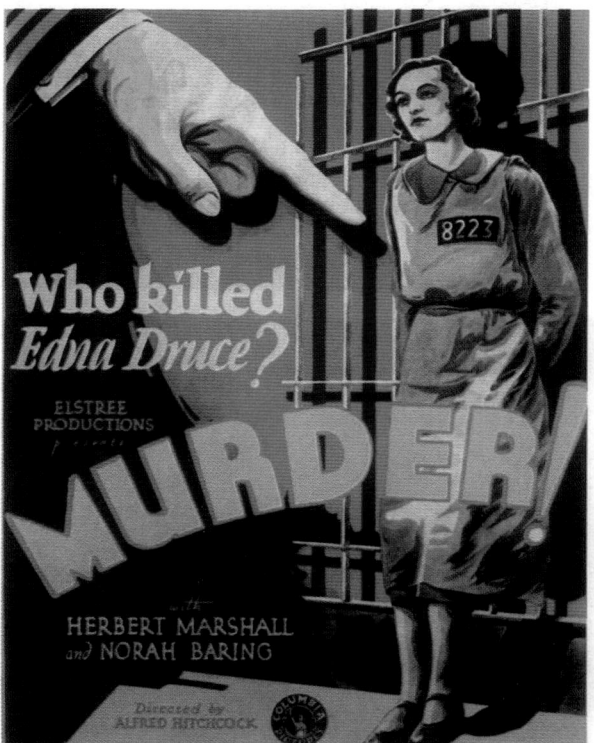

In Alfred Hitchcock's early films, he never shows a killing, just allows his viewers to imagine it. This is the victim in *The Lodger: A Story of the London Fog* (1927), the story of a serial killer with many similarities to 'Jack The Ripper'.

Hitchcock's film *Murder!* (1930) was his only foray into the conventional 'whodunit' of detective fiction's Golden Age. His work, morally ambiguous, had more in common with the sensation novelists of the 1860s, or the post-war thriller.

that she had destroyed it because it had been stained with blood during the throat-slashing. It's poignant to learn that the missing nightgown was identified as Constance's because it was plainer than those of her more favoured, younger half-sisters. Yet Constance herself was protected, in court, from questioning on the matter because of the undesirability of talking in public about what a well-born young lady wore in bed.

Meanwhile, her father, Samuel Kent, as head of the household, was apparently above suspicion. He was invited to take part in a police trap to identify the female member of the household who had placed another nightgown, covered in blood, in the scullery boiler. It could have been evidence of violent, sanguinary night-time activities. But it could also have been just a discarded item of clothing that had been used as a sanitary towel.

Under Samuel's supervision, a roomful of policemen, provided with cheese and beer, planned to spend the night staking out the scullery containing the boiler in the hope that its owner would come down and retrieve her nightclothes. But unfortunately Samuel accidentally locked the door of the room where they were waiting and watching, so that even if they had heard the nightgown's owner coming down to the scullery to recover it, they would not have been able to catch her. And – doubly embarrassing for the policemen – during their incarceration the nightgown did indeed disappear.

None of this actually emerged in the official inquiry into the case. The story of the bungling policemen, locked into the kitchen while the clues vanished, only came out after the official investigation had failed, and local residents gathered in the Temperance Hall for an informal, community-based attempt to solve the crime.

Because of the inability of the local authorities to crack the case, Jack Whicher, a celebrated member of the original team of eight Scotland Yard detectives formed 18 years previously, was brought in to investigate. He suspected, but could not prove, the guilt of the sullen, unwomanly, teenage Constance, who had previously run away from home dressed in boy's clothes, and who had told her friends that she was treated cruelly. She was described as 'lacking in delicacy', and it was clear she 'wished to be independent'.

Constance Kent, who eventually confessed
to slitting her half-brother's throat.

There was a good deal of sympathy, locally, for Constance, but little in her own home. Despite Mr Whicher's failure to make the case against his prime suspect stick, the following year a friend of Constance's father's published a book that seemed to point the finger at this child of a mad mother. 'It is in the woman's soul,' he begins, 'that poets and moralists have sought and found the most frequent and disastrous examples of revenge.'

Five years later, Mr Whicher was proved correct, for Constance made a confession to the crime. However, Kate Summerscale, in the most recent book on the Road Hill House Murder, argues that she was just an accomplice. Perhaps she had indeed taken part, but she could equally well have been covering up for her beloved brother William, both of them united in their dislike of the second family who had made them cuckoos in the nest.

After the official investigation petered out, the Kent family were left in a state of stasis. They were offered no solution at all to the mystery that had unfolded as they slept. They commemorated their son Savill with a gravestone that still stands in the churchyard of St Thomas's Church, East Coulston, in Wiltshire. Its epitaph baldly announces that he had been 'cruelly murdered' and that the killer's capture seemed unlikely:

SHALL NOT GOD SEARCH THIS OUT? FOR HE KNOWETH THE SECRETS OF THE HEART.

Enormous efforts still continued in the hope of untying the knot, and this particular murder contributed to a new craze among members of the public, for *detecting crime themselves*. Novelist Wilkie Collins described this fresh enthusiasm for clues and mysteries, and the fervid search for solutions, that sprung up in the wake of the Road Hill House mystery, in terms of a new illness: 'Do you feel an uncomfortable heat at the pit of your stomach ... and a nasty thumping at the top of your head? ... I call it the detective-fever.'

Collins was not the only one to find the sensation painful and yet enjoyable at the same time. 'I like a good murder that can't be found out,' said one character in a novel of 1859, voicing the feelings of many in Victorian Britain. 'That is, of course, it is very shocking, but I like to hear about it.' The Road Hill House case became a touchstone for these sensations due to the 'deepened and prolonged' mystery attached to the crime. As a result, wrote one observer in 1861, 'suspicion has become a passion'.

The evidence that Britain in the 1860s became afflicted by this 'detective fever' can be seen at the National Archives. It lies in the thick stacks of letters, written by ordinary people during the course of the Road Hill House investigation, to both the police and the Home Office. Each letter contains the writer's own personal solution to the mystery.

With complete and minute accounts of the crime scene, along with full transcripts of the inquest published in the newspapers, the players of this real-life guessing game were much better informed than their equivalents would be today. One of the great attractions of the Road Hill House mystery was the way that a solution seemed tantalizingly within the reach of anyone who might devote the necessary time to weighing up the evidence.

Poor old Jack Whicher was obliged to read each letter, and indeed to write notes assessing the value of each suggestion. The letters of the nation's armchair detectives were taken surprisingly seriously. The people sending in these suggestions did not yet entirely trust the police to do their job properly, and, indeed, the bumpy progress of the investigation would not have reassured them. They expected their letters to be answered.

'I fancy that step by step I can trace the crime,' wrote one lady, who lived in Westbourne Grove, London. 'The murderer is the brother of [local resident] William Nutt, and the son in law of Mrs Holly the laundress.' Her letter was just one among many. And so Mr Whicher is to be found writing that, no, he did not think that chloroform had been used, because no trace of it was found in the victim's body, and that, yes, he had indeed considered the possibility that the nursemaid and the master had been having an affair.

When I interviewed Kate Summerscale, the author of the best-selling *The Suspicions of Mr Whicher*, about these letters, she pointed out a fascinating trend among them. The most popular solution to the crime, the one mentioned most often by members of the public, was indeed the theory that Samuel Kent had been having an adulterous relationship with his nursemaid (just as he had done previously with his children's governess before he married her). People were quick to suggest that the murdered child had seen something that he shouldn't, and had been silenced permanently so that the secret should not come out.

Our popular image of Victorian life, to this day, is of sexual secrets buried beneath hypocrisy, the head of a respectable household with a double life, the vulnerability, and the silencing, of his women. Many historians have sought to overturn, or at least to nuance, such a bald view of Victorian domestic life. And yet, as Summerscale suggests, the letters written to Mr Whicher suggesting that Samuel Kent was sleeping with his nursemaid really do place the very worst construction that the writers could imagine upon events and relationships. The cliché exists because it was – and remains – powerful. The strangers who wrote these letters show that our stock image is how Victorian society indeed saw itself. Detective fever involved assuming the worst, trusting no one and ferreting about for dirt. No wonder the residual middle-class fear and dislike of the professional detective lingered on, even while people came reluctantly to admire his achievements.

What did this mean for professional detectives like Jack Whicher? Like Inspector Field, his fellow member of the original Detective Branch of the Metropolitan Police, Whicher was far from well born. He was the son of a gardener, and worked as a labourer before he joined the police. This lowly background is one of the reasons he was looked upon askance by the family at Road Hill House.

As was the case for Inspector Field, working for the police allowed Whicher to better himself through using his brains. He was regarded with high esteem by journalists: Dickens described him as possessing 'a reserved and thoughtful air, as if he were engaged in deep arithmetical calculations'. Another journalist simply labelled him as 'a man of mystery'. He was considered to be the best, and was certainly the best-known, detective on the force when he was sent down to Road Hill House. Yet his failure to pin the blame firmly on Constance Kent would gravely bruise Whicher's reputation. Many of the letters in the National Archives criticize Whicher personally, for failing to make the pieces fit together, for a lack of subtlety in his investigations, even for originating from the wrong social class.

Dickens had done much, in journalism and fiction, to boost the image of the Detective Branch. But Jack Whicher's failure and public humiliation at Road Hill House did even more to set back their cause. So, too, did a great scandal uncovered in 1877, when most of the detectives on the force were discovered to have been complicit in a betting racket they were supposed to be investigating.

Kate Summerscale points out that the damage done to the standing of the professional policeman in the 1860s and 1870s was transferred to their image in literature as well. All the great fictional detectives until the Second World War – Sherlock Holmes, Lord Peter Wimsey, Hercule Poirot, Albert Campion – are amateurs or private investigators. And, indeed, the Detective Branch had not replaced the private sector – far from it. A boost to the private eye business was provided in 1857 when an Act was passed 'to amend the Law relating to Divorce and Matrimonial Causes'. This made divorce a matter for the civil, rather than the ecclesiastical, courts, and – for the first time since the seventeenth-century Commonwealth period – marriage was made a contract between two citizens as well as a divine sacrament. Before this, if you'd wanted a divorce you either had to seek a religious annulment, or a Private Bill in Parliament. This had effectively limited divorce to the wealthy and well connected. In the year before the passing of the Act, there had been three requests for divorce. In the year after it, there were 300.

The so-called 'Matrimonial Causes Act' meant that marriages could now be dissolved on the production of 'evidence' of adultery, and an army of private investigators would be kept busy hunting it down on behalf of wives with adulterous husbands. In Wilkie Collins's novel *Armadale* (1866), the characters spend an awful lot of time spying upon each other, often using a paid inquiry agent, and exchange views illustrating that detection was still seen as a dirty business: 'the Confidential Spy of modern time ... There he sat – the necessary Detective attendant on the progress of our national civilisation ... a man professionally ready on the merest suspicion (if the merest suspicion paid him) to get under our beds, and to look through gimlet-holes in our doors.'

Meanwhile, Whicher himself was fictionalised by Collins in his next novel, *The Moonstone* (1868), as Sergeant Cuff, the unsuccessful detective. Like Mr Whicher, Sergeant Cuff is a man of mystery who lacks the social status to mingle easily with the family he is investigating. Nobody knows what he is really thinking as he prattles on about his beloved hobby of growing roses. Like so many fictional detectives, Sergeant Cuff is given a hobby to cover up this essential blankness at his centre. Just as Inspector Morse is really little more than a hyper-intelligent and grumpy collection of hobbies (beer-drinking, opera and crossword puzzles), Sergeant Cuff's central preoccupation is gardening. He is treated as a mere mechanic by the snooty household who have called him in. And yet, at the same time, they don't understand him and fear the searching beam of his gaze. His eyes 'of a steely light grey, had a disconcerting trick when they encountered [you] of looking as if they expected something more from you than you were aware of yourself'.

He is an ambiguous, incomprehensible, possibly dangerous character, and, as such, he reflects the status of the detective himself in society in the 1860s. Although Jack Whicher is today the most celebrated detective of the Victorian age, it took him many years (and Constance's eventual confession) to recover anything like the standing he had held before Road Hill House.

14

——◦——

A New Sensation

'We look upon the detective officer as the magician of modern life.'

Mary Elizabeth Braddon

A respectable family, a country house, a limited number of suspects, a lower-class investigator lurching in from outside: the crime and setting of the Road Hill House Murder seemed like a real-life equivalent of a rather thrilling new form of literature: the 'sensation' novel. And as this new genre developed, details of the Road Hill House Murder would crop up time and time again in its plots.

In the 1860s, the 'sensation' novel would come to supersede both the 'Newgate Novel' and melodrama as the nation's favourite form of crime story. Instead of featuring lowlifes and criminals, black and white passions and interventions by Providence, 'sensation' novels were set in ordinary domestic situations, often involving the middle- and upper-middle-class families who believed themselves to be too grand to be investigated by the police.

Mary Elizabeth Braddon, one of the 'sensation' novel's greatest authors, pinned down a definition of the type of murder that would now arouse maximum interest in the reading public. It has to be 'uncommonly cruel, cowardly, and unmanly,' she wrote, but, most importantly, it had to take place 'in a respectable rank of life'. The implication that even the best families might have secrets was a pleasantly scandalous notion, and there was something more than a little shocking and improper about a good 'sensation' novel. 'Indications of widespread corruption,' the philosopher Henry Mansel called these books in 1863, 'called into existence to satisfy the cravings of a diseased appetite.'

But perhaps the best known of the 'sensation' novelists was Wilkie Collins. Henry James later described Collins as 'having introduced into fiction those most mysterious of mysteries, the mysteries that are at our own doors'. 'Instead of the terrors of "Udolpho",' he continues, 'we were treated to the terrors of the cheerful country-house and the busy London lodgings.' Collins's first success, *The Woman in White* (published in serial form, 1859–60), has many of those telltale sensational qualities: a country house, a conspiracy and a mystery solved by an amateurish alliance between the hero and a friend, first-time detectives both.

It was *The Moonstone* eight years later, however, that became his best-known work, and his first to feature a professional detective. Even though it lacks an actual murder, *The Moonstone* has nearly everything else one might require from a detective story: a substantial country property as a setting, a closed circle of suspects, a professional investigator, hidden clues, even a style of writing that reads like the presentation of a file of evidence to a court. The solution to the

Wilkie Collins, opium addict
and 'sensation' novelist.

puzzle will defeat all guesses, but it is in fact scrupulously signposted by clues that you will pick up on rereading. This is why T. S. Eliot made the claim that *The Moonstone* is 'the first, the longest, and the best of the modern English detective novels'.

It also has the special *domestic* quality that Henry James saw as the secret of Wilkie Collins's success. The theft of a famous jewel, the Moonstone itself, took place in a country house in Yorkshire. The exact layout and decoration of each of its rooms is conjured up for us by Collins, down to the painted door and Indian cabinet in the young female heroine's boudoir.

At the same time, though, the country house could have been in any county of England. It was the archetypal, comfortable, prosperous Victorian home. And the wellspring of the plot was a very everyday domestic detail. The hero of the story, Franklin Blake, wishes to give up cigar smoking, because the girl he loves dislikes the smell. Deprived of nicotine, he feels uncomfortable and cannot sleep. The solution to this minor inconvenience will come as no surprise: of course, it is that Victorian cure-all, laudanum. The opiate helps Franklin Blake to get through the night, and ultimately, it explains the whole mystery of *The Moonstone*.

Yet what people remember most from their first reading of *The Moonstone* is its addictive, page-turning, brain-teasing, feverish quality. 'Sensation' when applied to novels had two meanings. Firstly, the subject matter was 'sensational' in the sense of lurid and gripping. But the 'sensation' novel was also supposed to arouse real 'sensations' in the reader. The style was hard-hitting and jagged. 'Sensation' writers often employed characters' first-person recollections, scraps of conversation, or their transcribed letters or diaries. Ideally, a 'sensation' novel will accelerate the heart, quicken the breath and constrict the blood vessels so the reader grows pale – experiences to be had today watching a horror film at the cinema.

The Moonstone also has much in common with the case at Road Hill House. In both, a maidservant becomes the chief suspect, but the detective prefers to think it was the respectable daughter of the house. In both cases, a nightgown provides an important clue. Even the style of the nightgown is similarly important: in *The Moonstone*, it is notably plain, as a servant's would be, and at

Road Hill House the item's simplicity showed it belonged to one of the older, less loved children. And, in both cases, the detective was treated by the family as somebody rather like a tradesman. He still was not quite yet a professional, socially acceptable person in middle-class circles. Geraldine Jewsbury, a contemporary critic for the *Athenaeum* magazine, noted that the strength of *The Moonstone* was the 'wonderful construction of the story' rather than the 'sordid detective element'.

Interestingly, although T. S. Eliot and others have argued that *The Moonstone* is 'the first' English detective novel, it actually breaks two of the cardinal rules that would develop in the coming 'Golden Age' of early twentieth-century detective fiction: that the narrator himself must not have done the deed, and that the solution should not be a powerful drug that compels people to act out of character. In a magnificently unexpected twist, Franklin Blake, one of the narrators, discovers that he'd been dosed with opium without his knowledge and that under its influence *he himself* had stolen the jewel.

———

The committing of a crime in a drug-induced dream may provide the thrillingly unpredictable ending of *The Moonstone*, but it was also yet another example of the ubiquitous, unsensational presence of narcotics in Victorian daily life. What seems jarring, and indeed criminal today – the spiking of someone's drink with a heavy-duty drug – is presented by Collins as little more than a foolish (albeit dangerous) prank. It's not surprising to learn, then, that Wilkie Collins was himself writing *The Moonstone* under the influence of opium.

By 1869, he was describing serious attempts to give it up: 'I am stabbed every night at ten with a sharp-pointed syringe which injects morphia under my skin – and gets me a night's rest without any of the drawbacks of taking opium internally', he wrote. 'If I only persevere with this, I am told I shall be able, before long, gradually to diminish the quantity.'

But this was a wish made in vain. Collins's obituary recorded that he still depended daily upon 'more laudanum than would have sufficed to kill a ship's crew or company of soldiers'. No wonder opiates appear in so many of his books.

Collins's addiction wasn't the only unconventional feature of his life. He was the son of an artist, a hedonist, and a life-long indulger in food and drink. He worked in his youth for a tea merchant in the Strand, and found it boring, though the job gave him plenty of time for writing stories and essays. He was called to the bar, but never practised; his family money meant that he didn't have to.

Collins became great friends with Charles Dickens, 12 years older, who gave him excellent editorial advice but sometimes despaired of his protégé's unconventional habits. Everyone addressed him very informally as 'Wilkie' (his middle name, rather than his first name, William), he wore flamboyant clothes and – infamously – maintained two separate establishments with two women, neither of whom he married. Dickens worried that his gifted young friend was 'unnecessarily offensive to the middle class'.

Collins was adamant that he didn't draw his plots from true crime, but literary critics have certainly discovered enough clues to prove that he was being disingenuous in his claims of complete novelty. It was a round-up of celebrated French crimes that provided the inspiration for *The Woman in White*. The plot hinges on a dastardly deed: a young woman committed to a madhouse so that her fortune could be stolen. This is to be brought off on the basis of her physical similarity to her illegitimate half-sister who has already been imprisoned.

The crime is solved by a young drawing master working in tandem with the splendid Marian Halcombe, another half-sister of the heroine. Marian identifies the two villains, eavesdrops upon them, is captured, falls ill of fever, recovers, bribes the attendant to let her half-sister out of the asylum and discovers that the villain himself was born out of wedlock and is therefore not entitled to his fortune or position in society. She does all this with vigour, charm and good humour despite – O tragedy! – being 'ugly'. She has a 'large, firm, masculine mouth and jaw', down on her upper lip that was 'almost a moustache' and a waist 'undeformed by stays'. Despite all these supposed defects, her expression is 'bright, frank, and intelligent'. The critic John Sutherland calls her 'one of the finest creations in all Victorian fiction'.

'Sensation' novelists were particularly good at showing women stepping outside the normal conventions of behaviour, and, among them, Wilkie Collins was best at it. Just as he used current events to shape his work, he also used his own experience of women. This is perhaps best seen in *Armadale*, with its evil but impressive heroine, Miss Lydia Gwilt. To make it absolutely clear of her wickedness, not only is her surname a mere letter away from 'Guilt', she also has wickedly red hair.

The plot of *Armadale* is really quite ludicrous. But this story, too, was related to contemporary events, however much Collins may have claimed otherwise. In it, two men both named Allan Armadale, one rich, one poor, become friends. (They are related, but don't know it.) Lydia Gwilt's plan is to marry the poor one, thereby legally becoming 'Mrs Armadale'. Then, having bumped them both off, she would pose as the widow of the rich one in order to claim his estate.

This sort of thing was in fact no stranger than the real-life affair of the Tichborne Claimant. In 1854 Roger Tichborne, heir to a baronetcy and fortune, was lost at sea and presumed dead. His devoted mother, however, believing that he might have survived, advertised widely in Australia, his supposed destination, and heard back from a butcher from Wagga Wagga. The butcher came to see her in England, and despite his uncouth ways, was accepted as the missing man by Lady Tichborne, and by many of his friends. (The family doctor claimed that both the missing man and the butcher shared an unusual deformation of the genitals.) But the rest of the family scented fraud and refused to accept him. Eventually the Tichborne Claimant was accused of perjury, and died destitute.

This idea of using a false identity to claim an inheritance is central to *Armadale*. But one of the most enjoyable aspects of the novel is found in the relationship between the two central female characters. The plot depends upon a passionate, though quite frankly unbelievable, friendship between Allan Armadale and the other Allan Armadale (of mixed race), who goes by the assumed name of Ozias Midwinter. Far more engaging is the rivalry for the rich Allan's affections between Neelie Milroy, the teenage daughter of one of his neighbours, and the thirty-something Lydia Gwilt, who contrives to be engaged as Miss Milroy's governess specifically for the purpose of meeting and snagging him as a husband.

The character of Lydia Gwilt shocked and horrified readers upon her first appearance, but from today's vantage point she is much more sympathetic, coping rather valiantly with the setbacks of life (albeit, like Collins himself, with the help of her bottle of laudanum). Born illegitimate, she spent the first eight years of her life in the care of a 'baby farmer', or paid foster mother, Mother Oldershaw. When the money from Lydia's family mysteriously stopped, Mother Oldershaw put Lydia out to work, sending her, at twelve, to become a servant in a large Norfolk household. Here, her employer gets her to forge a letter on his behalf, because of her 'wicked dexterity' with the pen. John Sutherland points out that, of course, this wasn't the real reason: Lydia's wicked master knew that forgery was a capital offence, and wanted the actual crime off his hands. Also, the sub-text is that he seduced his maid as well. The family get rid of this inconvenient girl by sending Lydia to France, where she is next accused of seducing her music teacher and thereby sending him mad. Lydia goes into a convent for a while, before becoming a pianist in Brussels then being recruited by a female criminal baroness as bait for a gambling scam. After five years of this, Lydia marries a rich young Englishman, but her by now heinously corrupt nature causes her to take a lover. Her husband horsewhips her for this; she poisons him. She is caught and convicted, but is pardoned on the basis that people feel sorry for her. All this takes place before the story of *Armadale* even starts.

At its opening, Lydia's plan is to support herself by marrying Allan Armadale. After having exhausted so many other options, it's hard to see how else she might be able to earn a living. But the plan is eventually foiled when Lydia falls in love with her victim. It is her only weakness. In every other respect, she is a female Victorian Jason Bourne, employing the latest technology to achieve her ends. She aims to poison her victim by wafting carbonic acid into a bedroom through the air-conditioning in a new and purpose-built mental asylum. She also uses the facilities offered by London's smart new railway stations, carrying out a complex skein of manoeuvres to get her possessions, her correspondence and her travel arrangements lined up without being detected:

> to the cloakroom of the Great Western, to get the luggage which I sent there ... next to the cloak-room of the South Eastern (to leave my luggage) ... to wait for the starting of the tidal train on Monday. Next to the General Post Office, to post a letter to Midwinter at the Rectory, which he will receive to-morrow morning.

The most enjoyable passage of the book concerns the battle for Armadale's affections between Lydia, with all her splendid mature beauty (maintained by artifice), sophistication and wily ways, and, on the other, the peachy and unstudied attractions of her young rival, Neelie. The pull between these two different types of woman was something that Wilkie Collins had experienced at first hand. Among his many unconventional views was the belief that marriage was unfair to women, and he campaigned vigorously against what he saw as the injustices of the law regarding it. He avoided marriage all his life, but certainly did not live alone and celibate in consequence.

When he began *Armadale*, Collins was cohabiting with Caroline Graves, a woman in her mid-thirties, and her daughter, Harriet, whom Caroline had had with another man. (Wilkie loved Harriet and acted as her father.) Although they were not married, Caroline was the wise and worldly woman to whom he introduced his friends and with whom he discussed his work. In 1864, though, after ten years with Caroline, Wilkie Collins met the 19-year-old Martha Rudd, from Norfolk, the daughter of a shepherdess. He encountered her in Great Yarmouth as he was researching the East Anglian location of the action in *Armadale*, and persuaded her to come to London. He set her up in a house in Bolsover Street (only a ten-minute walk away from his and Caroline's home in Gloucester Place) and she bore him three children.

The competing charms of Wilkie's two mistresses are paralleled, in *Armadale*, by Lydia and Neelie's rivalry. 'Am I handsome enough, today?' Lydia asks her diary. 'Well, yes. Handsome enough to be a match for a little dowdy, awkward, freckled creature, who ought to be perched on a form at school.'

And yet, Allan Armadale would chose dim, dumpy little Neelie, malleable and easy-going, instead of the splendid Lydia.

In real life, Caroline's response to the arrival of Martha upon the scene was almost worthy of Lydia herself. She didn't poison anyone, but she finally decided that she'd had enough, left Collins and married someone else. And yet, despite this, Wilkie and Martha never married, and he never introduced her to his friends as his 'official' consort. Something went wrong with Caroline's new relationship and, within a couple of years, she was back in residence with Collins, even though he now had three children in the other home he shared with Martha. It was Caroline who nursed him in his final sickness, and Caroline was the 'wife' with whom Wilkie Collins was buried – in life, if not in literature, the older woman beat the younger.

Victorian readers, however, didn't take to Lydia at all, finding her immorality revolting – 'a woman fouler than the refuse of the streets' – and *Armadale* was something of a disappointment in sales terms. Another of Lydia's defects was the attention she paid to maintaining her striking good looks, a type of duplicitous vanity considered to be rather wicked.

This disapproval carried over to minor characters like Mother Oldershaw, whom contemporaries would have recognized instantly as the fictional equivalent of the beautician, con woman and procurer of abortions known as 'Madame Rachel'. Born in the East End as Sarah Rachel Levison, Madame Rachel of Bond Street promised those who visited her salon that she would make them – in the words of her advertising slogan – 'Beautiful for Ever'. Her cosmetic secrets included a process called 'enamelling', which involved plastering the face with a white paste designed to tighten, brighten and smoothen the skin. Today, we would presumably think it looked rather like the make-up of a clown, but to rich ladies – including the Princess of Wales herself – it was highly desirable.

Distinctly unnatural, though, an 'enamelled' or made-up face became easy to spot, and was the target of the sort of moral disapproval aimed at Botox today. 'We feel alarmed,' wrote a journalist in the *Glasgow Herald*,

> when a beauty looks as if she were going to be betrayed into a smile lest her cheek should suddenly become fractured. We shall watch with tremendous apprehension when some beauty applies her pocket handkerchief to her nose, lest four or five guineas worth of its exquisite proportions should come away with it.

The historian Helen Rappaport has discovered that some of Madame Rachel's clients required ever more personal services. One Mrs Esdaile, for example, embarked upon a course of Arabian Bath treatments at Madame Rachel's salon. She complained that her diamond earrings had gone missing from the changing room. Mrs Esdaile's husband marched her along to a solicitor: he believed that the earrings had been stolen, and wanted Madame Rachel's salon investigated. However, as the couple concluded their meeting with the solicitor, Mrs Esdaile nonchalantly left her gloves on his desk. Returning later, alone, to pick up the gloves, she admitted that she'd been using the salon to meet up with a lover in a private cubicle.

Madame Rachel's fees for this extra service and for her continued discretion had escalated over the months to the level of blackmail. It was no good Mrs Esdaile refusing to pay, Madame Rachel had threatened: 'I know who you are. I have had you watched. I know where you live.' But Mrs Esdaile quietly asked her husband's solicitor to abandon the case. She knew that she had even more to lose than Madame Rachel if he brought about a successful prosecution.

The fraudster and blackmailer was eventually indicted in 1865 for a poignant crime: she'd undertaken to remove the smallpox scars from the face of a client who had, in return, promised to give Madame Rachel all her jewellery. Madame Rachel was finally exposed in a trial conducted under a glare of publicity, and was confirmed as a celebrity criminal when her waxwork entered Madame Tussaud's.

The fictional Madame Rachel, Mother Oldershaw, the nearest person Lydia has to a mother, lends the anti-heroine money and helps her with her schemes, but is ready to turn and stab her in the back on the slightest provocation. Collins ran the risk of libel in creating such similarities between Oldershaw and Rachel, although Helen Rappaport has discovered no evidence to prove that the real-life Madame Rachel had links with backstreet abortionists, like her fictional equivalent. Setting the novel in 1851, ten years before its date of publication, Rappaport suggests, was a deliberate strategy that Collins came up with to defend himself from accusations of feeding upon the distress of real people.

Despite the scandal caused by characters like Lydia Gwilt and Mother Oldershaw, the sympathy that Collins showed for women and the engaging complexity that he gave to his female characters ensured that he had many devoted female readers. A manual for women published in 1889 told them how they ought to react to the disappointments of life: 'Perhaps you are unhappy; perhaps your heart is bursting. But do not look for consolation, even in the realm of ideas, these are dangerous if they can become sinful. Resign yourself. Lose yourself completely in your children.'

'Sensation' novels like *Armadale* – or Ellen Wood's *East Lynne*, or Mary Elizabeth Braddon's *Lady Audley's Secret* – provided an alternative to this. In them women were often bad, mad, dangerous and murderous. 'Female anger, frustration and sexual energy' bursts out of these stories, writes the critic Elaine Showalter, and often 'the death of a husband comes as a welcome release, and women escape from their families through illness, madness, divorce, flight and, ultimately, murder'.

The 'sensation' novel has retained its admirers ever since its emergence in the 1860s. The magnificent detective novelist of the 1930s Dorothy L. Sayers was devoted to the form. In her masterpiece *Gaudy Night* (1935), her bluestocking heroine Harriet Vane returns to her old Oxford college to research a very appropriate pet project: the work of 'sensation' novelist Sheridan Le Fanu.

And Collins and his contemporaries still influence writers today. Sarah Waters was inspired by the hits of the 1860s for her fabulous novel *Fingersmith* (2002). 'I was hooked on the "sensation novels" of writers such as Wilkie Collins, Sheridan Le Fanu and Mary Elizabeth Braddon', she wrote in the *Guardian* in 2006, 'novels whose pre-occupation with sex, crime and family scandals had once made them runaway bestsellers.' In *Fingersmith*, Sue, the child of an urban baby farmer (like Mother Oldershaw), is sent by her family of thieves to a remote country house. Her mission is a plot against Maud, an isolated, strange young lady, who lives with her uncle, a noted collector of pornography. The plan is that Sue will persuade Maud to elope with a man who's really a fraudster. He will then place her in a madhouse and claim her fortune.

It's a story Wilkie Collins would have loved.

15

———◆———

'It is worse than a crime, Violet ...'

'Harrowing the Mind, making the Flesh Creep, Causing the Hair to Stand on end, Giving Shocks to the Nervous System ... and generally Unfitting the Public for the Prosaic Avocations of Life.'

Punch, *describing the novels of Mary Elizabeth Braddon*

Like many of her contemporary writers, and many of her own heroines, Mary Elizabeth Braddon would probably have preferred to live a less lurid life. But she had little choice. She desperately needed the money to be made by exploiting the British weakness for crime.

The daughter of a solicitor, she grew up in Frith Street, Soho. In 1839, when she was four, her parents broke up. Braddon's father's infidelity and spend-thriftery drove her mother to leave him, taking her daughter with her, and to set up home in Kensington. Here the future novelist received a good education at a girls' school.

Yet cash was short. In her early twenties, Braddon was forced to find work, to make ends meet, and she chose to go on the stage.

With her mother in tow, she toured the Midlands as an actress. Suitably for a girl forced by circumstances to act older and wiser than her years, she often took the part of a middle-aged matron rather than the ingénue.

Even during her theatrical years, though, Braddon had an alternative career in mind. Eventually she picked up an admirer who was willing to fund her to write, full-time, for six months. Her earliest published efforts were Penny Dreadfuls, which were published weekly, and cheaply, in serial form – 'Dreadfuls' were aimed at a slightly younger market, particularly boys. Judith Flanders

Mary Elizabeth Braddon.

points out that, in 1861, 9 out of the total population of 20 million were aged 18 or under, so 45 per cent of the potential reading public were children. Feeding their demand for entertainment as a serial writer involved sustained, disciplined work, which evidently suited Braddon: 'I have never written a line that has not been written against time.' And yet, as she began to find success, she also found herself constrained by her genre, complaining: 'the amount of crime, treachery, murder, slow poisoning and general infamy required by the halfpenny reader is something terrible'.

Braddon lost her generous patron, because she had set herself up with another man. She became a literary assistant to John Maxwell, publisher of fiction magazines. He was married, and had five children, and in a turn of events that would not be out of place in one of Braddon's own novels, his wife had been locked away in a lunatic asylum.

Braddon (her faithful and long-suffering mother still in tow) now moved into John Maxwell's house in Bloomsbury, and began to act as his wife and as stepmother to his five children. She would live with him, unmarried, for many years, and have a further five children with him, giving her many critics ammunition for accusations of impropriety.

And bigamy formed the central theme of Braddon's first great triumph, *Lady Audley's Secret*. Published in serial form in 1861, it sold enormously well. The story of Lady Audley's infamy unfolds through the investigative work of her husband's nephew, a handsome, lazy and unemployed barrister called Robert Audley. As the book progresses, he toughens up, becomes increasingly dedicated to his task, and finishes up as the rather high-handed arbiter of retribution.

At the very end, once it has become clear that Lady Audley was indeed guilty of attempted murder, Robert Audley takes it upon himself to imprison her in a mental institution rather than drag his family name through the scandal of the criminal courts.

At the heart of *Lady Audley's Secret* is the ancient mansion of Audley Court. Braddon's model for the house was Ingatestone Hall in Essex, dating from the 1540s. It was the secondary home of its owners, the Catholic Petre family, who rented it out as a series of apartments. It seems that John Maxwell rather than Braddon herself was their tenant, and it's unclear whether his landlords knew that the lady writer whom he installed for a while in the apartment was his lover. Braddon's description of Audley Court still applies to Ingatestone Hall to this day:

> The house ... occupied three sides of a quadrangle. It was very old, and very irregular and rambling. The windows were uneven; some small, some large, some with heavy stone mullions and rich stained glass; others with frail lattices that rattled in every breeze ... the principal door was squeezed into a corner of a turret at one angle of the building ... a glorious old place. A place that visitors fell in raptures with; feeling a yearning to have done with life.

Running alongside a sluggish green canal behind Ingatestone Hall is the celebrated Lime Walk. In the story, the Lime Walk leads to the infamous well down which Lady Audley pushes her first husband. Braddon claimed later that it was walking beneath the Ingatestone limes that inspired the whole story. Only to a 'sensation' novelist like

Robert Audley and Lady Audley at the well
down which she has pushed her husband.

Braddon would this peaceful and secluded spot have suggested (in her words) 'something uncanny' and 'a history of domestic crime'.

Middle-class reaction to this scandalous book (and to its equally scandalous author) was predictable. 'She has temporarily succeeded in making the literature of the kitchen the favourite reading of the drawing room,' sniffed one critic. She satisfied only 'the cravings of a diseased appetite,' huffed another, while a third marvelled at her invention, 'which could only have been possible to an Englishwoman knowing the attractions of impropriety'.

Much of the impropriety of the book lay in its anti-heroine, Lady Audley. She looked good as gold with her china-doll, passive prettiness, and yet she was quite capable of murder. The heroine in Braddon's next book, *Aurora Floyd* (1862), would be even less womanly: she actually horse-whips her blackmailer, in a celebrated scene, which deranges her clothing in a manner that suggests that she enjoyed the sadism.

But it was *Lady Audley* who made her creator a fortune, and with it Braddon purchased a grand house in Richmond where she wrote many of the rest of her 80 novels. Lichfield House (dating from the eighteenth century, and demolished in the 1930s) was grand and substantial, not quite as grand as the ancient Audley Court but more than respectable. Braddon's publisher, William Tinsley, built himself a villa at Barnes, Audley Lodge, with his own share of the profits.

Reading *Lady Audley's Secret* today, one is struck by how unfair the contemporary vilification of the heroine seems. We know that Helen (alias Lady Audley) is a villainess by the repeated references to her beautiful, ethereal, feathery *golden* curls: the sub-text is that she (shamefully) dyes her hair. Just as with Lydia Gwilt, though, it's hard to dismiss Lady Audley as a truly evil character.

She was parted as a child from her own mad mother to grow up with her alcoholic father. Once married, and with a young baby, she is deserted by her husband George Talboys, who goes off to Australia without a word. It is the action of a heartless villain, though contemporary readers found him a paragon of virtue. It may have been his intention to seek – and in fact he did succeed in finding – a fortune in Australia for the benefit of his wife and child, but Helen is abandoned to a life of poverty. I find it quite understandable that she should give him up as a bad lot, find work as a governess and then marry the aged and wealthy baronet Sir Michael Audley. But then she has a stroke of bad luck: it turns out that Robert Audley, Sir Michael's nephew, was also a friend of her first husband. Robert grows increasingly suspicious about what might have happened to George Talboys, and who the new Lady Audley might really be.

Helen's greater crime was the abandonment of her child to the not-so-tender mercies of her drunken father, although her husband George – held up as a hero – does exactly the same thing when he returns from Australia and the boy becomes his responsibility. Even Robert Audley, inheriting the problem of what to do with the child after his friend's supposed murder, does nothing more than pack the poor boy off to school. I like to think that Lady Audley finally saves her own life by *pretending* to be mad, thereby persuading the stuffy Robert Audley that she should live, at his expense, in Belgium for the rest of her life rather than face trial for attempted murder.

Despite the resetting of our moral compasses, one of the enduring pleasures of the story of Lady Audley is working out who's good and who's bad, and changing one's mind as new facts emerge. Mary Elizabeth Braddon was instinctively aware of what her readers would praise and blame, and managed to walk the tightrope between the two in a manner that kept people reading even if they didn't approve. 'It is worse than a crime, Violet, it is an impropriety' is a celebrated line spoken by a character in one of her later works, which could only have been written by a clear-eyed observer of contemporary society.

Jennifer Carnell, Braddon's biographer, points out that contemporaries would have judged many of Braddon's characters more harshly than their creator did herself. Those who commit murders and other crimes (and there are many of them in her many books) are often allowed to escape hanging or death, and Braddon sends them off instead to a long life of quiet repentance. This enraged her more moralistic readers, but, from a modern vantage point, it looks as if Braddon had more insight into human weakness than many of her male fellow writers. Life had not treated her kindly, and she therefore understood what circumstances could drive people to do.

Indeed, in the midst of her wealth and achievements, the past caught up with her. When John Maxwell's legal wife eventually died in the psychiatric institution in Ireland, Braddon's detractors made sure that the death was announced widely in the press. Letters of condolence began to arrive at Braddon and Maxwell's house in Richmond, as everyone assumed that it was Braddon herself, his presumed wife, who was dead. When it became clear that she was still very much alive, the respectability of this apparently affluent couple living in Richmond was shredded, and all but one of their servants left. Yet, even if Braddon wasn't immensely respectable, when she died in 1915, she was immensely successful and immensely rich, the reward of a career providing Victorian readers with exactly the stories they desired most.

16

Monsters and Men

'Strong men shuddered and women fainted and were carried
out of the theatre.'

Richard Mansfield's obituary describes the
effect of his performance as Mr Hyde

In 1888, a serial killer was terrorizing the East End of London.
The few undisputed facts about him are rather grubby and shop-
soiled from so much handling, and the identity of the murderer
is still a complete mystery. Over the summer and autumn, several
killings of prostitutes on the streets of Whitechapel and Spitalfields
became linked – at least in the public's imagination – with a
single perpetrator. The removal of internal organs from three of
the women led people to think that he must have had medical
knowledge, and be experienced in dissection. The final touch came
from a hoax letter, purporting to be from the killer but probably
written by a journalist aiming to stir up the story. He signed it
with the name that stands today as shorthand for a whole ragbag
of half-facts and inferences: the assumption that there was a single

killer and mutilator, trained as a doctor, who called himself 'Jack the Ripper'.*

The case was recreated in fiction almost immediately. *The Curse Upon Mitre Square* is a novelette inspired by one of the Ripper killings and published by John Francis Brewer as early as October 1888. And, of course, its influence is felt to this day, with TV dramas like *Whitechapel* and *Ripper Street*.

But historians have recently pointed out an extremely interesting relationship that goes in the other direction, from fiction to real life.

Robert Louis Stevenson's story *The Strange Case of Dr Jekyll and Mr Hyde* (1886) was inspired by a nightmare – 'I was dreaming a fine bogey tale', as he put it – and he wrote it in three furious days. The short novel is about a respectable doctor with a split personality. By day, he is a fine, upstanding member of his profession and community. At night, though, he is transformed into a terrible, dark inversion of himself. Through the consumption of a magic medicine, he would 'turn into' the other, baser, half of his character: the monstrous killer Mr Hyde. The story opens with a description of Mr Hyde, rampaging down a London street at night, and in a blind fury trampling down and crushing a little girl who had been sent out by her family to run for a doctor for a sick relative. His evil actions are particularly terrifying because they appear to be random and without motive.

---

* When I interviewed Judith Flanders about the 'Ripper', she pointed out that of the many hundreds of Victorian murders she investigated in her research, only four remained unsolved. Of these, three had a closed group of suspects of whom the guilty party must have been one. Only the 'Jack the Ripper' case remains completely open. More than one hundred different named suspects have been put forward during the course of the century that has followed.

Accosted by spectators, Mr Hyde agrees to pay compensation to her family for hurting the child, but the cheque he makes out is in the name of the highly respectable Dr Jekyll. This is the first hint that the evil, deformed and violent Mr Hyde – he later bludgeons someone to death with a walking stick – has some sort of relationship with the virtuous doctor. It's initially assumed that Mr Hyde is blackmailing Dr Jekyll, but the two of them are never to be seen in the same place at the same time. Eventually, when Hyde is suspected of having murdered Jekyll, the secret comes out that they are one and the same person. Along with it the source of the transformation is revealed: it lies in the potion and the special salt with which it must be mixed. Dr Jekyll had been performing chemical experiments to explore the 'thorough and primitive duality of man', and, through a batch of contaminated drugs, had stumbled upon unforeseen and tragic consequences.

Once again the Victorian love/fear of poisons raises its head, as does the idea that darkness lurks in the heart of the respectable doctor, like William Palmer. The theme of a man's being able to present two very different faces to the world runs through Victorian literature: it would be seen again in *The Picture of Dorian Grey* by Oscar Wilde (1890).

Stevenson's book was enormously successful and soon became a stage play, which opened at London's Lyceum Theatre on 5 August 1888. The murder of Martha Tabram, a crime some people think is the first in the series committed by 'Jack the Ripper', took place just two days later. Other murders followed swiftly on.

Every night at the Lyceum, in front of a couple of thousand people, an actor named Richard Mansfield (1857–1907) played both of the characters, the good Dr Jekyll and the evil Mr Hyde. The climax of the play came when he transformed himself, on stage, from Mr Hyde back into Dr Jekyll. The film versions of the story show the transformation going the other way, from good to bad, from Jekyll to Hyde. But the original stage version showed the monster turning into the man.

Stevenson's story described the transformation as:

the most racking pangs ... a grinding in the bones, deadly nausea, and a horror of the spirit that cannot be exceeded at the hour of birth or death. Then these agonies began swiftly to subside, and I came to myself as if out of a great sickness. There was something strange in my sensations, something indescribably sweet.

This was what Richard Mansfield had to convey – and he was an extraordinarily skilled actor. His background had been in Gilbert and Sullivan operettas, and he would go on to be a hugely popular Shakespearian performer. When he died, the *New York Times* called him 'the greatest actor of his hour, and one of the greatest of all times'.

Dr Jekyll/Mr Hyde was the role that made Mansfield's reputation. The *Daily Telegraph* claimed that 'his nervous electricity caused silence throughout the house – the surest test of power'. (This also shows that audiences were not yet expected to sit in the well-mannered, attentive silence that we know today.) 'Mr Mansfield,' the reviewer continued, 'has come, he has been seen, and he has conquered as an actor of remarkable power and intelligence.'

How did Mansfield achieve the changeover from Hyde to Jekyll? There was much speculation about his use of make-up, trap doors and secret lighting effects. 'Every one speculated on the secret of the transformation which they saw yet could not believe', Mansfield's obituary would claim. 'He was accused of using acids, phosphorus and all manner of chemicals.' Indeed, one witness 'declared it was "all perfectly simple. He uses a rubber suit which he inflates and exhausts with pleasure!"'

Mansfield was understandably reluctant to reveal the secrets of his craft, but it does seem that the transformation was achieved through the physical body alone. He did, however, receive help from the swelling music of the orchestra, and some nifty lighting. As Mr Hyde, he was lit from below, to darken and deepen the eye sockets. As Dr Jekyll, he was lit, flatteringly, from above, as the conventional, handsome, juvenile lead in any play would have been. (The critics generally preferred Mansfield as the twisted Mr Hyde rather than as the much more straightforward and run-of-the-mill hero, Dr Jekyll.) But most of the effect he achieved by himself. The moment Mr Hyde swallowed the magic potion, Mansfield would turn his back on the audience, writhing and grimacing as it went down his throat. Then, as he completed his circuit, he faced them once again as the smiling doctor. The *Evening Standard* described how: 'It is the puny fiend that swallows the draught, then the figure straightens itself, actually seems to increase in stature, passes its hands upwards over its face, and Jekyll stands revealed. The change is amazing in its completeness and rapidity.'

Mansfield would have adopted the overblown, melodramatic acting style necessary for two thousand people to be able to see clearly what he was doing, and they found it thrilling and terrifying in equal measure.

It was a remarkable performance, and people were amazed partly because they had simply never seen anything like it before. The effect on the audience's nerves was so deep as to be almost dangerous. One newspaper reported:

> I was attracted by a crowd in the Strand the other night, and on investigating the matter, found that they surrounded a well-dressed young man who had bolted out of a ' bus while it was going at a rapid rate, and then fallen down in a fit. It appeared that he had been to see Mr Mansfield as Dr Jekyll, and on getting into the 'bus found himself beside a most repulsive-looking man, whom he immediately concluded must either be the Doctor himself or the Whitechapel Murderer. In a fit of fearful nervousness, he jumped from his seat, and came to grief as mentioned.

The press were reporting that 'Jack the Ripper' had been removing internal organs from his victims with some skill, suggesting that he, too, had a medical training – and it wasn't long before people began to mix up fact and fiction. In an article for *The Ripperologist* (the journal for historians of 'Jack the Ripper'), Alan Sharp analyses the links the media made between the 'Ripper' and Mr Hyde during London's fearful summer of 1888. He notes how the *Freeman's Journal* began in a sober, comparative note, reflecting that 'these atrocities and apparently causeless murders show that there is abroad at the present time in the East End a human monster even more terrible than Hyde'. Meanwhile, another gentleman wrote to the *Telegraph* with a stronger connection, suggesting that 'the perpetrator [of the 'Ripper' killings] is a being whose diseased brain has been inflamed by witnessing the performance of the drama of "Dr Jekyll and Mr Hyde"'. Others went still further than the facts warranted. A correspondent to *The Star* insisted that: 'You, and every one of the papers, have missed the obvious solution of the Whitechapel mystery. The murderer is a Mr Hyde, who seeks in the repose and comparative respectability of Dr Jekyll security from the crimes he commits in his baser shape.'

There were even those who insisted that the actor Richard Mansfield was himself the killer. After all, every night, on stage, he showed that he had the capacity to be both a healer and a killer: 'I do not think there is a man living so well able to disguise himself in a moment as he does in front of the public,' claimed the *Pall Mall Gazette* under the headline 'Mr Hyde at large in Whitechapel'.

As Judith Flanders has pointed out, the story of Dr Jekyll and Mr Hyde has had a powerful effect upon people's understanding of who 'Jack the Ripper' might have been. The killer is never assumed to be a local East Ender with a history as a ne'er-do-well. He's always judged to be a man out of place, flipping between high society by day and the dark and dirty streets of Whitechapel by night. The suspects put forward include the artist Walter Sickert, the writer Lewis Carroll, and Edward VII's eldest son, the Duke of Clarence, all of them embodying the idea that within a respectable man may lurk a monster.

Reality and fiction seem to become entangled even further when one considers the interrelationship between 'Jack the Ripper' and another character who began walking London's streets around the same time, the brilliant detective Sherlock Holmes. Holmes made his first appearance in a Christmas album in 1887, and the same story, *A Study in Scarlet*, was published as a novel in 1888, the same year that the 'Ripper' terrorized the nation.

The 'Ripper's' crimes had not yet taken place at Holmes's debut, but as his character developed during the numerous stories that followed, Holmes seems to become almost a mirror image of 'Jack the Ripper'. Where 'Jack' is uncontrollable, mysterious and motiveless, a creature of the night, Sherlock is rational, reassuring and brilliant, shining a light into the darkest places. Where the police fail – both in the real-life Whitechapel murders and in the many fictional cases described by Sir Arthur Conan Doyle – Holmes is always successful. And in a strange intertwining of our images of 'Jack' and Sherlock, one of the very few eyewitnesses thought to have actually seen the serial killer reported that he was wearing a deerstalker hat.

Fittingly, it is to Sherlock Holmes that government ministers, successful businessmen and the royal families of Europe turn for solutions to their knottiest problems. On the whole, though, Holmes's clients aren't the great and the good. They also include vicars, typists, engineers, landladies, governesses ... the very sort of people who had to walk home along the streets at night, who read Sir Arthur Conan Doyle's stories in magazines and who were encouraged by them to imagine that 'Jack the Ripper' might yet be caught.

There is something solid and reassuring about both Sherlock Holmes and his world. At the same time, though – exactly in common with many people's conception of the 'Ripper' – Holmes is an oddball, somebody standing outside normal society. Lacking close family ties, subject to spells of deep depression, dependent on morphine and other drugs to carry him through periods of boredom and lassitude, he is so unfailingly devoted to what he sees as justice that it sometimes causes him to act thoughtlessly or even dangerously.

It makes for a thrilling, if occasionally unsettling, reading experience. Holmes is the hero of the story, taking hansom cabs and chasing criminals through the Pool of London by boat. But he also haunts opium dens, and the very first time we see Holmes, in *A Study in Scarlet*, he is indulging in a suitably 'Ripper'-ish activity: beating a corpse with a stick.

This, of course, was part of his work as that latest of Victorian inventions: the forensic scientist.

17

The Adventure of the Forensic Scientist

'A medical man, when he sees a dead body, should notice everything.'

Alfred Swaine Taylor, A Manual of Medical Jurisprudence *(1844)*

What was it like to enter a Victorian mortuary?

It was a room in a hospital likely to look out upon an internal courtyard, so that members of the public couldn't see in. Its windows would be rubbed with soap or tallow to obscure the view, but natural light was preferred. In the centre of the room would stand a stone table, without a rim or drain: any fluids ran off it to be soaked up by the sawdust on the floor.

Sometimes there was a secret chamber above the fireplace, where a dubiously acquired corpse would be lifted, via hooks and pulleys, to evade any investigation. The notion that medical students needed to hone their skills by dissecting corpses caused great distress, and in previous centuries had been condemned by the Church.

Since the seventeenth century, doctors' practice had been to use the bodies of condemned criminals, and, when the supply ran short, to use the services of the 'Resurrection Men'. These murky characters robbed fresh graves of their corpses, and sold them to medical schools for a profit. (It wasn't illegal to steal a body, but body snatchers could be prosecuted for the theft of the clothes in which corpses had been buried.)

The 1832 'Anatomy' Act was an attempt to make it easier for medical students to acquire the bodies they needed without breaking the law. From then on, corpses of the inmates of workhouses left unclaimed by their families for 48 hours or more could be sent on to the hospitals. But problems remained. Sometimes families were not told that the body released to them for burial had already been dissected at a hospital, and such was the authority and stature of the workhouse that some relatives did not dare claim their dead at all, and gave them up to dissection silently and unwillingly.

The cadavers required for dissection by medical students would arrive in barrels labelled 'pork' or 'beef', and preserved in alcohol. Firstly, any identifying features would be removed. Then a body would be arranged on its back on the table, a block of wood raising the head, the chest presenting itself for the initial cut down from the chin to the pubic bone. Before electric saws, it required extremely energetic work to cut open a ribcage. The oscillating surgical saw was only invented in 1947 by the Dr Homer Stryker who gives it its name.

In these smelly rooms, medics risked exposure to infectious diseases, working as they did with bare hands and faces, their bodies protected only by aprons. But they were gradually establishing the details of how a human being was made – and how it might have died.

They were learning how to read a body.

Over the course of the nineteenth century, the art of interpreting the medical evidence of a crime developed in two related but separate arenas. First, there was the reading of the body itself, in the mortuary, or through chemical analysis of the type used in the case of William Palmer. Second, there was the reading of the minute evidence left at the scene of the crime itself, which was slower to become established.

It is in both of these contexts that we first meet Sherlock Holmes, though his work in the latter field is much more innovative. In his very first appearance in print, *A Study in Scarlet* (1887), Dr John Watson hears that a friend of friend – 'a fellow who is working at the chemical laboratory up at the hospital' – is looking for a lodger. Dr Watson himself wants to rent a room, so is keen to meet the unknown chemist.

The mutual friend takes Dr Watson to St Bartholomew's Hospital, where the as-yet-unknown Sherlock Holmes spends much of his time. Dr Watson's friend warns him that Holmes is a crank, 'a little queer in his ideas'. He has been seen, for example, pounding a human corpse, apparently to establish how far bruises may be created post-mortem. We learn that Holmes is unnaturally interested in poison:

> I could imagine his giving a friend a little pinch of the latest vegetable alkaloid, not out of malevolence, you understand, but simply out of a spirit of enquiry in order to have an accurate idea of the effects. To do him justice, I think that he would take it himself with the same readiness. He appears to have a passion for definite and exact knowledge.

Dr Watson discovers Holmes at work in a chemistry laboratory, in high spirits because he has just discovered a new way of identifying bloodstains. 'I've found it! I've found it!' Holmes cries, as he comes running to meet his visitors 'with a test-tube in his hand'.

Sherlock Holmes then shakes John Watson's hand: '"How are you," he said cordially, gripping my hand with a strength for which I should hardly have given him credit. "You have been in Afghanistan, I perceive."'

Dr Watson is astounded by this, and only some time later, after an appropriate build-up of suspense, do we learn about the thought process by which Holmes pulled off this feat of deduction:

'Here is a gentleman of a medical type, but with the air of a military man. Clearly an army doctor, then. He has just come from the tropics, for his face is dark, and that is not the natural tint of his skin, for his wrists are fair. He has undergone hardship and sickness, as his haggard face says clearly. His left arm has been injured. He holds it in a stiff and unnatural manner. Where in the tropics could an English army doctor have seen much hardship and got his arm wounded? Clearly in Afghanistan'. The whole train of thought did not occupy a second. I then remarked that you came from Afghanistan, and you were astonished.

In the very first few pages, then, of Holmes's life in print, we're introduced not only to the character of the detective himself but to the business of applying science to detection. We see him at work in the laboratory, researching toxicology and inventing a new chemical test for the identification of blood, 'the most practical medico-legal discovery for years', as Holmes himself puts it. And then we see his process of step-by-step, deductive reasoning at work when he flabbergasts Dr Watson by reading the evidence hidden in Watson's own appearance to conclude that he has done military service in Afghanistan.

Arthur Conan Doyle, the creator of Sherlock Holmes, was himself trained as a doctor, and it was one of his own teachers, Dr Bell, whose methods inspired Holmes's. In an audio recording made shortly before his death in 1930, he describes the process by which his detective was brought to life. Speaking slowly and clearly in his Scottish/Northumbrian accent, with his rolled 'r's providing the occasional flourish, Conan Doyle explains how he had been, at the time of writing *A Study in Scarlet*:

> a young doctor ... educated in a very severe and critical medical school of thought, especially coming under the influence of Dr Bell of Edinburgh, who had most remarkable powers of observation. He prided himself that when he looked at a patient he could tell not only their disease but very often their occupation and place of residence.

Bell was prominent among the younger generation of forensic medical scientists following on from Alfred Swaine Taylor and William Herapath. He had risen high in his field, was invited to attend upon Queen Victoria when she was in Scotland, and in later years would take considerable satisfaction in his reputation as the inspiration behind Sherlock Holmes.

Conan Doyle's genius was to combine Bell's scientific approach with his own love of storytelling. His original plan had been to settle down happily into general practice as a doctor. Waiting in his surgery for the patients who failed to arrive, he started writing stories, and sent many of them off to magazines in a variety of genres: horror, mystery, ghost. But he struck gold only when he turned to detection.

'I thought I would try my hand,' he explains, in his audio recording, 'at writing a story where the hero would treat crime in the way Dr Bell treated disease – and where science would take the place of chess. The result was Sherlock Holmes.' A scene in *A Study in Scarlet* that swiftly follows the initial introductions shows Holmes as the heroic scientist, this time at work at the scene of a crime. The body itself had long been the site of study, but the location of the deed had only more recently come under scrutiny as a legitimate part of the work of a detective. Here Holmes was in his element, and ahead of his peers. He castigates the police detectives on site for trampling all over the muddy path outside the house and spoiling the evidence of the footprints of the murderer. 'If a herd of buffaloes had passed along,' he tells the policeman in charge, 'there could not be a greater mess.' It sets a pattern he would follow throughout the whole of his fictional career, railing against the blundering, ignorant, plodding professionals around whom he runs rings.

Once inside, Holmes looks at the body in exactly the manner advised by Alfred Swaine Taylor, whose work Conan Doyle had read closely. Broadening out the study of material evidence, Holmes has also made a deep study of the different types of cigar ash, bicycle tyres and mud, all the better to read clues. When Holmes studies the corpse, Conan Doyle shows us his 'nimble fingers were flying here, there, and everywhere, feeling, pressing unbuttoning, examining'. This is quite in line, as the medical historian E. J. Wagner points out, with Taylor's exhortation that:

> The first duty of a medical jurist is to cultivate a faculty of minute observation ... He should observe everything which could throw a light on the production of wounds or other injuries found upon it. It should not be left to a policeman to say whether there were any marks of blood on the dress or on the hands of the deceased, or on the furniture of the room.

Once the body is removed, Sherlock Holmes gets to work on the room itself, looking at every inch of the floor and ceiling for evidence:

> He whipped a tape measure and a large round magnifying glass from his pocket. With these two implements he trotted noiselessly about the room, sometimes stopping, occasionally kneeling, and once lying flat on his face ... I was reminded of a pure-blooded well-trained foxhound ... in one place he gathered up carefully a little pile of grey dust from the floor, and packed it away in an envelope.

The idea of a SOCO, or 'Scene of Crimes Officer', is very familiar today, but in 1887 it was a novelty. It had never been seen before in literature, nor were readers even familiar with the theory behind the collecting of hair, dust and other seemingly trivial traces of evidence. The Sherlock Holmes stories would do a great deal for the popularization and professionalization of forensic science, so much so that the great French forsensic scientist Alexandre Lacassagne, who set up one of the first police labs at Lyons, would tell all his new recruits to read the great detective. 'Fascinating technique' was his verdict.

But the most gripping thing about Sherlock Holmes is not so much his strength as his weakness. The supremely rational detective would have led a sad and arid life without his firm friend, admirer, cheerleader and chronicler, Dr Watson, who devoted himself to Holmes from the moment of their first meeting to the last.

In one of the later Sherlock Holmes stories, 'The Adventure of the Devil's Foot', a near-perfect paradigm of the form published in the collection *His Last Bow* (1917), we see both Dr Watson's warmth and Holmes's coolness: it is the combination of the two that's irresistible. In one immensely tender scene, the two friends stagger out of a room that Holmes has, in the interests of research, filled with poison gas. Sherlock Holmes may appear at first glance to be indomitable, but without his much more human friend he cannot navigate life:

> I dashed from my chair, threw my arms around Holmes, and together we lurched through the door ...
>
> 'Upon my word, Watson!' said Holmes at last with an unsteady voice, 'I owe you both my thanks and an apology. It was an unjustifiable experiment even for one's self, and doubly so for a friend. I am really very sorry.'

'You know,' I answered with some emotion, for I had never seen so much of Holmes's heart before, 'that it is my greatest joy and privilege to help you.'

He relapsed at once into the half-humorous, half-cynical vein which was his habitual attitude to those about him. 'It would be superfluous to drive us mad, my dear Watson,' said he.

Coming as it does toward the end of their lengthy friendship, truths long unspoken are at last expressed.

———

O nce the science of preserving and examining a crime scene had been established, the stage was set for new techniques to be employed in determining the identity of criminals and suspects. From 1871, the Prevention of Crimes Act decreed that convicted criminals should be photographed for the purpose of future identification. But the huge volume of paper produced proved impractical for storage and record-keeping. Five years later, the rule was relaxed so that only 'habitual' criminals had mug shots taken.

Yet this initiative to keep records of criminals would bear fruit in other ways. Prisoners leaving jail had to have their appearance and distinguishing marks recorded on cards, including the inky prints of their fingers. (Many convicts left poignantly faint imprints, the skin of their hands having been worn down by hard labour in jail.) These record cards contained a good deal of information intended to allow offenders to be identified if they went back to their old tricks. The cards employed a French technique of recording a set of standard body measurements. Under this Bertillon system of 'anthropometric measurement', the distance between the outside of the elbow and the tip of the middle finger, for example, or the diameter of the head, was recorded with metal callipers or gauges. The more measurements you took, the less the probability of two suspects having exactly the same ones.

However, a team of British civil servants working in India refined the system down to its essential core. Exploiting the existing knowledge that every person has a unique pattern to his or her fingerprints, Edward Henry, the Inspector-General of the police in the province of Bengal, headed a team which established a system of classifying prints so that new ones could be matched to those in an existing database. He already knew that every person's print was different. The innovation that made the discovery useful to the police lay in the record-keeping that allowed the information to be stored and accessed. Henry's book on the new system was published in 1897, and it was adopted across the British Raj, though today credit is usually rightly given to Hemchandra Bose and Azizul Hacque, Henry's Sub-Inspectors, for devising the means by which prints were given a numerical value, based firstly upon the main types of shape – loops, whirls and arches – then upon the variations in the curves and spacing of the lines.

Henry's work began to make a stir in law enforcement circles, and when he came back to London to become a commissioner at Scotland Yard in 1901 he established a new Fingerprint Bureau for the Metropolitan Police. (During Henry's time as commissioner, he also oversaw the introduction of typewriters and police dogs to the force.) At this time, fingerprints were already being taken and stored, but only from prisoners.

The earliest murder actually to be solved through the identification of fingerprints came in 1905, when two shopkeepers were found murdered in their shop in Deptford. A fingerprint on their cash box was linked to Alfred Stratton, one of two brothers suspected of the crime, and was used to place him firmly at the scene, and to convict him. But Sherlock Holmes, once again, was ahead of the police. A bloody fingerprint was central to the case in 'The Adventure of the Norwood Builder', published two years earlier.

However, the real strength of fingerprinting would lie in identifying whether or not suspects had previous criminal records. With the establishing of the Fingerprinting Bureau, all the pre-existing prints of the prisoners taken under the Bertillon system had to be classified so that they could form a huge database which would now be added to every time suspects were brought in. The system survives to this day: every person arrested and charged with a serious offence has to give fingerprints, and the police are allowed to use reasonable force to make him or her do so. Only if the person is found 'not guilty' is the record destroyed.

Methods continued to improve and resources to increase as the police instructed their rank and file in how to become better detectives. A training museum opened at Scotland Yard, a collection of artefacts, samples, weapons and even human remains compiled for the purpose of educating junior officers. It was modelled after a similar venture by Eugène François Vidocq (1775–1857), the former criminal-turned-investigator who was responsible for the Sûreté, the French Security Brigade.

Vidocq was a thief-turned-thief-taker in the eighteenth-century mould, and first went to prison at the age of 13. He made a living through fencing, working in a puppet theatre and playing the part of a cannibal in a travelling show before joining and then deserting the French army. At the age of 34, he decided to change sides, and gave up a life of crime to become a police informer. His background helped. 'Adored by the thieves,' he claims, 'I could always rely on their devotion to me.'

Within the police, Vidocq set up the Sûreté, a unit of investigators, or secret agents, that brought about many improvements in the science of detection, through the wearing of disguises, the keeping of records on criminals and even the casting of 'footmarks' in plaster (the term 'footprints' was only settled upon much later). However, Vidocq was tainted by his continued involvement in frauds and forgeries, and the French police were not keen to trumpet his achievements.

He nevertheless found fame and fortune through his best-selling, if unreliable, 'memoirs'. He was particularly celebrated for his skill in disguises. Vidocq could easily turn himself, for example, into 'one of those good sexagenarian citizens whom all the old ladies admire' with the help of 'some false wrinkles, a pig-tail, snowy-white ruffles, a large gold-headed cane, a three-cornered hat, buckles, breeches and coat to match'. Detail was all: 'if you would play a peasant, there must be dirt under the nails'. He also insisted that his operatives carry a number of different hats and scarves so as to change their appearance frequently, a technique still adopted by undercover policemen today. Sherlock Holmes, likewise a master of disguise, seems to have studied Vidocq's methods.

The Frenchman was also a born teacher, instructing his secret agents in ballistics and record-keeping as well as disguises. In later life, he visited London with his travelling exhibition of murderous weapons designed both to instruct and amuse. The poet Robert Browning went to see the show in 1851, and was taken round personally by Vidocq himself. He saw the 'museum of knives & nails & hooks that have helped great murderers to their purposes ... one little sort of dessert-knife *did* only take *one life* ... "but then" says Vidocq, "it was the man's own mother's life, with fifty-two blows"'.

Obviously a detective could learn a lot from such a man and such a museum, and in 1874 the Metropolitan Police at Scotland Yard established a collection of their own. The passing of the Prisoners' Property Act five years previously had given the police the right to retain the possessions of criminals, and by 1875 the appointment of an inspector and a police constable to permanently man the 'Prisoners' Property Store' suggests that the Scotland Yard museum had become something of a fixture. Its surviving visitors' books show a steady stream of users between 1877 and 1894.

It contained earlier exhibits, such as a letter written by Dr William Palmer, but the bulk of the collection was built up as cases were solved. There still remains, for example, evidence used to accuse John Robinson of the murder of Minnie Bonati in 1927. Robinson had boldly placed his victim's dismembered body in a black wickerwork trunk deposited in the left-luggage room at Charing Cross station. The cloakroom ticket was put in the museum, as was a bloodstained matchstick. This latter was spotted in the wastepaper basket of the office where John Robinson had cut up the body. The evidence it provided of blood having been spilt on the premises, combined with the testimony of an acquaintance who'd been told that Robinson wanted his help to move an extremely heavy trunk 'of books', was Robinson's undoing. No young detective who had heard the story would overlook a clue like a bloody matchstick in a wastepaper basket at the scene of a suspected crime.

The Metropolitan Police today are understandably very careful about whom they let into their gruesome collection. After all, it does contain two death masks of Heinrich Himmler, a fridge belonging to the serial killer and necrophiliac Dennis Nilsen, and other objects destined to attract unwholesome interest. From the very start journalists and film crews (including our own) have been distinctly unwelcome, and even though the museum is officially called 'The Crime Museum', everyone uses quite a different name: 'The Black Museum', its colloquial title coined by a writer from the *Observer* in 1877, who had, like so many others, been refused access.

18

---◆---

Revelations of
a Lady Detective

'I had not long been employed as a female detective, and
now having given up my time and attention to what I may
call a new profession, I was anxious to acquit myself as well
and favourably as I could.'

W. S. Hayward introduces his character Mrs Paschal in his story
'The Mysterious Countess' (n.d., probably 1864)

In describing the origins of his famous detective Mma Precious
Ramotswe, Alexander McCall Smith has written that he chose
a female as his lead because, if she were a man, 'the conversation
would be less interesting ... less personal, less subjective – and less
emotionally engaging'. McCall Smith is a compelling contemporary
advocate for the pleasure to be found in following the success of a
female detective. Readers take satisfaction in 'seeing women, who
have suffered so much from male arrogance and condescension,
either outwitting men or demonstrating that they are just as
capable as men of doing something that may have been seen as a
male preserve'.

He sees the female detective as often 'the outsider in the male world of policing and criminal investigation', a fertile place for a character to come up against the difficulties and tensions which provide the germ of fiction. And she can use her position on the margins to good effect: 'We suddenly realise that it is the woman who has seen and understood what is happening without ever being suspected of being a threat to anybody.'

While all this holds true of the great Mma Precious Ramotswe, though, it also applies to the earliest female detectives, who existed in fiction long before they did in real life.

A great deal of debate has developed about the exact moment the first fictional female sleuth made her debut. It's generally agreed that *The Female Detective*, published in 1864 (or possibly in 1861) by Andrew Forrester (the pen-name of James Redding Ware) was the first work in this new genre. His character, Mrs Gladden, investigates crimes in a professional capacity, and is paid for her services.

Mrs Gladden tends to get all the attention, but she was preceded by earlier, if amateur, female detectives, characters who accidentally fall into the role of solving a mystery. Some scholars make the case for a maidservant named Susan Hopley. Catherine Crowe published *The Adventures of Susan Hopley, or Circumstantial Evidence*, a novel in which the heroine solves a murder, as early as 1841. As an amateur female investigator, Susan Hopley developed out of the heroines of Gothic novels who had sought a means of exposing or escaping the evil villains who harassed them, just as Emily does in *The Mysteries of Udolpho*.

But Hopley, the sleuthing maidservant, also looks forward to the fully-formed detective genre. She follows correct procedure in the gathering of evidence: 'her most earnest desire', for example, 'was to go over the house that had been the scene of the catastrophe, and inspect every part of it'. She solves the crime with apparent effortlessness – the *Athenaeum* magazine noted that 'through all the intricacies of the story, she winds her way with preternatural ease – the *Dea Vindix* ['Avenging Goddess'] who unties all knots'. And Susan occupies the classic marginal position of a female detective: working as a servant, relatively powerless, she usually passes unnoticed and unsuspected. She is devoted to her duty of finding out the truth: at one point in her story, she is rewarded for her efforts by being sacked from her day job.

Susan Hopley was a bestseller, and inspired a stage version, but in many ways she was ahead of her time, and aroused consternation as well as admiration. Detective fiction, let alone detective fiction with a female heroine, was not yet well understood. 'We hardly know what to say of this book', wrote one critic:

> It perplexes us extremely. It is powerful, beyond all question; but unsatisfactory ... precisely as in real life, facts and recollections of apparently the most trivial kind, which have got remotely away in some inaccessible corner of the memory, come gradually out into more and more prominence, until, some last link in a long chain of occurrences wanting, they suddenly and thoroughly supply it. The writer, in a word, has the art of *reality*. You are struck with the trifling minutenesses, yet find them not so trifling as you first supposed.

Today we recognize that sensation of satisfaction that good detective fiction produces. When *Susan Hopley* came out, however, the Detective Branch had yet to be established, 'detective fever' had yet to infect the public in the wake of the Road Hill House case and the 'sensation' novel had still to open up the home and all its minute and everyday details as the site of drama.

So why, then, has this groundbreaking author and her character, warmly admired by Mary Elizabeth Bradden among others, been forgotten? The answer lies partly in the fate of her creator, Catherine Crowe, whose reputation dimmed quickly after she produced a much derided work on spiritualism and quack science. She eventually fell into neglect and remains so today, to the extent that her detective fails even to appear in *The Penguin Book of Victorian Women in Crime* (2011).

Crowe was curious and mysterious. Quite a figure on the literary scene in Edinburgh, she and a friend were observed inhaling ether, or laughing-gas, at a dinner party held in 1847 for Hans Christian Andersen, which gave another guest 'the feeling of being with two mad people'. She was interested in phrenology, was described as 'a very clever, eccentric person' and believed that one day the supernatural world would find itself 'within the bounds of science'.

She became deeply involved with seances and spiritualism until she suffered some sort of mental breakdown in 1854. Charles Dickens, who heard about it, thought she had gone:

> stark mad – and stark naked – on the spirit-rapping imposition. She was found t'other day in the street, clothed only in her chastity, a pocket-handkerchief and a visiting card. She had been informed, it appeared, by the spirits, that

if she went in that trim she would be invisible. She is now in a madhouse, and, I fear, hopelessly insane.

This picture, however, was so false that Catherine Crowe had to write to the newspapers defending herself. She had experienced, she protested, only a brief 'state of unconsciousness' and hallucination, but the prejudice against female writers and spiritualists translated this into crazed nakedness on the Edinburgh streets.

And so Crowe and her work fell into obscurity, and the crown for producing the first female detective is generally awarded to two men: Andrew Forrester, marginally the winner, and W. S. Hayward in close pursuit. To be fair, their two books, *The Female Detective* and *Revelations of a Lady Detective*, both feature professionals, heroines who, unlike Susan Hopley, are employed purely – and paid accordingly – to solve crimes.

Kathryn Johnson, curator of the British Library exhibition 'Murder in the Library: An A to Z of Detective Fiction' (2013), points out that Andrew Forrester most likely decided to try a female lead as a logical next step in a lengthy writing career. He'd started out, and had great success, producing fictionalized 'memoirs' of various real-life Bow Street Runners. These works were so realistic and convincing that the genuine Runners had to write to the papers, pointing out that what were apparently their memoirs had actually been made up. Forrester also wrote on the murder at Road Hill House, in both non-fiction and fictional form. There was obviously a market for crime, and a female detective could be seen as an exciting and original angle.

Forrester and Hayward's female detective novels were published in a new and specialized form called the yellowback. These small, flimsy and semi-disposable novels took their name from their glossy covers with bright yellow borders. Costing 6d. (when a hardback novel would cost 10s.) they were sold mostly on the railway stations that had by now sprouted up all across 1860s Britain. Promising a soothing interval of cheap entertainment, a yellowback from the bookstall seemed the perfect purchase for a traveller about to start, say, the ten-hour journey to Edinburgh.

Because they were made from such thin and cheap paper, very few have survived in good condition, but the British Library does have a copy of Hayward's *The Revelations of a Lady Detective*, with its rather racy cover still intact. It could be that the author never selected or even saw the cover art, and, on the basis that 'sex sells', it shows a lady rather more racy than the detective herself featured in its pages. A nattily dressed lady is *smoking*, a very fast habit, and she's also lifting up her skirts to reveal her ankles. The image bears a close resemblance to the Victorian 'Haymarket Princess', the ladies of the night who worked around the theatres of London's Haymarket, the revelation of the ankle beneath the skirt being the age-old indication of a prostitute.

This salacious image was obviously intended to tempt readers into buying a saucy tale, and it is true that the female detective of the story does some rather unladylike things. At one point, while chasing a villain, she finds it necessary to drop down through a hatch into a cellar. Her crinoline won't fit through the hole, so she simply takes it off and abandons it. It's a wonderful moment of female emancipation: freed from the 'obnoxious garment', as she calls it, she is able to get on with her work. She also carries a silver Colt revolver.

This is strikingly modern behaviour, and both the *Lady Detective*, Mrs Paschal, and the *Female Detective*, Mrs Gladden, are forceful, impressive characters. Mrs Paschal possesses great skill and knows it: verging upon forty years old, she has found a life-long calling in detection. She tells us that her brain is 'vigorous and subtle', and that she concentrates all her energies on her work. 'I was well born and educated,' she says, and

for the parts I had to play, it was necessary to have nerve and strength, cunning and confidence, resources unlimited [and] numerous other qualities of which actors are totalling ignorant. They strut, and talk, and give expression to the thoughts of others, but it is such as I who create the incidents upon which their dialogue is based and grounded.

The *Female Detective* is varyingly either Mrs or Miss Gladden – perhaps another editorial lapse or perhaps a deliberate part of her shadowy, elusive identity – and elucidates for us the advantages that women possess in detecting crime. Like Mrs Paschal, she possesses the ability to pass invisibly through life. 'The woman detective,' says Mrs Gladden, 'has far greater opportunities than a man of intimate watching, and of keeping her eye upon matters near where a man could not conveniently play the eavesdropper.' Both heroines illustrate this point in rather melodramatic terms, one of them taking the job of a servant in order to penetrate the household of 'The Mysterious Countess', the other dressing up as a nun in order to infiltrate a convent. But here an important new strand of detective fiction is being spun: the crime-solver who blends into the background, like G. K. Chesterton's Father Brown, or, ultimately, Miss Marple.

And yet these two impressive women of the 1860s did not set a lasting trend. After them, female detective characters faded away until the 1890s. The reason for this is that they were just a little too advanced for the taste of the times. Both characters have to justify taking on such dirty, unwomanly work. Mrs Paschal tells us: 'It is hardly necessary to refer to the circumstances which led me to embark in a career at once strange, exciting and mysterious, but I may say that my husband died suddenly, leaving me badly off.'

Mrs Gladden, meanwhile, defends her actions by saying that when a women turns to criminality, she's much worse than a man, and it takes a woman to catch her.

And yet, women would not be employed as police officers until just after the First World War. This was not a sudden decision, but a slow change in attitudes triggered by the war itself. During it, of course, women had proved their capacity for driving and making munitions and other work formerly left to men. In 1916 Scotland Yard was forced, by a shortage of male staff, to employ female typists for the first time. Neither were there enough fathers and brothers left in Britain to chaperone wives and sisters on the streets to pre-war standards. In London's public spaces, voluntary groups of special female police auxiliaries were formed for the protection of other women.

The experiment caused some concern, but was ultimately a success. In 1918, women over 30 were allowed for the first time to vote in elections. On 22 November of the same year, an order was written for 110 permanent female police officers to be appointed, albeit with fewer powers than male constables. The nascent female force was the victim of financial cutbacks in 1922, but in 1923 they were back for good. Fifty females were sworn in, and this time it was with the power of making arrests. Lillian Wyles (1885–1975), one of the first female sergeants from 1919, was by 1923 working on murder cases, and would end up as a Chief Inspector.

It's much harder to find evidence that women in real life worked as paid detectives in a private capacity, but they do re-emerge, triumphantly, in post-war fiction, not least in the 'cattery' of old ladies employed by Lord Peter Wimsey. It was the beginning of a Golden Age.

Part Three

The Golden Age

19

—◆◇◆—

The Women
Between the Wars

'It's not the crisis, it's the Christie, that is keeping people
awake at night.'

Newspaper advertisement for Murder is Easy,
by Agatha Christie (1939)

B y the 1930s, the murder rate had fallen to the lowest level
Britain had ever seen. Those crimes that did take place were
usually linked to poverty, alcohol or domestic violence. And yet it
seemed that more and more killings, usually in genteel and pleasant
surroundings, were taking place in the pages of books. In 1934,
about one-eighth of all the books published were crime novels.
The decades between the two world wars saw a great explosion
of fictional death by the novelists of the so-called 'Golden Age' of
detective fiction. Their stories were ever more remote from real-
life violence and true crime. In them, murders became tidy and
domesticated, apparently causing little more upset than a lost cat.

And they wrote a great number of them. Edgar Wallace
(1875–1932) is little known today, and primarily as the man who

created King Kong. In his time, though, he was a hugely popular and enormously prolific author who produced no less than 175 novels, including many detective stories. (It was said that if Wallace refused to take a telephone call on the grounds that he was writing a new book, the caller would gaily ask the operator to put him on hold: 'I'll wait until he's finished!') The size of Wallace's output was extreme, but many of his colleagues had similar stamina. Some authors produced as many as three books a year. Dorothy L. Sayers did not work that fast – ten novels in twelve years – although she recognized that others had good cause: 'There are many reasons which may prompt an author to produce books at this rate, ranging from hyper-activity of the thyroid to the grim menace of rates and taxes.'

She certainly read them at an alarming rate, though. In just two years, between June 1933 and August 1935, she reviewed 364 detective novels. Among those she covered for the *Sunday Times* were *Crime at Guildford, Poison in Kensington, Death on the Oxford Road, A Dagger in Fleet Street* and *Death at Broadcasting House*.

What was the cause of this fictional crime wave? The American critic Edmund Wilson, writing in *The New Yorker* in 1944, argued that the detective story had declined in inventiveness and creativity since the days of Dickens. But he noted that reading writers like Agatha Christie made people feel slightly better about living in an ever more dangerous world:

The world during those years was ridden by an all-pervasive feeling of guilt and by a fear of impending disaster which it seemed hopeless to try to avert ... Nobody seems guiltless, nobody seems safe; and then, suddenly, the murderer is spotted, and – relief! – he is not, after all, a person like you or me. He is a villain ... and he has been caught by an infallible Power, the supercilious and omniscient detective, who knows exactly where to fix the guilt.

It seemed the pleasures of Golden Age detection were just the thing to steady the nerves after the First World War. At the turn of the twentieth century, old hands like Sherlock Holmes were still in business, but only just. His last full-length outing was published in serial form in 1914–15, and his absolute final appearance in a short story came in 1927 in the *Strand Magazine*.

Sir Arthur Conan Doyle's best work had been done within the constraints of the short-story format forced upon him by publishers such as the *Strand*. With the honourable exception of *The Hound of the Baskervilles* (1901–2), Sherlock is always sharpest in the short stories rather than the novels. His cases are not necessarily long-drawn-out murder investigations, but snappy little frauds, thefts and blackmails that can be neatly wrapped up in a few thousand words. The *Strand* gave Conan Doyle and Holmes a readership reaching half a million monthly.

Conan Doyle brought Holmes's career to a halt in 1893 by killing him off after a tussle with his arch-enemy Professor Moriarty, falling to his death over a waterfall. Holmes's creator had simply wanted to write something else: 'I must save my mind for better things', as he put it. It was commercial pressure from his publisher that caused Conan Doyle to bring his hero back from the dead in 1901 to solve the case of *The Hound of the Baskervilles*. This story, published in serial form in the *Strand Magazine* once again, had readers queuing up at the magazine's offices to get their hands on the next number as soon as possible.

In the story, Sherlock Holmes lives secretly for several days in a prehistoric stone hut on the moors where a dangerous killer and a 'supernatural' hound roam at will, and ends up shooting the latter dead. Holmes had always had a wiry strength, despite his cerebral appearance, and he is very much a man of action as well as thought. His gallantry and heroism in *The Hound of the Baskervilles* belongs to the jolly variety of derring-do also to be seen in the Scottish politician and administrator John Buchan's adventure stories: *The Thirty-Nine Steps*, set just before the First World War, and *Greenmantle*, set during it. So devoted to their duty are Buchan's heroes with their stiff upper lips that it comes as no surprise to learn that Buchan also helped to write propaganda for the British war effort in 1914. Conan Doyle was likewise on the side of the British bulldog. Another later excursion of Holmes's, 'His Last Bow', has him unmask a German spy on the very eve of the war. As Holmes puts it: 'There's an east wind coming all the same, such a wind as never blew on England yet. It will be cold and bitter, Watson, and a good many of us may wither before its blast. But … a cleaner, better, stronger land will lie in the sunshine when the storm has passed.'

This combination of valour, patriotism and sportsmanship can also be seen in the exploits of Raffles, the daring gentleman thief and adventurous hero of the *Strand Magazine*. Raffles was created by E. W. Hornung, Sir Arthur Conan Doyle's brother-in-law. He's a criminal, rather than a detective, but he has the physical prowess to represent England at cricket, and eventually volunteers for the Boer War. (In a nod to the importance of Scotland Yard's Black Museum, Raffles attempts to steal from it the items relating to his own career.) These, and other, adventure writers of the 1890s and 1910s seem to express and celebrate something of the blithe fighting spirit that convinced many to sign up for the trenches. As one sapper wrote to John Buchan of *The Thirty-Nine Steps*, 'the story is greatly appreciated in the midst of mud and rain and shells, and all that could make trench life depressing'.

But what followed four years of fighting couldn't have been more different. One could never imagine Hercule Poirot trekking across Dartmoor, sleeping rough or shooting anybody. ('The neatness of his attire was almost incredible; I believe a speck of dust would have caused him more pain than a bullet wound.') Sherlock Holmes, Raffles and Richard Hannay, Buchan's all-round action hero, would seem a little too butch for the more sinuous and hedonistic 1920s. The new-style detective novels of this era were deliberately unsensational, a better fit for a nation in mourning, where nearly every house had lost a son.

Even beyond the annual commemoration of Remembrance Day, the lasting effects of the Great War could not be ignored or avoided. Children were left orphaned, the surviving young men left wounded in ways both seen and unseen, young women left without partners. This is the background that should be born in mind when the Golden Age writers are criticized – as they often are – for being limited or sterile or boring. They were writing not to challenge society or to stir things up. They were using their pens to heal.

By contrast to the bold, grand gestures of Richard Hannay's or Raffles's stories, the texture of *The Murder of Roger Ackroyd* (1926), Agatha Christie's first success, is like a tightly woven tapestry. The *New York Times* summed up its demure appeal:

> There are doubtless many detective stories more exciting and blood-curdling than *The Murder of Roger Ackroyd*, but this reviewer has recently read very few which provide greater analytical stimulation ... the author does not devote her talents to the creation of thrills and shocks, but to the orderly solution of a single murder, conventional at that, instead.

Character, plausibility, violence and romance were not an important part of books like this. Their attraction was chaste and cerebral. *The Murder of Roger Ackroyd* is all about the plot, the clues and the pay-off: the pleasure and satisfaction felt when an elegant solution to the puzzle is revealed at the end. Christie herself explained that 'a detective story is complete relaxation, an escape from the realism of everyday life. It has, too, the tonic value of a puzzle – it sharpens your wits'.

Christie's breakthrough coincided with changes to reading habits and to the publishing industry that saw the short story published in magazines like the *Strand* being replaced by the longer novel, and very often the novel involving crime. In Britain, the 1920s also saw the development of commercial libraries, such as those run by W. H. Smith or Boots, and publishing imprints such as Victor Gollancz's 'Gollancz Crime' or William Collins' 'Crime Club' met their voracious appetite for new books for circulation. Our archetypal image of a Sherlock Holmes reader is a man reading a magazine on the train on his way to work. By the 1920s, Everyman may well have driven to his place of employment, his opportunity for reading having been lost with the acquisition of a car, while his wife spent the afternoon reading a detective novel by a female author from the library.

While the literary marketplace could be lucrative, it was also crowded. With the exception of Agatha Christie, the writers of these crime novels of the 1920s and 1930s were not, on the whole, made vastly rich by their detectives. Dorothy L. Sayers left a very moderate estate of £36,277 when she died in 1957 and even Conan Doyle left an estate of only £63,491. And these were writers who mainly hailed from a middle-class background. Conan Doyle trained as a doctor; G. K. Chesterton (1874–1936) was a journalist; the very successful Freeman Wills Crofts (1879–1957) was a railway engineer.

One of the most distinctive features of the Golden Age is the fact that its longest lasting and best remembered writers were female. Agatha Christie, Dorothy L. Sayers, Margery Allingham and Ngaio Marsh – the four Queens of Crime – came, at least in retrospect, to dominate our picture of crime-writing in the 1930s. Why did these women come to the fore, and why are they still read today more often than their brilliantly talented male counterparts Nicholas Blake and G. K. Chesterton? In part, it could have been the subject matter towards which they leaned: the detailed and the domestic, stories with lots of female characters, the layering up of a densely constructed plot through a process rather like knitting. Perhaps a more feminine view of the world was welcome after the violence of the First World War. Then there was the 'problem' of what the 'spare' women, left widowed or unmarried by the loss of a generation of males, should do with themselves in the absence of potential husbands. This sometimes turned out to be an opportunity to try new professions. Women (at least those over 30) now had the vote. They'd experienced the world of work while contributing to the war effort. They were stepping forward boldly in many areas of public life, and not least into publishing, and they brought their own experience with them. 'To read the detective novels of these four women,' P. D. James has written, 'is to learn more about the England in which they lived and worked than most popular social histories can provide, and in particular about the status of women between the wars.'

What impresses about the four Queens is not so much their work (although I would make the case for Dorothy L. Sayers as one of the great writers of the twentieth century) but the way in which they set about doing it. They were all writing to make a living, of course; Christie herself makes very modest claims, calling herself 'an industrious craftsman'. But more than that, she and her colleagues were also writing to make themselves heard, to stake a claim, to win an independence and a place in the world. They also all used their writing, as P. D. James has pointed out, to keep secrets. All four women were in some way scarred by the earlier parts of their lives, and were reinventing themselves, through writing, into the successes that they later were.*

Ngaio Marsh (1885–1982), for example, born in New Zealand, was a person who moved easily between worlds. The actual year of her birth was in some doubt for many years as her father failed to register it at the time, and Marsh failed to elucidate matters. She studied art before travelling to England and embedding herself into a circle of aristocratic friends. Yet she was only observing, rather than participating, in debutante circles: her real passion was for the theatre. Her experience of country house life would transform itself, when she was nearly 40, into her first published novel, *A Man Lay Dead* (1934). It was one of many to follow featuring Roderick 'Handsome' Alleyn (he takes his name from the stage, being called after the Elizabethan actor Edward Alleyn), a detective from Scotland Yard who often investigates crime in upper-class circles.

Marsh wrote her books at night, using green ink and sitting in a deep armchair. Spending her time between Britain and New Zealand, hanging out with theatrical folk, pretending to be younger

---

* James's insight into the motivation of these four hard-working writers seems equally revealing of her own. She left school at 16 because her family needed her to work; she told me that she would have liked to have studied history instead. She has had to deal, in her own family life, with a mother, and then a husband, damaged by psychiatric illness. She never felt secure enough, even in her great success as a novelist, to give up her day job at the Home Office. She maintained a punishing schedule as a civil servant and an author, exhibiting exactly the same qualities of steely determination and dedicated craftsmanship – as well as the creativity – of the Queens of Crime.

than she really was, this woman from a colonial background seemed constantly to reinvent herself. 'For an incurable & unrepentant traveller,' she wrote, 'a landfall, a foreign port, the great white lights of a foreign city still unexplored, or the modest lamps of a strange village at the end of a darkling road – these things are happiness.'

Margery Allingham (1904–66), creator of Albert Campion, led a similarly unconventional life. She was the child of professional hacks, who swapped plots among themselves as valuable commodities, and published her first novel at 19. Allingham's mother was the creator of Phinella Martin, 'the beautiful and famous lady-detective', who appeared in the *Woman's Weekly* from 1916 onwards. One of her family's housemaids found it very odd to be part of this household of writers, based in an Essex village, with frequent visits from other authors. She once grabbed a notebook from the young Margery's hands in disgust, saying: 'Master, missus and three strangers all sitting in different rooms writing down lies and now YOU startin!'

But Margery did fall back on writing as a back-up plan, having overcome a terrible childhood stammer and a failed career as an actress before settling down to her work. In some ways it seemed unavoidable because of her heritage. 'I have been trained to remark since I was seven,' she wrote, 'and must always be watching and noting and putting experience into communicable form.' Yet she wrote away diligently for the money, too, to support an illustrator husband – who went on to have a secret and unacknowledged child with another woman.

According to Pip, Allingham's husband, 'sex was of minor importance' in their marriage and this is another theme of the four. Ngaio Marsh never married, but is buried beside a long-standing female partner, Sylvia Fox. Dorothy L. Sayers did marry, but not the father of her child, and Agatha Christie sought refuge from a failed marriage to a damaged First World War pilot in a companionable relationship, like Allingham's, with a much younger archaeologist.

None of them was what their 1930s contemporaries would have called a conventional wife or mother. And yet this did not stand in the way of a career as a writer. A crime novelist is not obliged to expose too much of him or herself in her work, and an air of privacy, indeed mystery, still shrouds each of the four. 'Nobody cared what the mystery writer *thought*,' wrote Margery Allingham, 'as long as he did his work and told his story.'

20

The Duchess of Death

'Perhaps her greatest strength was that she never over-
stepped the limits of her talent. She knew precisely what she
could do and she did it well.'

P. D. James on Agatha Christie

During the First World War, a young woman was training
to be a pharmacist's assistant in a Torquay chemist's shop.
One day, her boss showed her something he always carried in his
pocket: a dark-coloured lump of curare, the poison used on the
tips of arrows by certain exotic tribes. He warned her that if curare
reached her bloodstream it would kill her. Understandably, the
young woman asked the pharmacist why he kept such a deadly
substance on his person. The answer was striking and intriguing.

'Well, you know,' he said thoughtfully, 'it makes me feel powerful.'

This was a taste that Agatha Christie, known by her American
fans as the 'Duchess of Death', would develop for herself: a taste
for power and for control over her own destiny. She ended up with
a much younger and amenable husband (she contributed financially

to his archaeological investigations), substantial property including country houses in Oxfordshire and Devon, and an almost reclusive lifestyle that allowed her to avoid strangers and publicity.

And despite all her sales, and biographies, and TV adaptations, something about Christie's success still seems mysterious, its explanation elusive. The criticisms made of her books are long-standing and valid. Her characters are wooden and she cannot conjure up atmosphere, even while her plots and dialogue are excellent. While her two main detectives, Poirot and Marple, are memorable and lovable, they can hardly explain the remarkable popularity of her work.

It's widely accepted by historians that Christie was a particularly well-loved and cosseted child, living a life of comfort and leisure with her parents in Torquay, or staying with her numerous relatives (she sometimes entertained her grandmother by reading the crime stories aloud from the newspaper). Christie moved smoothly on from teenage dances and country house parties to a loving marriage with a handsome hero, an aeroplane pilot of the First World War. They had two children, a boy and a girl, and travelled round the world together.

They looked like the perfect family, and it seems that nothing went wrong at all for Agatha Christie until she reached the age of 35. She had even, egged on by a challenge from her sister, become a moderately successful detective novelist.

Then, in 1926, she touched down upon adult life with a bump, finding herself stuck, with two children, in a large house near a golf club in Surrey. Her beloved mother had recently died and she was married to a man who worked all week in the City, spent his

Agatha Christie's pharmacy training as a young lady during the First World War gave her experience of drugs and poisons that showed in her first detective novel, *The Mysterious Affair at Styles* (1921).

weekends with his mistress and who never seemed to open up to her at all. Probably he couldn't: his experiences in the war had seen to that. 'His own determined casualness and flippancy – almost gaiety – upset me,' she wrote, years later, about Archie's demeanour when on leave from France.

> I was too young then to appreciate that that was for him the best way of facing ... life. I, on the other hand, had become far more earnest, emotional, and had put aside my own light flippancy of happy girlhood. It was as though we were trying to reach each other, and finding, almost with dismay, that we had forgotten how to do so.

Christie responded to her feeling of being trapped in a frozen, lifeless marriage in a way that seems in some lights to be bold and dramatic, or in others to be remarkably emotionally immature. She simply ran away, in the middle of the night, leaving her car on the edge of a chalk pit in the North Downs. The event would become known in Christie circles as 'The Disappearance'.

Some people thought that this was a publicity stunt by a professional novelist. Others assumed suicide, or else thought that Christie herself had been the victim of crime. Countryside and ponds across southern England were searched, and Christie's fellow writers did not neglect to help out. Sir Arthur Conan Doyle consulted a medium, and Dorothy L. Sayers joined the crowds of hundreds of people trying to find her, or at least her body. The police issued a description of the missing woman: 'hair reddish and shingled, eyes grey, complexion fair ... dark grey cardigan, small

THE DAILY NEWS, SATURDAY, DECEN

MRS. CHRISTIE DISGUISED.

Mrs. Agatha Christie as she was last seen (centre), and (on left and right) how she may have disguised herself by altering the style of her hairdressing and by wearing glasses Col. Christie says his wife had stated that she could disappear at will if she liked, and, in view of the fact that she was a writer of detective stories, it would be very natural for her to adopt some form of disguise to carry out that idea.

At the time of 'The Disappearance', *The Daily News* printed an image of Agatha Christie in various disguises in the hope that someone would recognize her.

green velour hat, wearing a platinum ring with one pearl, but no wedding ring'.

But it turns out that Christie was alive, and well, and staying in a hotel in Yorkshire. The missing wedding ring shows what was on her mind: she had even checked into the hotel under the name of her husband's mistress, Nancy Neele. Eventually Christie was recognized in her Harrogate bolthole by a maid who had been alerted by the endless newspaper articles illustrated with her picture.

239

Amid huge publicity, and complaints about the waste of police time and money, the search for her corpse was called off.

In her autobiography, Christie herself describes her state of mind at this time as some kind of mental breakdown, while her family and ex-husband posited a period of amnesia brought on by mental stress. Her most recent biographer, Laura Thompson, stoutly defends Christie, pointing out that she had written a letter to her brother-in-law telling him that she was going away for a while, and that she had been taken completely by surprise by what she thought an unwarrantable level of interference and concern.

Christie enthusiasts seem united in their inability to talk about what was quite clearly a period of mental illness. But 'The Disappearance', embarrassing, pointless and perhaps painful as it might have been, had a silver lining. It propelled the fame of this already successful crime novelist to stratospheric heights. Margery Allingham drew a conclusion about the popularity of the detective novel of the Golden Age that also seems to apply, in miniature, to the private life of Agatha Christie: 'When the moralists cite the modern murder mystery as evidence of an unnatural love of violence in a decadent age, I wonder if it is nothing of the sort, but rather a sign of a popular instinct for order and form in a period of sudden and chaotic change.'

When I interviewed Christie's grandson, Mathew Pritchard, about his grandmother, he painted a picture of a woman quite lacking the flamboyance of Ngaio Marsh or the theatrical ambitions of Margery Allingham. He described her as shy, almost reclusive, generous to a fault with family and friends, but quite the opposite of gregarious. In 2008, he came across a Dictaphone machine and tapes into which Christie had dictated notes towards her published autobiography. Once recordings were converted into a digital format, he told me that the greatest shock of hearing her voice once again was hearing her say *quite so much at once*. In person she was briefly and softly spoken, never gave a speech or a monologue and always refused to appear on television. This shunning of the limelight and retreat into domesticity stemmed, Mathew has said, 'from the unhappy time in her life when she lost her first husband and mother in quick succession … she felt rather hounded by the press'.

Writing seems to have provided Christie with a different and much more satisfactory world, where the confusion, dismay and broken relationships she had experienced are simplified into the more straightforward world of detective fiction. 'Each book was a kind of catharsis,' P. D. James has said, 'all of them, a little catharsis.' 'At times of great sorrow,' her grandson says, 'what she held on to was her ability to write.'

Much of the skill of Christie's detective, Hercule Poirot, lies in predicting what people will think and feel, and in this he is aided by his own minute understanding of the rules and regulations of social behaviour. 'Poirot, you old villain,' cries his sidekick Captain Hastings on one occasion. 'What do you mean by deceiving me as you have done?' 'I did not deceive you, *mon ami*,' Poirot replies. 'At most, I permitted you to deceive yourself … you see, my friend, you have a nature so honest, and a countenance so transparent, that – *enfin*, to conceal your feelings is impossible!'

Poirot can read other people exceptionally well, and Christie's own autobiography discusses the training in psychology and courtesy that she had received from her family as a well-brought-up

Edwardian girl. She knew 'back to front' the rules of flirtation, the inadvisability of ever showing an open preference for a man, but the satisfaction of knowing that oneself was preferred. Like Poirot, Christie seems an arch-assimilator of the rules of society. But also like him, she was an observer, not a follower. Quietly scrutinizing the social scene of her family, friends and middle-class contemporaries, she purified it down to its essence and transformed it into words.

One of Christie's ladylike tricks was to minimize or disguise the amount of time she put into her work. During summers at Greenway, her house in Devon, her grandson Mathew never saw her writing: 'she could manage to write a book almost without one noticing'. That's partly because it was a holiday home, and there she took a break, but even her publishers were astonished by her productivity.

Christie described getting ideas for plots from newspaper accounts of crime, but also from everyday experiences such as looking into a hat-shop window. Her own first book, *The Mysterious Affair at Styles* (1920), an affair of poisoning, reprocessed Christie's own experience in the pharmacy:

'What a lot of bottles!' I exclaimed, as my eye travelled round the small room. 'Do you really know what's in them all?'

'Say something original,' groaned Cynthia. 'Every single person who comes up here says that. We are really thinking of bestowing a prize on the first individual who does not say: "What a lot of bottles!" And I know the next thing you're going to say is: "How many people have you poisoned?"'

Of course, although Cynthia distracts us from them, these bottles hold the clue to the crime. According to P. D. James, Christie's clues are 'brilliantly designed to confuse. The butler goes over to peer closely at a calendar. She has planted in our mind the suspicion that a crucial clue relates to dates and times, but the clue is, in fact, that the butler is short-sighted.'

And yet, despite all this, something about Agatha Christie's success still seems odd. Just why has she been translated into more languages than Shakespeare? Barry Forshaw, editor of *British Crime Writing: An Encyclopaedia* (2008) ascribes her continued saleability to the lowest common denominator: 'There is no single author … who manages to translate so well into so many different languages. She keeps the language fairly straightforward and simple but the plots are constructed incredibly well, like a finely-tuned machine.'

Christie, though, tells us her own views on the secret of her success, on one of the Dictaphone recordings that I listened to in the company of her grandson, in the drawing room at Greenway. 'I was eminently a writer for entertainment,' she says. She did not set out to be 'serious' or 'worthwhile', and, in this aim, her work falls firmly into the grand British tradition of art inspired by crime.

21

———◦◦◦———

A Life Less Ordinary

'What would those women say to her, to Harriet Vane, who had taken her First in English and gone to London to write mystery fiction, to live with a man who was not married to her?'

Dorothy L. Sayers of her character Harriet Vane
(or perhaps herself) in Gaudy Night *(1935)*

At first sight, Dorothy L. Sayers (1893–1957) looks indomitable: full of certainty, self-confidence and strong opinions. A born newspaper columnist, she seemed to hold trenchant views on nearly every subject under the sun. But above all, her passion was for clarity of language and thought. She concluded her (often damning) reviews of other crime writers for the *Sunday Times* with a section of her column called 'The Week's Worst English', and described the abuse of grammar as 'treason'.

Ngaio Marsh described Sayers as 'robust, round and rubicund', a cross 'between a guardsman and a female don with a jolly face (garnished with pince-nez), short grey curls, & a gruff voice'. Sayers herself claimed that her life was 'far too humdrum to be worth writing about'. And yet this was far from true, and smacks of deflection. She was a woman far more complex than her projected public image as a busy, even bossy, figure, organizing a club for her fellow fiction writers and directing the future of the Church of England.

Given the circumstances in which she was born, Sayers played her hand boldly and bravely. From today's vantage point, her life seems crowded and rich with friends and incidents and projects, and yet at the same time painfully lacking in love. She used her gregariousness, and her pen, to create substitutes for the husband and children she would dearly love to have had. It seems impertinent to feel sorry for someone so impressive in so many ways, and yet she left enough of a record of her inner thoughts to show that in some ways she would have liked a life that was more conventional.

Physically, Sayers had strong features and a heavy body; mentally, she was combative and steely. And life did nothing to soften her edges. Her father was in the Church, and she was brought up in the bracing atmosphere of a vicarage. In 1893, when his only child was born, Henry Sayers was a chaplain at Christ Church Cathedral in Oxford, but the family soon moved to the small village of Bluntisham-cum-Earith in Huntingdonshire. It sounds like a made-up place from a detective novel, and indeed Dorothy L. Sayers would turn it into one, in *The Nine Tailors* (1934), many peoples' favourite among her novels, with its plot revolving around the intricacies and eccentricities of bell-ringing and bell-ringers.

After rather a lonely Fenland childhood, Dorothy found fun and friends at Somerville College, Oxford. Here she made lifelong connections – 'The Mutual Admiration Society' – sang in the

Dorothy L. Sayers during her time
at Somerville College, Oxford,
where she arrived in 1912.

Bach choir, flirted with unsuitable men and was truly happy. The nostalgic tone of *Gaudy Night* (1935), her finest novel, set in an Oxford college, suggests that this was the only period of her life of which this could be said.

Sayers earned herself the equivalent of a first-class degree, but it was not until 1920, five years later, that women were allowed to become full members of the university. The precariousness of the position of the women of Somerville College, tolerated rather than welcomed by their male peers, is another theme of *Gaudy Night*. A note from Sayers' tutor warns her against being 'smart': it was not a quality then required or even desired in a female.

Her first works in print were poetry produced in the few years following her degree. Lacking the strength to tear herself away from the scenes of her undergraduate bliss, she found a job with the publisher Blackwells, and published some rather terrible verses about her favourite town:

Oxford! Suffer it once again that another should do
    thee wrong
I also, I above all, should set thee into song.

Her career as a junior editor was short-lived – her boss called her 'a race-horse harnessed to a cart' – and Sayers knew that she wanted to write for a living. She moved to London in search of work. This was a low period, during which she often feared that she would have to give up and find permanent paid employment as a teacher. She was genuinely hard up and short of money for food.

At the eleventh hour, in terms of her finances, Sayers found a job she seemed born to do, and it involved writing of a sort. She became a copywriter at Benson's, an advertising agency in Holborn. Living in a Bloomsbury flat and walking to work in the busy office, Dorothy's life became almost a 1920s version of *Mad Men*. She felt at home among the male copywriters, who valued her sharp brain and gift for words. The noisy, competitive, jokey atmosphere of the advertising agency would be lovingly recreated, years later, in *Murder Must Advertise* (1933). Its plot is preposterous, but what every reader remembers is its vivid picture of office life between the wars. At Benson's, Sayers created memorable campaigns such as 'The Mustard Club' and a celebrated jingle for Guinness involving a toucan:

If he can say as you can
Guinness is good for you
How grand to be a Toucan
Just think what Toucan do.

Finally, in her thirtieth year, she sold the detective novel upon which she had been working in her spare time. *Whose Body?* (1923) introduced Lord Peter Wimsey, the man who would lead Sayers out of her wilderness years and into financial security, and a career as a full-time novelist.

This is Lord Peter Wimsey, Amateur Detective, and quite a new character in fiction.—

—He is not nearly so foolish as he looks, as this refreshing story will show you.

The Problem of Uncle Meleager's Will

By DOROTHY L. SAYERS

An illustration accompanying Lord Peter Wimsey's
first appearance in a magazine story of July 1925

Lord Peter Wimsey saw Sayers through these difficult times. He was a financial – and, one suspects, an emotional – support to her. For a start, she took great pleasure in spending his money. 'After all, it cost me nothing,' she later explained,

> and at that time I was particularly hard up ... when I was dissatisfied with my single unfurnished room, I took a luxurious flat for him in Piccadilly. When my cheap rug got a hole in it, I ordered an Aubusson carpet. When I had no money to pay my bus fare, I presented him with a Daimler double-six, upholstered in a style of sober magnificence, and when I felt dull I let him drive it.

The ease and luxury and implausible grandness of Lord Peter's life certainly contributes to the divided response he provokes. Many people find him ridiculous: too suave, too aristocratic, expert in too many fields (incunabula, cricket, international relations), sentimental and embarrassing when he has scruples (as he always does at the end of the story) about sending the murderer to the gallows.

At the same time, though, he has a gift for speaking the truth to everybody, peer and charlady alike. He never spares himself in pursuit of a criminal, and he has an attractive understanding of the lot and toils of the women of his age. Sayers has Wimsey bankroll an agency, for example, that specializes in sending 'surplus' women out to useful work. Run by Miss Climpson (a spinster herself, of course), the employment agency gives its women workers money and purpose, and provides Wimsey with all the adjutants he might need for his cases. Miss Climpson, rather like Miss Marple, is a particularly capable secret agent: in *Strong Poison* (1930) she insinuates herself into cafés and households – in her unthreatening way – to pick up vital information. She's even capable of pretending to be a medium, and of tricking a nurse into thinking that the spirits of the dead require her to reveal the hiding place of a vital missing will.

The sympathetic side of Wimsey emerges only slowly as he opens himself up to his mother, and to his faithful 'man' Bunter, his former batman from the trenches. He eventually reveals himself to be suffering from survivors' guilt and what we would call post-traumatic stress disorder from his experiences in the First World War. Beneath the suave exterior, he is a deeply damaged person.

Despite that, one feels that Sayers would have been better off sticking to Lord Peter. In real life, however, she became entangled with John Cournos, a Russian Jew working in London as a journalist. He liked interviewing literary figures, and Sayers described him as the kind of man 'who spells Art with a capital A'. It was not an easy relationship. 'It's such a lonely dreary job having a lover,' she wrote: 'One has to rely on him for companionship, because one's entirely cut off from one's friends ... it's so dirty to be always telling lies, one just drops seeing them. One can't be open about it, because it would end by getting round to one's family somehow.'

After a long, slow struggle, Cournos finally talked Sayers into sleeping with him, much against her religious principles. Disaster followed. 'I dare say I wanted too much,' she wrote, bitterly, after he had deserted her: 'I could not be content with less than your love and your children and our happy acknowledgement of each other to the world ... you went out of your way to insist you would give me none of them.'

After the split with Cournos, she consoled herself with a very different character. Easy-going, fond of dancing and cars, Bill White was merely a stand-in. She slept with him, too, almost casually this time, and became pregnant. But White was no more cut out for fatherhood than Cournos had been, and Dorothy was left on her own. The first royalties from *Whose Body?* came in handy for doctors' bills. She took just eight weeks off from the office and – fearful of telling her parents – travelled to Hampshire to give birth in a private nursing home.

Once her son was born, Dorothy arranged for him to be looked after by a cousin. It seems that no one else suspected what had happened. Flush with funds to spend on food, Dorothy had been putting on weight, which disguised the pregnancy. Her parents would never know their grandchild, because Sayers' moral standards did not allow her to brazen things out. Above all, Sayers was a principled, conventional member of the Church of England, and this would cause her, for the rest of her life, publically to deny her son.

In fiction, too, P. D. James rightly points out that Dorothy was conventional, 'an innovator of style and intention not of form'. She stuck to the rules of the Golden Age in her novels: a limited circle of suspects, a frequently implausible method of murder and a neat denouement at the end. The ever more bizarre and complex methods of the killing in Sayers' novels were in fact part of their attraction. 'Those were not the days of the swift bash to the skull followed by sixty thousand words of psychological insight,' James adds. 'The murder methods she devised are, in fact, over ingenious and at least two are doubtfully practicable. A healthy man is unlikely to be killed by noise alone, a lethal injection of air would surely require a suspiciously large hypodermic syringe.'

However, Sayers did move away from convention through the development of the character of Lord Peter Wimsey, and particularly through the relationship he formed with the plucky and vulnerable Harriet Vane.

Vane, Sayers' fictional alter ego, was another writer of detective stories. Like Sayers, Harriet was independent and bold and yet had been wounded by men. When she first appears in *Strong Poison*, it is in the dock. In an echo of Sayers' relationship with Cournos, Harriet had agreed to live, unmarried, with a man. She too paid a high price for it, being accused of his murder.

Harriet's salvation from the gallows comes in the form of the brainy and wealthy Wimsey, who, while clearing her name, falls in love with her. After a suitably prolonged period of disputations and misunderstandings, Harriet ends up united with him in wedded bliss and material splendour. Sayers' tragedy was that there was no such happy ending for her.

Gaudy Night is the book in which Harriet finally realizes that her lover will never attempt to subdue or stifle her, and that she can relax into this relationship. The sparkling fairy on top of the tree of Sayers' work, *Gaudy Night* is a beautiful love story and a serious exploration of whether it was possible, in the 1930s, for women to combine work and marriage. The reader who has accompanied Harriet and Peter through hundreds of pages in which Harriet refuses to surrender her hard-won independence and pride will cheer when they finally kiss, in New College Lane, rather shyly and foolishly speaking to each other in Latin. It's a heart-warming if exasperating end (what took them so long?) to a very curious love story, in which the head plays as great a part as the heart. Typically of Sayers, she argues that the intellect brings her two lovers together. As she put it in her own words, she had at last found a plot in *Gaudy Night* that exhibited 'intellectual integrity as the one great permanent value in an emotionally unstable world'. This was the book in which she found herself saying 'the things that, in a confused way, I had been wanting to say all my life'.*

S ayers did eventually get married, to Captain Oswald Fleming, a divorced journalist. James Brabazon, Dorothy's biographer, who knew her, wasn't able entirely to pin down the nature of the relationship with her husband:

> Conventional comic images of the tiny henpecked husband alternated with more melodramatic versions of the mad monster chained in the attic. Slightly closer to the truth was the theory of the unpresentable alcoholic. But what seemed quite clear was that this was by no means what we in those days regarded as a normal marriage.

Fleming was kept at home in the house Sayers bought in the Essex village of Witham. He was not introduced to her friends, and was

---

* To hear *Gaudy Night* written off as the critic Julian Symons does in *Bloody Murder* (1972) is not unusual, but it remains infuriating. When I read the page where he states that '*Gaudy Night* is essentially a "woman's novel" full of the most tedious pseudo-serious chat between the characters that goes on for page after page', I threw Mr Symons's book on the floor, and stamped upon it.

apparently unable, through ill health, to earn a living himself. All he seemed to have in common with Lord Peter was his inability to recover from his experiences in the First World War.

As the years went by, Sayers dropped detective fiction, having apparently felt that she had exhausted its possibilities. She wrote increasingly for the radio and the stage, and became a noted translator of Dante's *The Divine Comedy*. Her ever-present Christian beliefs also inspired her to retell Bible stories simply, for a new generation, in the new medium of radio. Their success reinvigorated the faith of many of her fellow churchgoers, and the Church of England was so pleased that she was offered an honorary doctorate in Divinity. But Sayers turned it down, perhaps fearing that her private life would not withstand scrutiny.

It seems possible that, had she continued husbandless, or if she had married a more understanding man, Sayers may have eventually felt able to have her son come to live with her. But it never quite happened. Decades later, she was still using the presence of her Aunt Mabel, a surviving and possibly censorious relative, to argue that the time was still not ripe.

Sayers' son knew her as 'cousin Dorothy', and received regular money and visits, but never any public recognition of their relationship. He eventually discovered the mystery for himself, when he sought out his birth certificate to apply for a passport: it seems that seeing Sayers named as his mother was not a surprise. It seems rather shocking that Sayers, literate to a fault in her work and in public, was so emotionally illiterate that this was the way she felt forced to introduce herself, as a mother, to her child.

But when Sayers threw herself behind a cause – as she often did, having a stable-full of pet hobbyhorses which she liked to exercise

– she had a voice and authority that could achieve considerable change. Whether she was exhorting the Church of England to make itself more accessible, or universities to give degrees to women, she would use her heavy guns: rhetoric, passion and humour. Here she is in 1938 answering the question 'Are Women Human?'

> When the pioneers of university training for women demanded that women should be admitted to the universities, the cry went up at once: 'Why should women want to know about Aristotle?' The answer is NOT that all women would be the better for knowing about Aristotle ... but simply: 'What women want as a class is irrelevant. I want to know about Aristotle. It is true that many women care nothing about him, and a great many male undergraduates turn pale and faint at the thought of him – but I, eccentric individual that I am, do want to know about Aristotle, and I submit that there is nothing in my shape or bodily functions which need prevent my knowing about him.

In its quicksilver cleverness, its comedy and its belief in the importance of intellect, it is the unmistakable voice of Dorothy L. Sayers.

22

The Great Game

'Should you fail to honour [this oath], may your publishers
cheat you, may total strangers sue you for libel, may your pages
swarm with misprints and your sales continually diminish.'

From the 'Ritual' performed at the entry
of new members to the Detection Club

In the late 1920s, many of the Golden Age's crime novelists
became members of a group called the Detection Club. Starting
out simply as an informal gathering of friends who liked to have
dinner together, by 1930 the Club's members were well enough
organized to write a joint letter to the *Times Literary Supplement*,
and they went on to publish three collaborative novels together,
with chapters each written by a different author, to raise Club
funds. In 1932 a proper Constitution with rules was devised
and printed in a little booklet. Club premises were established
in Gerrard Street, and a magazine shows a picture of members
enjoying themselves there. (Dorothy L. Sayers, in one of them, is
smiling broadly, and downing half a pint of beer.)

The entrance requirements for the Club, taken from the 1932 Constitution, were:

> That he or she has written at least two detective-novels of admitted merit ... it being understood that the term 'detective novel' does not include adventure stories or 'thrillers' or stories in which the detection is not a main interest, and that it is a demerit in a detective-novel if the author does not 'play fair' by the reader.

More than a dining society but less than a trade union, the Detection Club showed how the output of the Golden Age had coalesced into a genre both recognizable and definable. Its members included Agatha Christie, Dorothy L. Sayers, G. K. Chesterton, Baroness Orczy and A. A. Milne (in addition to creating *Winnie the Pooh*, Milne wrote an excellent detective novel, *The Red House Mystery*).

As Sayers said of the Club: 'If there is any serious aim behind the avowedly frivolous organisation ... it is to keep the detective story up to the highest standards that its nature permits, and to free it from the bad legacy of sensationalism, clap-trap and jargon with which it was unhappily burdened in the past.'

Monsignor Ronald Knox, another member, conceived the inter-war detective story as a kind of game with rules, rather like tennis, which was to be played out between 'the author of the one part and the reader of the other part'.

He laid out the regulations of this game in a (tongue-in-cheek) set of Ten Commandments, and advised that they should be followed as strictly as the rules of cricket:

1. The criminal must be someone mentioned in the early part of the story, but must not be anyone whose thoughts the reader has been allowed to follow.

[Agatha Christie broke this rule, with tremendous effect, in *The Murder of Roger Ackroyd*, by making her narrator the perpetrator. But some readers were quite genuinely affronted and aggrieved by what they saw as a betrayal of trust on her part as an author. It's a reaction that's difficult to understand without getting back into the mindset that took the Ten Commandments terribly seriously.]

2. All supernatural or preternatural agencies are ruled out as a matter of course.

3. Not more than one secret room or passage is allowable.

[Knox added that even one secret passage was on the edges of acceptability: when employing one himself, he was careful to plant a clue, pointing out 'beforehand that the house had belonged to Catholics in penal times'.]

4. No hitherto undiscovered poisons may be used, nor any appliance which will need a long scientific explanation at the end.

5. No Chinaman must figure in the story.

6. No accident must ever help the detective, nor must he ever have an unaccountable intuition which proves to be right.

[That's Maria Marten's stepmother's dream ruled out: the old conventions of melodrama were by now completely superseded.]

7. The detective himself must not himself commit the crime.

8. The detective must not light on any clues which are not instantly produced for the inspection of the reader.

9. The stupid friend of the detective, the Watson, must not conceal any thoughts which pass through his mind; his intelligence must be slightly, but very slightly, below that of the average reader.

[Conan Doyle himself said of his second most famous creation: 'Watson never for one instant as chorus and chronicler transcends his own limitations. Never once does a flash of wit or wisdom come from him.' This is fundamentally unfair to Watson, and all his sidekick colleagues, though. Of course what he offers is not intellectual intelligence but emotional intelligence. Watsons bring warmth and humanity to their cerebral but cold-hearted superiors. A. A. Milne had a more charitable and fairer definition of a Watson: 'a little slow, let him be, as so many of us are, but friendly, human, likeable'.]

10. Twin brothers, and doubles generally, must not appear unless we have been duly prepared for them.

This idea of detection as a game, played out more often than not in an upper-class, country house setting, would take its final physical form in the board game Cluedo, which was produced in 1949 by the Leeds-based company Waddingtons. The game's setting, the Tudor mansion, and its players – Miss Scarlett, Colonel Mustard, Mrs White, Reverend Green, Mrs Peacock and Professor Plum – are instantly recognizable. But Cluedo had its forerunners in the 1930s, a decade which also saw the flourishing of brain-teasers such as crossword puzzles, jigsaws and publications such as *The Baffle Book.* *

What sort of relationship did the work of the Detection Club have with the real-life crimes of their day? It was certainly not such a close intertwining of fact and fiction as we saw with Charles Dickens or Wilkie Collins. In fact, the murders that caught the attention of the detective story writers were those which accidentally seemed to embody the spirit of the Ten Commandments, and which presented an intricate puzzle. One of these was the murder of Julia Wallace, in Liverpool, in 1931.

Julia's husband, William Herbert Wallace, was an agent for an insurance company. One day he received a telephone message calling him to a meeting at a potential client's house. He spent the evening of 20 January 1931 searching in vain for the address he'd been given, asking directions of various people who could (conveniently) later confirm his presence in the area. He'd been

---

* Containing 15 detective puzzles, charts, maps and lists of clues, *The Baffle Book* (1930) was basically a set of parlour games for a family to solve together, including vital questions such as 'Who stole the emerald?'. A series of 'Crime Dossiers' took the concept one stage further, and into three-dimensional form, with case files of letters, testimonies, and even evidence (hair, for example, or a piece of bloodstained wallpaper) provided for the players. The solution came in a sealed envelope at the back. *Herewith the Clues* and *Who Killed Robert Prentice?* in the 'Crime Dossiers' series were the forerunners of the kinds of boxed multi-player mystery games that can still be bought today.

instructed to go to a house in Menlove Gardens East. Despite the existence of Menlove Gardens West, and Menlove Gardens North, there was no such street. Once Wallace had finally established this, he returned home – only to find his wife, Julia, bludgeoned to death in her own sitting room.

The case against Wallace was highly circumstantial. It depended on persuading the jury that he had constructed the whole Menlove Gardens business as an elaborate alibi to get him clear of his home at the time the deed was done. However, Wallace had the misfortune to dress habitually in black, to look impassive in court, and to have been overheard stating his views that the jurors were all fools. They found against him. In an unprecedented fashion, though, their verdict was overturned by the judge, who thought it quite unacceptable to condemn a man to death on such flimsy evidence.

In the spirit of Thomas De Quincey in the previous century, many novelists praised this particular crime for providing them with entertainment and inspiration. The case caught the interest of the Detection Club because so much of the argument rested on timings and telephone calls and tram rides and the asking of directions – all common ingredients of the classic whodunit. Dorothy L. Sayers even wrote an article setting out all the possible suspects and motives for the killing of Julia Wallace that reads very much like the denouement 'in the library' at the end of a detective novel. She pointed out that the evidence in the case could be read in two completely contrasting ways: either William Herbert Wallace was the culprit, or else he was framed: 'it is like a web of shot silk, looking red from one angle, and green from another'. 'The Wallace case,' wrote Raymond Chandler, 'is the *nonpareil* of all murder mysteries.' As a brain-teaser, he thought, it 'is unbeatable; it will always be unbeatable'.

But the final piece of evidence to emerge seems to confirm Wallace's innocence. He died only a couple of years after his wife. Despite his official discharge, his life had been ruined, and he'd had to move away from his old neighbourhood because of the suspicion with which he was treated by former friends. In a private diary discovered after his death, he had written about how much he missed his wife, and of his belief that the real murderer was still at large.

On his own front porch, Wallace wrote, he expected one day to see a figure 'crouching and ready to strike', and 'it will be that of the man who murdered my wife'.

———

The sociable, well-organized and commanding Dorothy L. Sayers seems to have been the prime mover behind the Detection Club, and its order of ceremonies bears her distinctive and ironic tone of voice. The Club possessed several props, including the red robe of the President, black candles and a human skull called Eric, with red bulbs in his eye sockets.

The first President of the Club, and first wearer of the robes, was G. K. Chesterton. At some point in the 1960s the original robe was damaged or lost at a meeting held at the Savoy Hotel, and the hotel itself took responsibility for providing a new one, which still remains in use today. Its generous size is said to have been dictated by the generous measurements of Chesterton himself.

During the 'Ritual' for the initiation of new members, 'Eric the Skull' would be carried into the darkened clubroom, his glowing eyes powered by batteries. Ngaio Marsh described one such initiation ceremony, which took place at Grosvenor House in 1937:

> A door at the far end opened (as all doors in detective novels open) slowly. In came Miss Dorothy Sayers in her academic robes lit by a single taper. She mounted the rostrum. Judge my alarm when I saw that among the folds of her gown she secreted a large automatic revolver ... in came the others in solemn procession bearing lighted tapers and lethal instruments. There was the warden of the blunt instrument – a frightful bludgeon, the warden of the sharp instrument – I think it was a dagger – the warden of the deadly phial, & last of all John Rhode* with a grinning skull on a cushion.

The meeting then began, as they all did (and still do) with the President calling out, 'What mean these Lights, these Ceremonies, & this Reminder of our Mortality?'

Candidates wishing to join the Club would have to make certain elaborate vows:

> 'Do you promise that your Detectives shall well and truly detect the Crimes presented to them, using those wits which it may please you to bestow upon them and not placing reliance upon nor making use of Divine Revelation,

---

* John Rhode was the pen-name of Cecil Street (1884–1965), a Club member and author of novels with a forensic scientist as the detective.

Feminine Intuition, Mumbo Jumbo, Jiggery Pokery, Coincidence or the Act of God?'

'I do.'

'Do you solemnly swear never to conceal a Vital Clue from the Reader?'

'I do.'

'Do you promise to observe a seemly moderation in the use of Gangs, Conspiracies, Death-Rays, Ghosts, Hypnotism, Trap-Doors, Chinamen, Super-Criminals and Lunatics, and utterly and forever to forswear Mysterious Poisons unknown to Science?'

'I do.'

On the occasion that Ngaio Marsh attended, high drama ensued. After the new member had sworn the oath:

> Without the slightest hint of warning, in a private drawing room at Grosvenor House at about 11 pm on a summer evening Miss Dorothy Sayers loosed off her six-shooter. The others uttering primitive cries, waved their instruments, blunt sharp & venomous, & John Rhode, by means of some hidden device, caused his skull to be lit up from within. And to my undying shame my agent laughed like a hyena.

All this was vastly amusing, no doubt, but Sayers in later years grew a little set in her ways, and was said to treat 'the whole thing with such solemnity as to deprive it of much of its fun'.

After the war, the Detection Club was forced to flow with the spirit of the times, and to accept as members the thriller writers who had been so clearly rejected at the time of its formation. Today, it has about 60 members, and 'Eric the Skull' makes his appearance at each meeting (although analysis by a doctor has suggested that 'Eric' is in fact female).

Simon Brett, the current President of the Club, told me how members recently held a debate about the ethics of Eric. Was it really right and respectful, they argued, to subject the remains of a dead person to the trauma of being a prop in a ridiculous ceremony, with bulbs in his (or her) eye sockets? The debate was closely fought, Eric's dignity being pitted against several decades of Detection Club history. But, as the minutes of that particular meeting proclaim, 'The Eyes Have It', and Eric remains in use.

The meetings of the Club itself, of course, seemed like something out of a detective story, and not even Agatha Christie could resist the temptation to fictionalize. In number 35 of the exercise books she used for notes she jots down an idea: 'Detection Club Murder – Mrs Oliver – her two guests – someone killed when the Ritual starts.'

Brett told me about another memorable recent meeting, held at the Garrick Club on a very hot and airless summer evening. A lady fainted, and all the authors present, having checked that she was still alive, collectively reached for their notebooks.

23

———⬦———

Snobbery with Violence

'In London anybody at any moment might do or become
anything, but in a village, no matter what village, they were
all immutably themselves, parson, organist, sweep, duke's
son and doctor's daughter, moving like chessmen upon
their allotted squares.'

Dorothy L. Sayers (1937)

I n Britain in the 1930s, three million people were unemployed. The
Great Depression saw economies brought low, and dictatorships
sprouting up, across Europe. Fascists were holding rallies in the East
End of London. The trauma of the First World War was barely over
before the rumblings of the Second World War began to be heard.
These topics were almost completely ignored by members of the
Detection Club and writers of Golden Age crime fiction.

In retrospect, the fact that all this is missing from inter-war crime
novels seems more than just ignorance. It looks like a deliberate
attempt to wish it out of existence. As Julian Symons, historian of
the form, writes:

It is safe to say that almost all of the British writers in the twenties and thirties, and most of the Americans, were unquestionably Right-wing. This is not to say that they were openly anti-Semitic or anti-Radical [although many of them were], but that they were overwhelmingly conservative in feeling ... the social order in these stories was as fixed and mechanical as that of the Incas.

And there's no doubt that the fiction of the Golden Age isn't to everyone's taste. 'The reading of detective stories,' wrote Edmund Wilson in 1945, 'is simply a kind of vice that, for silliness and minor harmfulness, ranks somewhere between smoking and crossword puzzles.'

It was the author of 12 crime novels Colin Watson (1920–1983) who introduced the term 'Mayhem Parva' to describe the work of the 1920s and 1930s writers who so often seemed to set their work in cosy English villages like St Mary Mead. Watson's own contribution to the school of criticism of the detective story was called *Snobbery with Violence* (1971). The phrase was originally coined by Alan Bennett to sum up the less attractive aspects of these books: the stultifying, repetitive, hide-bound and reactionary world whose values were only reinforced by the solution of the crime. In *The Murder of Roger Ackroyd*, Agatha Christie's narrator gives us a glimpse of the daily round in Mayhem Parva:

I made a few hurried remarks about the new sweet pea. I knew that there was a new sweet pea because the *Daily Mail* had told me so that morning. Mrs Ackroyd knows nothing about horticulture, but she is the kind of woman who likes to appear well-informed about the topics of the day, and she too reads the *Daily Mail*. We were able to converse quite intelligently until ... Parker announced dinner.

One reason for the great success of Golden Age detective fiction is that it reflected the values of its readers right back at them – and that image is not always an attractive one.

As well as Knox's Ten Commandments, other, unspoken, rules about class and hierarchy governed the genre. Even though the subject was murder, there was very little actual violence or blood in these novels. In *The Murder of Roger Ackroyd*, Christie describes the first glimpse of the victim in very low-key terms. 'Ackroyd was sitting as I'd left him in the armchair before the fire,' the narrator tells us. 'Just below the collar of his coat was a shining piece of twisted metalwork.' This was the dagger that had killed him, but there was no obvious sign of violence, and the weapon itself sounds rather like a piece of jewellery. In *Death at Broadcasting House* (1934) by Val Gielgud and Holt Marvell, a 'man's figure unnaturally crumpled' is found lying in a radio studio, but the next paragraph is all about the studio's 'special acoustic treatment removing all natural echo', the shaded light, the thick carpet, the padded walls and the excellent air-conditioning. This is quite typical of the Golden Age, where death seems to happen inconspicuously and with hardly any mess.

Knox's contemporary Willard Huntington Wright (1888–1939) was the creator, under the pen-name S. S. Van Dine, of the American detective Philo Vance. Like Knox, he was a commentator on the detective genre, which had both made his fortune and made a mockery of his earlier ambitions as an art critic. 'I Used to Be a Highbrow but Look at Me Now' was the title of one of his articles. Wright noted perspicaciously a second unwritten rule of the detective genre as it stood in the 1920s: that the killer could not be a servant, because that was 'too easy'. The culprit 'must be a decidedly worth-while person', as he put it. This snobbery about servants permeates the world of the Golden Age: they are either 'treasures', or 'bad 'uns' who indulge in a little mild theft or blackmail, but lack the class actually to commit a murder.

On reading 1920s and 1930s detective novels today, it is this attitude that servants are not really human that particularly jars. 'I believe him to be a perfectly truthful man, as such people go,' a lady says of her chauffeur in Dorothy L. Sayers' *The Nine Tailors*. Margery Allingham's detective Albert Campion casually refers to his manservant as 'the Cretin'. In *A Question of Proof*, Nicholas Blake (pseudonym for Cecil Day Lewis, the future Poet Laureate) very quickly writes off pretty much the whole of the below-stairs department. The policeman investigating the case: 'interviewed the whole staff of servants at Sudeley Hall. They were practically exempt from suspicion, having been underneath each other's noses – if not actually tumbling over each other – either in the kitchen or the garden.'

The 'well-trained servant' crops up literally countless times in Agatha Christie's work, but Captain Hastings does not know how condescending he is when he admires a notable example of the species: 'Dear old Dorcas! As she stood there, with her honest face upturned to mine, I thought what a fine specimen she was of the old-fashioned servant that is so fast dying out.' Captain Hastings was vaguely aware that changes to the labour market would cause domestic servants like Dorcas to become unaffordable for the middle classes, and like Agatha Christie's readers, he would strongly have deplored the fact.

In the Golden Age the detective, too, was usually of a specific social class, much more elevated than it had been in the days of Inspectors Field and Whicher, when detection was considered dirty work. 'It would have been unthinkable,' says Julian Symons, for these writers 'to create a Jewish detective, or a working-class one aggressively conscious of his origins, for such figures would have seemed to them quite incongruous'. Agatha Christie cleverly allowed Hercule Poirot to sidestep the issue of class by making him Belgian and therefore, notoriously, hard to categorize. But a great many of his colleagues sprung from the ranks of the aristocracy. Lord Peter Wimsey was the brother of a duke. Margery Allingham's detective, Albert Campion, 'well-bred and a trifle absent-minded', is the younger brother of some high-ranking aristocrat whose identity is kept firmly secret lest Campion's activities bring a noble house into disrepute. Campion also ends up marrying the annoying 'Lady' Amanda Fitton, following their first meeting on a case during which Campion re-establishes her family's ancient right to a title.

Ngaio Marsh's sleuth, Roderick Alleyn, is equally posh, having a mother called 'Lady Alleyn' who breeds Alsatians. In Marsh's most popular book, *A Surfeit of Lampreys* (1941), there are so many titled characters that the policeman investigating the case simply has to give up on correct form when a marquis dies, thereby passing on his title and, confusingly, changing the names of all his relations. Neither the police, nor the reader, nor even the author, can keep track.

The attitudes exhibited by these detectives are not always admirable. Lord Peter Wimsey, for example, casually lists the people not worth treating fairly: 'liars and halfwits and prostitutes and dagoes'. William D. Rubenstein, however, has argued that sinister Jews, a fixture of the 1920s (Agatha Christie's 'yellow-faced financiers') start to disappear from crime novels around 1930. As Nazi anti-Semitism grew more brutal, Jewish characters grew more likely to be sympathetic refugees from persecution.

In this respect, the ending of the Golden Age was inevitable as society became more liberal. The inter-war period saw a belief in science and rationality as central to the future of mankind. Trust in authority was still high: British justice surely never made mistakes and evil-doers should, of course, be sent to the gallows. As W. H Auden put it, 'the typical reader of detective stories is, like myself, a person who suffers from a sense of sin'. In 1945 Agatha Christie described 'the ethical background' of the detective story as 'usually sound. Very, very rarely is the criminal the hero of the book. Society unites to hunt him down, and the reader can have all the fun of the chase without moving from a comfortable armchair.'

The discovery, during the Second World War, that horrors such as the atom bomb and Auschwitz could exist shook this essential belief in order and hierarchy. As old values and convictions began to crumble away, the Criminal Justice Act of 1948 replaced the punitive ideal of justice with the concept of rehabilitation, or treatment and training intended to coach the criminal out of his ways. When hanging was eventually abolished in 1964, the certainties of the detective story had been replaced by the ambiguities of the spy thriller.

E ven as dusk was settling over the quiet, pretty but increasingly irrelevant village of Mayhem Parva, a new type of book was beginning to do exactly what the detective story could not: reveal to us the inner workings of the murderer's mind. Other writers were exploring alternatives to Mayhem Parva that would turn out to be just as readable, and just as profitable for their publishers.

The rival form to the detective story was the thriller, and by the late 1930s it had the brighter future ahead of it. In the thriller, the character of the villain would be central, and we see inside his or her head. Dorothy L. Sayers summed up the other main difference between the old and the new: 'The difference between thriller and detective story is mainly one of emphasis. Agitating events occur in both, but in the thriller our cry is "What comes next?" – in the detective story, "What came first?" The one we cannot guess; the other we can, if the author gives us a chance.'

Right up to the Second World War, though, traditional, mainly British, authors and readers preferred the older, more cerebral ways of crime. They disliked the violence, brashness and uncouthness of the American-led thriller movement. Dorothy L. Sayers found the thriller's aims 'trivial' compared with the nobility of the detective story, and most thriller writers' works to be full of 'bad English, cliché, balderdash and boredom'. And many thrillers were just as derivative as the worst Golden Age detective novels. It's disappointing to learn that even when the death-dealing spy James Bond appeared in 1952, many of his famous gadgets were simply cribbed from the works of Edgar Wallace.

This conservatism caused Sayers to overlook the earliest works of Graham Greene, but Mike Ripley, for ten years the crime fiction critic for the *Daily Telegraph*, argues that she was all too aware of the change in the tide and wisely stopped reviewing crime novels – and, indeed, writing them – just as they passed their peak. Her fellow Golden Age writer Ronald Knox, was also well aware that 'the game is getting played out'.

Raymond Chandler (1888–1959), a great crime writer himself but one of the vocal enemies of the traditional English detective story, also believed that Sayers had come to recognize the limits of her medium.

> I think what was really gnawing her mind was the slow realization that her kind of detective story was an arid formula which could not even satisfy its own implications. It was second grade literature because it was not about the things that could make first-grade literature ... Dorothy Sayers' own stories show that she was annoyed by this triteness; the weakest element in them is the part that makes them detective stories, the strongest the part which could be removed without touching the 'problem of logic and deduction'.

The most striking attack on detective fiction came in *The New Yorker* in 1944 and 1945, from Edmund Wilson, in two essays 'Why Do People Read Detective Stories?' and 'Who Cares Who Killed Roger Ackroyd?' In the first, Wilson criticizes the lifelessness of Agatha Christie's characters: she 'has to eliminate human interest completely, or, rather, fill in the picture with what seems to me a distasteful parody of it ... she has to provide herself with puppets'. Once he'd published this essay, Wilson was deluged with letters berating him for his lack of discernment, and imploring him to read other, classier, fiction writers: Dorothy L. Sayers was highly recommended. So he tried *The Nine Tailors*. His response misses the point almost laughably:

> One of the dullest books I have ever encountered in any field. The first part of it is all about bell-ringing as it is practised· in English churches and contains a lot of information of the kind that you might expect to find in an encyclopaedia article on campanology. I skipped a good deal of this, and found myself skipping, also, a large section of the conversations between conventional English village characters: 'Oh, here's Hinkins with the aspidistras. People may say what they like about aspidistras, but they do go on all the year round and make a background,' etc.

One can see what a distinguished New York man of letters may find offensive in this (he also called *The Lord of the Rings* 'juvenile trash'), but the bell-ringing and the aspidistras are part of the deepest charm of Dorothy L. Sayers, who makes the mundane seem so eccentric and amusing and, at the same time, so firmly rooted in a particular place and time. P. D. James agrees:

> In the Wimsey saga, the sounds, mood, speech, the very feel of the thirties seems to rise from the page: the resentful war-scarred heroes of the Bellona Club, the gallant or pathetic spinsters of Miss Climpson's agency, the ordered and hierarchical life of a few villages, now as obsolete as the

vast rectories round which it revolved, the desperate gaiety of the bright young things, the fear of unemployment which underlay the cheerful camaraderie of office life in *Murder Must Advertise*.

As you'd hope from a literary critic, Wilson does foresee what would replace the detective story. 'The spy story may perhaps only now be realizing its poetic possibilities, as the admirers of Graham Greene contend; and the murder story that exploits psychological horror is an entirely different matter.'

Raymond Chandler put a final nail into the coffin of Mayhem Parva in an essay of 1950 called 'The Simple Art of Murder'. Over 16 million of his fellow Americans had experienced military service in the Second World War, society had changed, but the conventional detective story had not. 'The murder novel,' Chandler claimed, 'has a depressing way of minding its own business, solving its own problems and answering its own questions. There is nothing left to discuss, except whether it was well enough written to be good fiction, and the people who make up the half-million sales wouldn't know that anyway.'

The English, he concludes, 'may not always be the best writers in the world, but they are incomparably the best dull writers'.

And yet, ultimately, such criticism of Mayhem Parva feels misplaced, revealing a snobbery about popular entertainment – fiction set out primarily to reassure, soothe and amuse – worthy of the middle-class people who wrote off melodrama as laughable or Mary Elizabeth Braddon as immoral. Even Sayers herself, much as she disliked the thriller, was well aware of the limitations of the classic Golden Age detective novel's form: 'It does not – and by hypothesis never can – attain the loftiest level of literary achievement. Though it deals with the most desperate effects of rage, jealousy and revenge, it rarely touches the heights and depths of human passion.'

She is saying, in other words, what Jane Austen had said more than a hundred years earlier: 'Let other pens dwell on guilt and misery. I quit such odious subjects as soon as I can, impatient to restore every body, not greatly in fault themselves, to tolerable comfort.'

You could call this an admirable philosophy for life.

24

The Dangerous
Edge of Things

'In everything that can be called art there is a quality of redemption.'

Raymond Chandler

In 1941, as the popularity of the detective story continued to wane, Philip Van Doren Stern, the American author of the story that inspired the film *It's A Wonderful Life*, made the case for change. 'The whole genre needs overhauling, a return to first principles,' he claimed. 'Writers need to know more about life and less about death.' And, indeed, for quite a long time by then, an alternative way of proceeding had been unfolding on his side of the Atlantic.

By complete contrast to the suave British sleuth, his American counterpart was tough. So-called 'hard-boiled' detectives made their first appearance in cheap, 'pulp' magazines, known as this because they were made from wood pulp, or recycled paper. They reflected the values of their unregulated, competitive Wild West society. 'Many people have their little peculiarities,' says a character called Race Williams, as hard-boiled as they come. 'Mine was holding a loaded gun in my hand while I slept.' Race uses his gun fairly frequently, because – as he explains – 'you can't make a hamburger without grinding up a little meat'. Usually a private eye rather than a policeman, the hard-boiled detective speaks his own language. 'Tell your moll to hand over the mazuma' (money), he might say, or 'Close your yap, bo, or I squirt metal'. He might call a black person 'dark meat', a car a 'bucket', or advise you to avoid wearing a 'Chicago overcoat' (a coffin).

The magazine *Black Mask,* founded in 1920, was the home of many of these characters. Its editor, Joseph T. Shaw, demanded that his writers tell simple, violent stories, without unnecessary description or affectation. And yet the action had to be motivated by character, and the 'hard-boiled' detective is flawed and fallible in a way that would be quite out of place in British crime fiction.

Dashiell Hammett (1894–1961), one of the *Black Mask* writers, and a Marxist, had even worked as a detective himself, for eight years, with America's famous Pinkerton agency. Another *Black Mask* writer was Raymond Chandler, who lived in London as a teenager. Chandler, creator of Philip Marlowe, the best-known 'hard-boiled' detective, explained that there were no 'hand-wrought duelling pistols, curare, and tropical fish' to be found providing arcane means of death in his stories. He thought that stories like his 'gave murder back to the kind of people that commit it for reasons, not just to provide a corpse'.

Chandler, who'd started out in the oil industry before being fired from his job in 1932, described how he came to end up as a writer:

Wandering up and down the Pacific Coast in an automobile I began to read pulp magazines, because they were cheap enough to throw away ... this was in the great days of the *Black Mask* (if I may call them great days) and it struck me that the writing was pretty forceful and honest, even though it had its crude aspect.

So he decided to try his hand at the genre, producing his classic story, the 18,000-word *The Big Sleep*, over a five-month period, and selling it for a mere $180. But 'after that I never looked back,' he claimed, 'although I had a good many uneasy periods looking forward.'

In *The Big Sleep*, Philip Marlowe tells his story in the first person, with the laconic, punchy, cynical language familiar to the ear from noir films:

I was neat, clean, shaved and sober, and I didn't care who knew it. I was everything the well-dressed private detective ought to be. I was calling on four million dollars.

And ...

Her eyes rounded. She was puzzled. She was thinking. I could see, even on that short acquaintance, that thinking was always going to be a bother to her.

And ...

'How do you feel?' It was a smooth silvery voice that matched her hair. It had a tiny tinkle in it, like bells in a doll's house. I thought that was silly as soon as I thought of it.

The Big Sleep is such a short novel, with short sharp punchy scenes, that reading it seems like watching a film, and Chandler himself explains that the people trying to write his sort of detective story 'had the same point of view as film makers'. When he first went to Hollywood, he recalled, 'a very intelligent producer told me that you couldn't make a successful motion picture from a mystery story, because the whole point was a disclosure that took a few seconds of screen time while the audience was reaching for its hat'.

Chandler set out to prove him wrong. All but one of his novels ended up as feature films, and some of them were made into several different versions of the same story.

The simplicity of Chandler's prose disguises deep, complex questions of life and death, and in Britain the most notable example of the same sort of thing was *Brighton Rock* (1938). Here again the fate of the soul is the motivating force beneath Graham Greene's story of the dirty Brighton underworld.

Greene (1904–91) suffered from bipolar disorder, lived a rootless existence all over the world and described himself as 'profoundly antagonistic to ordinary domestic life'. So, too, are his characters. *Brighton Rock* has an anti-hero, a violent gangster who nevertheless believes in God. The detective is a blowsy, immoral but kindly woman called Ida. But it's not clear that Greene admires her godless kindness more than the gangster Pinkie's cruel belief. J. M. Coetzee points out Greene's indebtedness to the movies, noting that Greene was also the *Spectator*'s film critic, and that his novels were like screenplays in their 'preference of observation from outside without commentary, tight cutting from scene to scene, equal emphasis for the significant and the non-significant'. Greene himself described how he imagined scenes as he wrote them, recreating in his mind the 'moving eye of the cine-camera ... I work with the camera, following my characters and their movements'.

As well as seeing the world in this novel way, Greene was far from seeing good and bad as two extremes, as they had been in Mayhem Parva, and was fond of quoting Robert Browning:

> Our interest's in the dangerous edge of things,
> The honest thief, the tender murderer,
> The superstitious atheist ...

Complexity rather than simplicity was the power and the glory of his work.

———

While Alfred Hitchcock (1899–1980) had little time for the writings of Graham Greene, the British films that he made before the Second World War also stand at the antithesis of the Golden Age. Hitchcock had some experience of real-life murder and retribution while growing up in Leytonstone with his strict, Catholic family. A blonde young lady was discovered dead in his neighbourhood; she had been poisoned. Edith Thompson, who would hang for murder in the celebrated Thompson–Bywaters case, was actually a customer at his family's fruit and veg shop. And one day, the shy, fat young boy was sent with a note by his father to the police station. The letter requested that Alfred Hitchcock be locked up, as a punishment, in the cells for a few minutes. 'That's what we do to naughty boys,' the policeman said. Hitchcock later admitted that this experience affected him powerfully.

Hitchcock loved reading about true crime in the newspapers, and after moving to Hollywood in 1939 he kept a series of bound volumes of *Notable British Trials* in the sitting room of his home in Bel Air. His favourite murder of all was the Thompson–Bywaters case, because of his personal connection to it. Edith Thompson was a buyer for a millinery firm, and lived with her husband in Ilford. With a career and income of her own, she felt secure enough to risk an adulterous relationship. At the age of 26, she had started an affair with Freddy Bywaters, an 18-year-old serving in the merchant navy. One night in 1922, Edith and her husband were walking home from the theatre when an assailant jumped out at them. Edith's husband was attacked and killed. Distraught, Edith accused Freddy Bywaters. But when her illicit relationship with him was exposed, Edith was charged alongside him for murder. It was considered that she had made common purpose with her lover to kill her husband.

The trial was reported with a good deal of sensationalism, and Edith did not help herself by giving inconsistent and unhelpful evidence. And yet, a huge popular movement started to save her from the gallows. There was no evidence that she had planned the murder, and witnesses heard her crying 'Don't, don't!' during the attack. On top of that, she was referred to in court as 'the adulteress', and was forced to be tried alongside Bywaters rather than being judged on her own.

A large segment of public opinion thought that these were rather Victorian assumptions to build into the justice system. Edith's adultery or immorality did not automatically mean that she was guilty of murder, and if there was no evidence that she had prior knowledge of the attack, why should she share a dock with the killer? She was, however, found guilty, and hanged at Holloway Prison in 1923.

The moral ambivalence of Edith Thompson, her composure, and her unknowable inner life all attracted Hitchcock. When he began to direct films, the behaviour of cool women under pressure formed a theme. So did murder. Yet only one of his films, *Murder!* (1930), is a classic whodunit in the mould of the Golden Age. In it, an actress is found sitting shocked, motionless and apparently redhanded next to the body of a murder victim. The story involves the slow realization, by a member of the jury at her trial, that she was in fact innocent.

Yet the slowly unfolding solution of a mystery like this was a format that Hitchcock found too limiting. He was much more likely to use a murder as what in film parlance is called the 'MacGuffin', a means of kicking off a series of events in which bystanders are forced to reveal something about themselves. Hitchcock himself described a MacGuffin as 'the mechanical element that usually crops up in any story. In crook stories it is almost always the necklace and in spy stories it is most always the papers.' What the MacGuffin might be is essentially unimportant. Hitchcock actually stated as much in an interview:

It might be a Scottish name, taken from a story about two men in a train. One man says 'What's that package up there in the baggage rack?', and the other answers, 'Oh, that's a MacGuffin'. The first one asks, 'What's a MacGuffin?' 'Well', the other man says, 'it's an apparatus for trapping lions in the Scottish Highlands'. The first man says, 'But there are no lions in the Scottish Highlands' ...

By then, the story has started. 'So you see,' Hitchcock concluded, 'a MacGuffin is nothing at all.' Murder, then, is essentially peripheral to Hitchcock's work.

Like Agatha Christie, Hitchcock did not depict actual murder or blood. In fact he couldn't, because the Motion Picture Production Code of 1930 (usually known as The Hays Code) had tried to clean up the image of the cinema by censoring the violence and sex that could be seen on screen. Yet Hitchcock built up a condition of suspense in his viewer even more effectively by allowing them simply to imagine the bloodshed he could not show them.

His first big success, *The Lodger, A Story of the London Fog* (1927), a silent film, already sowed the seeds of the classic Hitchcock films to come. It was based on a successful novel, loosely inspired by a 'Jack the Ripper'-like serial killer, and the opening scenes of gaslights glowing through the fog along the Thames Embankment have a powerful echo of the 'Ripper' panic of 1888. The very first scene in *The Lodger* shows the face of a blonde woman screaming in terror, while the captions repeatedly hammer us with the words of her mysterious killer: 'To-Night Golden Curls'. A series of blonde women have been murdered. But we see no more of her, or the killer. The emphasis is all upon the effects of murder, its ripples, and what happens to the witnesses, passers-by and to Londoners as a whole. Next, the woman who discovered the body is seen panicking, being reassured and being questioned greedily by a crowd.

In another classic Hitchcock trick, the opening scenes use humour to relax the viewer. A man in the crowd spooks the distressed lady by covering his face with his coat and creeping up on her from behind. It's amusing, but Hitchcock only makes us giggle in order to lull us into a state of relaxation so that the next shock will be more powerful.

The story of *The Lodger* is really the story of the jeopardy into which the hero – played by matinee idol Ivor Novello – is placed by being suspected of the crime, and the catching of a killer and the resolution of wrongs was never Hitchcock's concern. His authorized biographer, John Russell Taylor, told me that Hitchcock would have believed that 'messages are for Western Union', and that his films were not about good and evil, right or wrong. Instead, he simply aimed to extract maximum fear, horror and humour from his audience.

In this, Hitchcock, although he lived and worked at the same time as Agatha Christie, has nothing to do with the Golden Age of detective fiction. Consciously or not, his work looks back to the 'sensation' novels of the 1860s. Hitchcock saw the cinema seat, according to John Russell Taylor, as a machine for ministering a series of shocks, laughs, shivers and screams to its occupant. In this, he was following in the footsteps of Charles Dickens, Wilkie Collins or Mary Elizabeth Braddon.

And, indeed, while Agatha Christie may come second only to William Shakespeare and the Bible in terms of sales, fiction of the Golden Age does not seem to provide the strongest and most influential strand of British culture inspired by crime. The 'sensation' novel of the 1860s, with its aim of raising the hair and shivering the spine, would eventually give us the younger, stronger, vigorous and still-thriving genre of thrilling horror. The Golden Age knitting-type detective puzzle, for all its great commercial success, turned out to be a dead end.

Postscript

'The Decline
of English Murder'

In 1946, George Orwell published a celebrated essay lamenting 'The Decline of English Murder'. At the time, he was still better known as a journalist and an essayist. His novel *Animal Farm*, published the previous year, had not yet turned him into one of the giants of twentieth-century literature, and *1984* still lay ahead of him. Orwell's life, and writing career, was devoted to fighting totalitarianism on both the left and the right, and crime fiction interested him as an indirect expression of contemporary politics. 'The average man,' he claimed, 'is not directly interested in politics and, when he reads, he wants the current struggles of the world to be translated into a simple story about individuals.'

And he regretted what the new, nihilistic American hard-boiled thrillers indicated about the tastes of his contemporaries. In particular, Orwell took against the thriller *No Orchids for Miss Blandish*, by James Hadley Chase, a novel of 1939 which sold more than half a million copies. Although he was English, Chase modelled his style on the American writers of the *Black Mask*. Orwell complained that this novel, a runaway success in the first years of the Second World War, contained:

eight full-dress murders, an unassessable number of casual killings and woundings, an exhumation (with a careful reminder of the stench), the flogging of Miss Blandish, the torture of another women with red-hot cigarette ends, a strip-tease act, a third-degree scene of unheard-of-cruelty and much else of the same kind.

He was not alone in his dislike of the book, which displeased many moralists in its depiction of a masochistic gangster who experiences an orgasm in the moment he gets knifed, and the unfortunate kidnap victim, Miss Blandish, who is beaten with a hose-pipe and raped before falling in love with her captor.

Orwell thought this revealed an unhealthy taste for pain and inexplicable brutality that contrasted poorly even with the 'snobbery and violence' of the inter-war years. 'Snobbishness,' he wrote in another article, 'like hypocrisy, is a check upon behaviour whose value from a social point of view has been underrated.'

This is the background to Orwell's great elegiac essay. In it, he mourns the great murderers of the past in something of the same spirit of sardonic connoisseurship as Thomas De Quincey's essay nearly 120 years before. Assessing the greatest crimes of the period 1850–1925, Orwell concludes that a 'good' murder involved members of the middle class, and usually had a sexual motive.

And certainly it seemed to him that the elegant crimes of the past were being replaced by a more brutal present: 'the anonymous life of the dance halls and the false values of American film'.

He picked out one particular true-life crime of 1944 known as 'The Cleft Chin Murder' as being typical of his own debased times. A male deserter from the US army and a female, 18-year-old, would-be striptease artist struck up a casual partnership. They killed a cyclist by running her over with a stolen army truck, before murdering a taxi driver (he of the cleft chin) for just eight pounds, which they spent at the dog races the next day. The crime was full of meaningless, wanton, arbitrary violence, and Orwell thought that it could only have occurred in the wartime year of 1944, with its atmosphere of movie-palaces, cheap perfume, false names and stolen cars, and the 'brutalising effects of war'. One newspaper's account of the trial in the Old Bailey was immediately followed up with an article headed 'British Gangsterism Feared'. It was like a real-life version of *Brighton Rock*.

Thomas De Quincey had praised the artistry and industry of John Williams, the supposed perpetrator of the Radcliffe Highway Killings, with his tongue firmly in his cheek. But George Orwell was rather more serious as he now held up Dr Palmer of Rugeley, or Edith Bywaters and Frederick Thompson, as admirable murderers. For at the very least, he argued, they had committed their crimes out of conviction. He thought that a crime of passion could have 'dramatic and even tragic qualities which make it memorable and excite pity for both victim and murderer'. He regretted the passing of a stable, if unequal society, where people at least agreed that 'crimes as serious as murder should have strong emotions behind them'. For Orwell, the monumental destruction of human life that the twentieth century had seen was eclipsing and erasing the pleasure formerly to be taken in reading about a single crime in suburbia.

What Orwell feared would indeed come to pass. Pitiless, inhuman, random killings would be the flavour of fictional murder to come.

In the spring of 2013, a packed audience spent their Friday night at the British Library. They'd come to ask questions of an all-female panel of crime writers. Most exciting of all, people wanted to meet Piv Bernth, producer of the cult, slow-burning Danish TV series *The Killing*, with its investigation into the horrific abduction and murder of a child. It was the same week that the ITV crime drama *Broadchurch* had begun, a kind of home-grown version of *The Killing*, set in Dorset. Both drew huge audiences, and discussion of 'who did it' in each case formed the common currency of office, dinner table and classroom chat across Britain in the same way that the details of Maria Marten's death, or the details of Maria Manning's guilt, had done more than one hundred years before.

Equally, our interest in the characters and authors of the Victorian age is far from petering out. Sherlock Holmes has yet another new incarnation on the TV screen, so too do the events and players in the 'Jack the Ripper' case. Even the detective Jack Whicher has become the hero of a television drama series. But our modern depictions of violence have grown even nastier since the early days of the motion picture or even *No Orchids for Miss Blandish*. The first episode of 2012's *Ripper Street* saw women being stripped naked, violently dismembered, and made to appear in snuff movies. This is fiction in the thriller genre, the meaner, younger brother of the detective story that has dominated since the Second World War. Yet the detective story is not quite dead, either, even in its cosy, domesticated, Golden Age form. Hercule Poirot is still just about in business on TV, as is the cuddlesome *Foyle's War*.

While many people might argue that the violence in modern fiction shows that society is sinking fast into depravity, our story has shown that our thirst for blood is in fact at least two hundred years old. But we've also seen that it is *not* timeless. 'Scratch John Bull', the archetypal red-faced, beer-drinking patriotic Englishman, proclaimed the *Pall Mall Gazette* in 1887, 'and you find the ancient Briton who revels in blood, who loves to dig deep into a murder, and devours the details of a hanging.' While the ancient Briton might well have been of necessity a violent individual, though, he wasn't particularly anxious about murder. He, and his descendants for many centuries, lacked the luxury of being able to worry about such a comparatively rare event. Famine, disease or war were far more pressing concerns.

It was only with the turn of the nineteenth century that a new and awful significance became attached to the crime of murder, and that, in consequence, it took up its high position in art and culture. As we have seen, this fascination with murder can be ascribed to the limiting of the death penalty to fewer crimes, to the growth of literacy and to the creativity of writers like Thomas De Quincey. It came about because of city living, and with it the dissolution of the surveillance society of the village. It was due to the marvels of the modern age, such as easily available rat-poison and life-insurance. In other words, our elevation of murder above all other crimes and forms of violence was a consequence of what we like to think of as 'civilization'.

From 1800 onwards, with the birth of a recognizably modern world, enjoying murder became an increasingly profitable and commercial business. The character of the fictional detective is such a strong strand of modern life that the Victorians seem directly connected to us today in a way that the Georgians don't, with their cheerfully rapscallion highwaymen, implausible Gothic novels, and policing by elderly volunteers. The Victorians are, indeed, our blood relatives.

All through writing this book I've been worried about being too flippant about murder. It's not all good clean fun. There is horror here, and tragedy, beneath the puppetry and pageantry. But among the gore and horror, we've also glanced aside at the history of literature, of education, of women's place in society and of justice.

Our guilty pleasures reveal a lot about who we really are. As the mystery novelist C. H. B. Kitchin presciently put it in 1939:

If he wishes to study the manners of our age ... a historian of the future will probably turn, not to blue books and statistics, but to detective stories.

Acknowledgements

I would like to express my sincere thanks to everyone on the 'Murder' team at BBC Bristol: Michael Poole, Alastair Laurence, Gerry Dawson, Rachel Jardine, Matthew Thomas, Chloe Penman, Jo Verity, Michelle Soldani, Fred Fabre, Kinita Echeverria, Michael Robinson, Paul Nathan, Simon Pinkerton, James Harrison, Glenn Rainton, Natasha Martin and Deborah Williams, and to our commissioner, Mark Bell. Likewise, at BBC Books, I'm awfully grateful to Albert De Petrillo, Kate Fox, Claire Scott, Richard Collins, Sarah Chatwin and all their colleagues. I have been a happy client at Felicity Bryan Associates for nearly a decade now, and am indebted especially Felicity herself and to Michele Topham. I dedicate this book with love to Mark Hines, who will be glad when we no longer need share our house with a horde of murderers.

Thanks, finally, to the readers and other history-lovers who constantly contact me through my website. You're almost always a source of good cheer and encouragement. In the words of the oath of the Detection Club: 'May your only problems be fictional and of your own devising, and may many years pass before you write, for the last time, The End.'

Picture Credits

Sources

General books

Judith Flanders, author of the excellent *The Invention of Murder, How the Victorians Revelled in Death and Detection and Created Modern Crime* (2010), was a consultant to the TV series and provided us with a key interview. Her book (much more detailed than this one) is highly recommended, and the obvious place to turn next for the first two-thirds of the timescale covered here. At the same time, Rosalind Crone's *Violent Victorians* (2012) has been essential. Reading her research into the meaning of murderous entertainments is like pushing a spring-lock that opens up Victorian society. Moving onwards, time-wise, Matthew Sweet's provocative *Inventing the Victorians* (London, 2001) asks many stimulating questions about what we believe about Victorian life and its clichés, while P. D. James's *Talking About Detective Fiction* (2010) builds upon the essential work done by Julian Symons in *Bloody Murder: From the Detective Story to the Crime Novel* (1972), which is necessary reading even though I disagree with many of the author's interpretations. Two websites also fall into the general category: crimetime.co.uk, a site reviewing crime fiction, edited by Barry Forshaw and published by Oldcastle Books, and writersforensicsblog. wordpress.com produced by D.P. Lyle.

Part One: How to Enjoy a Murder

1. A Connoisseur in Murder

I'm grateful to the staff at Dove Cottage, The Wordsworth Trust, for access to their collections, and for a copy of Robert Woolf's catalogue to *Thomas De Quincey,* an exhibition staged at Dove Cottage, Cumbria in 1985. Grevel Lindop's *The Opium-Eater, A Life of Thomas De Quincey* (1981) provided extra detail.

2. The Highway

As well as Judith Flanders' and Rosalind Crone's work on the rise of policing in London, P. D. James's and T. A. Critchley's *The Maul and the Pear Tree, The Ratcliffe Highway Murders, 1811* (1971) was essential for the details of the crime.

3. The Watchmen

In addition to the sources for Chapter 2, Bob Jeffries, curator of the Thames Police Museum at Wapping, was a useful source of help, as was Simon Dell's *The Victorian Policeman* (2004) and the Open University's online resource called 'History From Police Archives'.

4. The Murder Circuit

I relied on Judith Flanders here, and the very full account provided by Albert Borowitz, *The Thurtell-Hunt Murder Case, Dark Mirror to Regency England* (1987), along with Angus Fraser, 'John Thurtell', *Oxford Dictionary of National Biography* (2004).

5. House of Wax

As well as help given by Charlotte Burford, the present archivist at Madame Tussaud's in London, two books were particularly useful:

Pauline Chapman, *Madame Tussaud in England, Career Woman Extraordinary* (1992) and, especially, Pamela Pilbeam, *Madame Tussaud and the History of Waxworks* (2003). On the earlier history of waxworks, *The Funeral Effigies of Westminster Abbey*, edited by Anthony Harvey and Richard Mortimer (1994), is essential.

6. True Crime

In addition to the sources already quoted, especially Rosalind Crone's *Violent Victorians* (2012), Richard Altick's *The English Common Reader: A Social History of the Mass Reading Public, 1800–1900* (1957) and V. A. C. Gatrell's *The Hanging Tree: Execution and the English People, 1770–1868* (1994) were also useful. The Richard Altick quotation is from *Victorian Studies in Scarlet* (1972). See also Andrew Brown, 'Lytton, Edward George Earle Lytton Bulwer', *The Oxford Dictionary of National Biography* (2004), and Neil R. Storey, *The Victorian Criminal* (2011), Robert Miles, 'Ann Radcliffe', *Oxford Dictionary of National Biography* (2004), and the wonderful online resource at <u>english.cam.ac.uk/pop</u> '*Price One Penny, A Database of Cheap Literature, 1837–1860*', produced by Marie Léger-St-Jean. The interpretation of Sweeney Todd comes, via Crone, from Sally Powell's article 'Black markets and cadaverous pies: the corpse, urban trade and industrial consumption in the penny blood', in A. Maunder and G. Moore (eds.), *Victorian Crime, Madness and Sensation* (2004).

7. Charles Dickens, Crime Writer

Simon Callow's *Charles Dickens and the Great Theatre of the World* (2012) was supplemented by his interview in person (which included a sensational performance as Bill Sykes killing Nancy). Claire Tomalin's *Charles Dickens, A Life* (2011), Philip Collins's *Dickens and Crime* (1962, 1994) and Haia Shpayer-Makov's *The Ascent of the Detective: Police Sleuths in Victorian and Edwardian England* (2011) were also useful. Rebecca Gowers has researched the case of Eliza Grimwood for her novel, *The Twisted Heart* (2009).

8. The Ballad of Maria Marten
Alex McWhirter, curator at Moyse's Hall Museum, Bury St Edmunds, was a terrific source of information on William Corder, as was Vic Gammon, now retired, but a guest member of staff at Newcastle University where he was director of the degree in folk music.

9. Stage Fright
Rosalind Crone's *Violent Victorians* (2012) was once again essential for this chapter, while the actor Michael Kirk gave me some practical coaching in the techniques of melodrama, onstage at the Old Vic. Kathy Haill, curator from the Victoria and Albert Museum, shared her knowledge of the collection's puppets. The webpage vam.ac.uk/page/p/puppets has more on the Victoria and Albert Museum's puppet collection, including the marionettes used to perform 'Maria Marten, or the Murder in the Red Barn'.

10. The Bermondsey Horror
In addition to all the general surveys of murder in the period, which uniformly mention the Mannings, Michael Alpert's *London 1849, A Victorian Murder Story* (2004) was the most detailed account consulted.

Part Two: Enter the Detective

11. Middle-Class Murderers and Medical Gentlemen

The William Salt Library, Stafford, holds many contemporary records of the Palmer trial, and I was also able to examine the medicine chest said to belong to William Palmer, courtesy of Sarah Williams and the museum at Tamworth Castle. There is more information on it in Fiona Sheridan and Nick Thomas, *Dr William Palmer, Trial by Media* (catalogue of the exhibition at the Ancient High House, Rudgeley, run by Staffordshire Council, 2004).

Ian Burney of the University of Manchester, author of several books on nineteenth- and early twentieth-century crime, shared his research published in *Poison, Detection and the Victorian Imagination* (2006) and the article 'Poison and the Victorian Imagination', *History Today* (March, 2008), pp. 35–41. Other useful publications included Noel G. Coley, 'Alfred Swaine Taylor, MD, FRS (1806–1880): Forensic Toxicologist', *Medical History*, vol. 35 (1991), pp. 409–27, James C. Whorton, *The Arsenic Century: How Victorian Britain was Poisoned, at Home, Work and Play* (2011) and Clive Emsley, 'Victorian Crime', published in *History Today* (1998).

12. The Good Wife

This is a richly researched and interesting area, where the key publications are: Mary S. Hartman, *Victorian Murderesses* (1977), Judith Knelman, *Twisting in the Wind* (1998), Virginia Morris, *Double Jeopardy: Women Who Kill in Victorian Fiction* (1990), Elaine Showalter, *A Literature of Their Own: British Novelists from Brontë to Lessing* (1977) and, for Florence Bravo,

I have relied heavily upon James Ruddick's extremely enjoyable *Death at the Priory, Love, Sex and Murder in Victorian England* (2001).

13. Detective Fever

Kate Summerscale's brilliant *The Suspicions of Mr Whicher* (2008) was supplemented by the interview she gave me for the programme. Haia Shpayer-Makov's *The Ascent of the Detective: Police Sleuths in Victorian and Edwardian England* (2011) stood out among the relevant books on the subject. Matthew Sweet also added to his published writings with an interview on Wilkie Collins, while Noeline Lyons' *A Greater Guilt: Constance Emilie Kent and the Road Murder* (2009) gives an alternative interpretation, and transcribes many useful documents, relating to the murder of Savile Kent. Michael Diamond's *Victorian Sensation* (2003) was also very useful. Stephanie Lyons and family welcomed us at Langham House, the modern name for Road Hill House, while James Dukes showed us Savil Kent's grave at St Thomas's Church, Coulston.

14. A New Sensation

Here, Andrew Gasson's *Wilkie Collins, An Illustrated Guide* (1998) was very useful, as was Helen Rappaport's *Beautiful for Ever, Madame Rachel of Bond Street, Cosmetician, Con-Artist and Blackmailer* (2010). As well as Wilkie Collins' own works, John Sutherland's introduction to the Penguin edition of *Armadale* (1995) is particularly recommended.

15. 'It is worse than a crime, Violet ...'

Lord Petre, the current inhabitant of Ingatestone Hall, showed us round the real-life 'Audley Court'. Katherine Mullin, 'Mary Elizabeth Braddon', *Oxford Dictionary of National Biography* (2004), provides an introduction to a life explored more fully in Robert Lee Wolff, *Sensational Victorian: Life and Fiction of Mary Elizabeth Braddon* (1979) and Jennifer Carnell, *The Literary Lives of Mary Elizabeth Braddon* (Sensation Press, 2000). Jennifer also gave an interview in person.

16. Monsters and Men

Judith Flanders' *The Invention of Murder* (2010) has an especially good chapter on 'Jack the Ripper' and Mr Hyde, also vital was Martin A. Danahay and Alexander Chisholm, *Jekyll and Hyde dramatized: the 1887 Richard Mansfield Script and the Evolution of the story on Stage* (2005). In addition, Michael Kirk, actor, showed me how Richard Mansfield did the transformation scene at the Lyceum Theatre. Alan Sharp's 'The Strange Case of Dr Jekyll and Saucy Jacky' was published in *The Ripperologist*, no. 55 (September, 2004), and online at casebook.org, a site produced by Stephen P. Ryder and Johnno.

17. The Adventure of the Forensic Scientist

E. J. Wagner's *The Science of Sherlock Holmes* (2006) gives an overview of the relationship between Holmes and forensic science, which is built upon by James O'Brien, *The Scientific Sherlock Holmes: Cracking the Case with Science and Forensics* (2013). Ken Butler, former Met fingerprint officer, explained the history of his profession in an interview, while Jonathan Evans, archivist of The London Medical College, now part of Queen Mary, University of London, elucidated early pathology for me in person. You can hear a recording of Sir Arthur Conan Doyle explaining how he came up with the character of Sherlock Holmes on the BBC website, in the BBC Radio 4 programme 'Great Lives' series 30, part 5, and Gordon Honeycombe is the author of *Murders of the Black Museum, 1875–1975* (2009).

18. Revelations of a Lady Detective
Kathryn Johnson, the curator at the British Library responsible for the exhibition 'Death in the Library' (2013), gave me an interview that was essential for this chapter. Alexander McCall Smith's quotations are taken from his article 'Why do we enjoy reading about female detectives?' published in *The Independent* (7 November 2012). Additionally, Haia Shpayer-Makov's *The Ascent of the Detective: Police Sleuths in Victorian and Edwardian England* (2011) was useful, as was Michael Sims, (ed.), *The Penguin Book of Victorian Women in Crime* (2011). Lucy Sussex, 'The Detective Maidservant', in Brenda Ayres (ed.), *Silent Voices: Forgotten Novels by Victorian Women Writers* (2003), puts the case for the forgotten Susan Hopley.

Part Three: The Golden Age
19. The Women Between the Wars
Here P. D. James's *Talking About Detective Fiction* (2010) was supplemented by her interview. The biographies of the 'Queens of Crime' include Joanne Drayton's *Ngaio Marsh, Her Life In Crime* (2008), Julia Jones's *The Adventures of Margery Allingham* (1991,

2009), James Brabazon's *Dorothy L. Sayers, A Biography* (1988) and Laura Thompson's *Agatha Christie, An English Mystery* (2007). I also used Clive Emsley's *Crime and Society in Twentieth Century Britain* (2011).

20. The Duchess of Death

Agatha Christie, *Agatha Christie, An Autobiography* (1977) reads well in conjunction with the analysis provided in Laura Thompson, *Agatha Christie, An English Mystery* (2007).

21. A Life Less Ordinary

Mike Ripley's article 'Dorothy L. Sayers as crime critic, 1933–35' was published in *Crime Time Magazine,* and James Brabazon, *Dorothy L. Sayers, A Biography* (1988) provided the biographical details.

22. The Great Game

Julian Symons' *Bloody Murder* (1972) was vital here, especially for details of the Club's writers. Simon Brett, today's Club President, gave me an informative and funny interview, while John Gannon, author of *The Killing of Julia Wallace* (2012), also contributed his expertise in person in an interview on William Herbert Wallace.

23. Snobbery with Violence

Colin Watson, *Snobbery with Violence* (1971), Julian Symons, *Bloody Murder* (1972) and T. J. Binyon's *Murder Will Out, The Detective in Fiction* (1989) will all get you reading detective stories with new eyes. Edmund Wilson's essay 'Why Do People Read Detective

Stories?' was published in *The New Yorker* (14 October 1944) and 'Who Cares Who Killed Roger Ackroyd?' in the same magazine on 20 January 1945.

24. The Dangerous Edge of Things

Graham Greene, *Brighton Rock,* Vintage Classics edition introduced by J. M. Coetzee (2004)

Index

Page numbers in *italics* refers to an illustration

307